BRONCOS!

BRONCOS!
The Team That Makes Miracles Happen

LOU SAHADI
Foreword by
RED MILLER

STEIN AND DAY/*Publishers*/New York

First published in 1978
Copyright © 1978 by Lou Sahadi
All rights reserved
Printed in the United States of America
STEIN AND DAY/*Publishers*/Scarborough House,
Briarcliff Manor, N.Y. 10510

Library of Congress Cataloging in Publication Data

Sahadi, Lou.
    Broncos!
    1. Denver Broncos (Football team)—History.
I. Title.
GV956.D37S23   796.33'264'0978883   78-7560
ISBN 0-8128-2504-7

Photographs on pages 60, 61, 62, 113, 116, 122, 126,
128, 132, 136, 142, 148, 152, 157, 159, 162, 176, 180,
and 182 courtesy Barry Staver.

Book Design/Dennis Peter Barnett
Inside Color/Mickey Palmer

For Alan and Paula,
two Texans who believed,
and to Denver's loyal Bronco fans
who waited 19 years.

ACKNOWLEDGMENTS

The author wishes to express his sincere thanks to Bob Peck, David Frye, and Lorraine Dieleman of the Denver Broncos organization and to Fran Connors of the National Football League.

CONTENTS

FOREWORD
by Robert "Red" Miller

After taking the head job with the Denver Bronco organization a year ago February, I met with each player individually and talked with him for at least an hour, and then met them as a team for the first time in our May Mini Camp. At both meetings, we stressed the teamwork concept and the idea of sacrificing the personal ego a little bit in order to fit it in with the team as a whole. They had tried winning the other way as groups and individuals, and knew they couldn't. I wanted to let them know that we could win in the NFL with a team concept. We also pushed the idea of being the best conditioned team in the NFL. When they reported to training camp in Fort Collins, I saw that an amazing transformation had taken place. They were shaved, they were lean, they were ready to play, and ready to make something happen. And as the sports world knows, something did.

I am most happy, not only about the winning, but also for the way our team played: for the enthusiasm they showed, the hard hitting, the clean play, the aggressive play, and the fact that we never gave up. This, plus the enthusiasm of the fans from our city, state and region, and of course our players and coaches, made it an incredible year. Just to be a part of it was one of life's greatest thrills.

Lou Sahadi has been familiar with the American Football League since its inception in 1960. He knows only too well the pains of survival teams like Denver had to endure. He has told the Bronco story well, from the early days of uncertainty to the fulfillment enjoyed last season.

INTRODUCTION

The sports fan is a paradoxical person—he can be fickle; he can be loyal. In 1960, the Denver Broncos were born under a cloud of doubt. They were the first major sports franchise in the history of Colorado: a new team, a new league, a new venture. Yet, not many people went to Bears Stadium and later to Denver University Stadium those early years to see them play.

The pains of losing were hard. It was clearly evident in the attendance. Denver did not exactly embrace the Broncos. Neither did the other American Football League teams. They despised going to Denver, not only because of the paltry crowds but also because of the inferior athletic facilities. The Broncos were easily the joke of the league with their ridiculous vertically striped socks and low player payroll. Nobody took them seriously, especially their opponents. Most of the first year players were former Canadian League imports.

There was even serious talk of the Broncos folding in 1961 after only one year of existence, but local interests succeeded in keeping them intact with a fresh infusion of working capital and new management. In 1962, the team discarded its sickly brown and gold uniforms for the brightness of orange, white, and blue. New hope and promise didn't last long. By the end of the 1964 season, the Broncos were on the open selling market. Three potential buyers were bidding to purchase the Broncos.

When it appeared imminent that the Broncos would be sold to out of town interests and relocated to another city, the tenacity of one person saved the franchise for Denver. With a welling of civic pride, Gerald Phipps, a local construction company owner, put a new group together at the eleventh hour and purchased the Broncos. Civic and business groups united behind Phipps's promise of keeping the Broncos in Denver. Before the 1965 campaign began, a spirited ticket drive produced over 18,000 season ticket sales, which was more than five other teams in the league.

The Phipps's era was a new awakening. Although the results weren't immediately shown on the playing field, positive things were happening. More important, Bronco fans believed. Their fierce loyalty was finally rewarded in 1977. The Denver Broncos became the American Football Conference champions. Another milestone, but a beautiful one.

This book is the story of the latest underdog to capture the imagination of every sports fan. Suddenly, derision changed to cheers; the Denver Broncos became the darlings of the sports world. The Orange Crush was part of the American mainstream. Bronco fans, this book is for you.

Lou Sahadi
March 1978

BRONCOS!

The Broncos were the joke of the American Football League when they began playing in 1960. Besides having second-hand uniforms with the strange colors of burnt gold and brown, they were the only team with vertically-striped socks.

1

THE BEGINNING

They were an ungodly looking bunch. If they looked somewhat out of place, it was understandable. The owner was a baseball man; the general manager and coach were from Canada, as was the quarterback; the uniforms were the dullest imaginable; a playbook was unheard of; and if the town drunk said he saw a football player wearing vertical striped socks, he would get a laugh. Fact is, so did everybody else when they got a glimpse of the 1960 Denver Broncos. They were something out of *Grimm's Fairy Tales.* Way out.

But then a lot of people laughed at Lamar Hunt when he first got the idea of starting the American Football League a year before. Only 26 years old, shy, and bespectacled, Hunt had the outward appearance of a choir boy; but he had guts and money. Early in 1959 Hunt wanted to buy a professional football team. He made a serious offer to purchase the Chicago Cardinals with the idea of moving the franchise to his hometown of Dallas. He encountered two obstacles. The first was that the Cardinal owners wanted to sell only twenty per cent of the stock. That would hardly qualify Hunt as the major stockholder. Then, too,

1

he had to confront George Halas, the owner of the Chicago Bears. The venerable Halas was the patriarch among the NFL owners; and as such, he was also the head of the league's expansion committee whose main concern was to accept or reject proposals for new franchises. Halas ruled with a strong arm; and whatever he decided was law, committee or no committee. He firmly informed young Mr. Hunt that the league was most definitely against any franchise shift to Dallas. He emphatically reminded Hunt that in 1952 a professional team had failed dismally there in the aborted four-year existence of the All America Conference.

But the quiet speaking Hunt was not discouraged. He had been a frustrated football player at Southern Methodist University, where he had graduated three years before and where he sat on the bench as a member of the varsity for the same number of years. He sat so far down on the bench that nobody knew him.

"I had received two letters at SMU," Hunt once recalled somewhat sheepishly. "The first letter came from Coach Matty Bell at the end of my senior year. It read, 'Dear Lamar: Please stay off our football field. You have cluttered it up long enough.'

"The second letter I got was also from Bell. It said, 'Dear Lamar: Please return to the Athletic Department the twelve T-shirts you have taken the past three years.'"

If Hunt couldn't play for a team, he could buy one. If he couldn't do that, then he would have to start his own league; and that's what he decided to do. Remembering one of the names that was mentioned in his dealings with the Cardinals, Hunt decided to approach K. S. "Bud" Adams, another wealthy Texan. They had never met. Late in January, Hunt went to Houston to meet Adams.

They were complete opposites. The only things they had in common were that they were both Texans and were both wealthy. Hunt is quiet, unassuming, dresses conservatively, wears glasses, and appears soft. He could easily pass for a librarian. Adams, on the other hand, is what a typical Texan is supposed to be, flamboyant in his ten gallon hat and cowboy boots—and with a barbecue pit in his office, no less!

Yet, their meeting was amicable. They talked for three hours but never mentioned football. Finally, as Adams was driving Hunt to the airport, the subject came up. Hunt was impressed with Adams. He told him about his idea of starting another professional football league.

"If I can get perhaps four other people in four other cities to sponsor teams, would you come in?" asked Hunt. Adams didn't hesitate in agreeing.

If there was one thing the embryonic league had going for them right at the start, it was Texas money and plenty of it. Besides owning the Ada Oil Company, Adams was a rancher, investor, cattle breeder, and real estate developer. He was one Texan who could put his money where his mouth was.

One time at a barbecue, Adams was among a group of others talking about land. One Texan bragged, "I own three thousand acres."

"I own five thousand," another said. Then they turned to Adams and asked, "How many do you own, son?"

"Just one hundred," answered Adams.

"Poor boy, and where is your spread?"

Members of the embryonic American Football League attend a football game early in 1959. From left, Bud Adams (Houston Oilers); Lamar Hunt (Dallas Texans); Harry Wismer (New York Jets) and Bob Howsam (Denver Broncos).

"Downtown Houston," Adams shot back.

These were the two pivotal individuals who launched the American Football League. As soon as Hunt returned to Dallas, he began contacting people he felt were interested in owning professional football franchises.

The first person Hunt talked to was Bob Howsam in Denver. Howsam had a background in professional sports and was then the owner of the Denver Bears baseball team of the Pacific Coast League, a high ranking minor league. He acknowledged to Hunt that he indeed would be interested in owning a football franchise, too, inasmuch as he had his own playing field, Bears Stadium. Howsam had received some national publicity because of the professional manner in which he operated the baseball club.

So, Howsam, along with his father Lee and his brother Earl, represented the first city outside of Texas in the still unnamed league. As it turned out, Howsam was not quite ready to expand into football due to an unexpected financial setback he had suffered in baseball the

year before. In 1958, Branch Rickey, the baseball sage of Brooklyn, had approached Howsam about joining a third major baseball league known as the Continental League. Howsam was excited and quickly accepted. The first thing Rickey advised him was to add more seats to his stadium, which Howsam did. Located just five miles from downtown Denver, Bears Stadium was an ideal location. Howsam added some 8,100 seats to the south stands, raising the seating capacity from 17,500 to 25,600. Howsam felt that by owning two sport teams he would get maximum use of the stadium, baseball in the summer and football in the fall. His setback came when plans for the Continental League fell through. Now all Howsam had was the construction costs of a newly furbished stadium and only a football team with the impending first year start-up costs.

Nevertheless Howsam would honor his commitment to the new American Football League, which began the 1960 season with eight teams. The first thing he did was to hire

3

a general manager. He didn't have to look far. Howsam named Dean Griffing, who had recently been released as the general manager of the Saskatchewan Rough Riders of the Canadian Football League. Griffing had served as the Rough Riders' general manager for seven years. Before that he had played in the Canadian League. It was only natural that Griffing looked to Canada to select the first coach in Denver's history. He didn't have to look far, either. He named Frank Filchock, who had been the coach under him during Griffing's seven years in Saskatchewan. Filchock had been a star quarterback at the University of Indiana and had gone on to play professional ball with the New York Giants in the late thirties and early forties.

Although most people wouldn't remember Filchock's exploits on the field, they easily recall his participation off it. Infamously, he was reported to be involved in a fix attempt by the New York Police, along with his teammate Merle Hapes, to throw the championship game against the Chicago Bears in 1946. Following an investigation by NFL Commissioner Bert Bell, Filchock was allowed to play in the game. Convinced of Filchock's innocence, Bell did manage to reprimand him for not taking any action in reporting the bribe attempt to the league.

If there was one thing that can be said of Griffing, and it was a trait that undoubtedly pleased Howsam, it was that he was frugal. Overly so, it turned out. Realizing that the club did not have sufficient cash to attract a first rate quarterback, he again turned to his Saskatchewan spa. He prevailed upon Frank Tripucka, who had been the quarterback during the Griffing-Filchock era there, and who ironically had replaced Filchock as coach during the final six games of the 1959 season, to play for the Broncos.

At least Tripucka had a national reputation. He was the star quarterback at Notre Dame for Frank Leahy's national championship teams in the late forties. He had played professionally with the Detroit Lions and the Chicago Cardinals before he and 14 other NFL players jumped to the Canadian League in 1953. He was an excellent T-formation quarterback and was regarded as a "coach on the field."

Griffing's telephone call to Tripucka came at a propitious time. Tripucka was in a squabble with the owners of the Rough Riders. It wasn't over money. Instead, the club owners felt that being a coach, Tripucka should put down some roots and reside in Canada on a year-round basis, not just during the football season. Armed with an offer from Denver, Tripucka was firm in his demands with the Rough Riders. When they wouldn't acquiesce to Tripucka's terms, he left. In his case, it was easy. He resigned his contract, which was that of a coach, in order to return to the United States as a player.

Tripucka was excited about the thought of a new league. He still felt that he could contribute as a player. He was certainly knowledgeable enough and still could throw the ball accurately. However, Tripucka was puzzled when he first reported to Denver and learned that he was getting $10,000 less than he earned in Canada. Griffing explained that the Broncos were not going to play him much. What they wanted him to do was primarily work with the other two quarterbacks, Tom Dublinski, a veteran NFL reserve quarterback, and rookie George Herring. Occasionally he might be asked to do some playing.

The Broncos' first training camp was at the Colorado School of Mines in Fort Golden. Only it wasn't so golden. The team was billeted on the fourth floor of an army-type barracks. Since the room was actually the top floor, it was extremely hot during the day when the sun baked down on the roof. The room itself was something else. There were no partitions or closets. The players had to hang their clothes on long pipes and virtually were forced to live out of a suitcase. The antiquated quarters caused one visitor to remark, "It should have been condemned long before this."

If anything, it was hoped that the food would make up for the primitive living quarters. It didn't. Hash was served practically every night, disguised in different shapes and forms. The players were allowed steak once a week, usually on Friday night, when the Catholic players had to bless themselves and assure themselves it was really fish. If anything, the menu change stopped the players' complaints, if only for a day at least.

Griffing didn't win any fashion design

Frank Filchock coached the Broncos during their first two years.

Frank Tripucka was Denver's first quarterback.

awards, either. He secured used equipment from one of the neighboring colleges. Then he purchased the most unbelievably drab uniforms from the Copper Bowl, a now-extinct post-season game that was once held in Tucson, Arizona. The uniforms featured dull gold shirts, brown pants, and vertically striped socks. It was the only set of jerseys the club owned, and they were used both for home and away games. Long before the season was over, they had become tight and torn from incessant laundering.

It was not surprising to see Filchock repairing the team's equipment. His staff was miniscule, to put it mildly. He handled the entire offensive phase and had only Dale Dodrill as defensive line coach and Jim Cason as defensive backfield coach. Things were so bad that Larry Elliott, a Denver fan, volunteered to help the Broncos with the equipment without pay. However, since Filchock was a close friend of Griffing, he didn't complain.

But Tripucka had a right to. Suffice to say, the exhibition season came and went, and the Broncos lost all five of their games. Griffing then cut Dublinski; and Tripucka, who was hardly going to play at all, was suddenly the number one quarterback. In fact the entire training camp scene was beginning to look like something out of a Marx Brothers movie.

"We had an exhibition in Little Rock," recalled Tripucka, "and Bud McFadin stopped by to see the game. The next thing you know, he's putting on a uniform; and the next thing, he's playing."

When the regular season opened, the Broncos made history. They not only participated in the first game ever in the history of the league; but they won it, too. On Friday night, September 9, 1960, in Boston, the Denver Broncos, 16-point underdogs to the then Boston Patriots, strode on to the Boston University field in their vertically striped socks before 21,597 curious fans. When the game was over, the strangely dressed Broncos had won, 13-10.

The stars of the game were Tripucka, who completed ten of fifteen passes, including a 59-yard touchdown pass to Al Carmichael, and unknown rookie Gene Mingo, who ran back a punt 76 yards for a touchdown in the third quarter.

"About three guys grabbed me, but I just

The first two years of Denver's existence in the American Football League was described as "The Early Futility" by this plaque that hands in the Pro Football Hall of Fame in Canton, Ohio.

ran past them," smiled Mingo after the game. Only months before while he was still in the Navy, Mingo had written the Broncos to ask for a tryout as a running back. Denver, desperate for any players, gave him the chance; and he made it.

Tripucka also acted as a coach during the game. Filchock didn't have a coach with a phone stationed high up in the stands to observe the opposing team's defense. As a result, Tripucka didn't know what the defensive line was doing to his backs. He would gather his offensive team near to one side of the bench and discuss strategy with them.

During the Boston game, the Broncos' only middle linebacker got hurt. When it appeared that he would be unable to play in Buffalo the following week, Tripucka beseeched Filchock to check waivers.

"Get out the waiver list and find out what middle linebackers are available," exclaimed Tripucka.

"We don't need any. We have plenty of players here," responded Filchock.

In spite of it all, the next Sunday the Broncos defeated the Bills 27-21. They had won their second straight game; and when they returned to their eastern base in Plainfield, New Jersey to prepare for their game against the New York Titans, they perhaps felt it wasn't so bad to play for Denver.

While they were practicing one day, they got another surprise. Lionel Taylor, a newcomer, joined them on the field, and without even being introduced was sent in to play as a defensive back. Later, when practice was over, the players became engaged in a touch football game. The star of the exercise was Lionel Taylor who caught every pass that was thrown near him. It was enough to cause Filchock to stop the game.

"I threw a pass that Lionel caught between three guys," exclaimed Tripucka. "Filchock yelled, 'Hold it. Let's look at this kid some more,' and he told me to throw him some passes. That was the end of the touch game.

8

UTILITY

HEISMAN TROPHY WINNER BILLY CANNON SIGNED WITH THE HOUSTON OILERS FOR 1960! MEANWHILE, THE DENVER BRONCOS WERE PLAYING IN SECOND-HAND UNIFORMS MADE FAMOUS BY THE VERTICALLY-STRIPED SOCKS THAT WERE LATER BURNED IN A PUBLIC CEREMONY. THUS, THE AFL'S GREAT HOPE AND ITS EARLY FUTILITY ARE GRAPHICALLY PORTRAYED AS CANNON GAINS YARDAGE AGAINST THE DENVER TEAM.

We had Lionel running some patterns; and I threw him some passes, and he caught everything I threw him. We had a receiver.

"Hey, son, you ever play offensive football?" asked Filchock.

"Yes, sir. I was a running back in college," he answered.

Filchock ordered a passing drill with Tripucka and the newcomer. Although he had been cut a few days before by the Chicago Bears, Taylor was so impressive that Filchock started him against the Titans. Although the Broncos lost in the final seconds, 28-24, Taylor caught eleven passes, including a 35-yard touchdown.

When the Broncos returned home for their first home game ever, a grand total of 18,372 fans greeted them. They were not disappointed either as Denver defeated the Oakland Raiders, 31-14. The surprising Broncos were off to a good start, winning three of their first four games. Still, the crowds didn't turn out; and then the team began to lose regularly. Griffing was beginning to get frustrated. His behavior reached a point where he once went into the stands and wrestled a football away

from a fan who had caught a ball that had been kicked there. The Denver fans booed Griffing something awful. The next day, Griffing invited the fan over for lunch and handed him a football that had been autographed by the team.

Tripucka was even more amazing. Surrounded with a weak offensive line, the veteran quarterback had the facility to improvise. He was a marvel in the huddle. He would actually diagram plays on the ground with his fingers. Then he would always tell his receivers to give him an escape valve in case he was rushed, as often was the case, and be ready for a makeshift pass. Being rushed was getting to be a way of life for Tripucka as the season went on. He looked back at all the "watch out" blocks he was subjected to. When Tripucka's blockers failed him on pass plays, as they did regularly, they would yell, "Watch out!"

"We would score," said Tripucka, "but we didn't have much of a defense. One time Filchock was moaning, 'Every time I look up, the other team has another seven points on the board'; and Bud McFadin told him, 'I know how to solve that problem. Don't look up.' "

When the season ended, the Broncos produced a 4-9-1 record. Only 91,332 fans had watched them, an average of 13,047 per home game. Tripucka, Taylor, Mingo, Carmichael, Goose Gonsoulin, and rugged Bud McFadin gave them some measure of respectability. The amazing Tripucka led the league in pass attempts, 478; completions, 248; yards, 3,038; and as expected with so many attempts, interceptions, 34. For someone who wasn't expected to play much, he had an outstanding year, running and coaching an offense that had no organized playbook. Most of his passes were caught by Taylor, who grabbed 92.

The draft after the season didn't help. Players coming out of college were afraid to sign with Denver which didn't have the money resources to battle the NFL for players. Tripucka knew that he would be in for another rough year. He asked for a new deal and got it. He was paid the $10,000 difference between his Denver and Saskatchewan salary and got an additional $5,000 on next season's contract.

One thing was certain, the Broncos did at least have a quarterback for 1961.

Red Miller was assistant coach with the Broncos during the 1962 and 1963 seasons.

2

THE FORMATIVE YEARS

It was obvious that Howsam couldn't undergo another season. He had lost $200,000 and facing any additional red ink was out of the question. He was openly receptive to selling the Broncos. A group of businessmen from San Antonio, Texas made serious overtures toward purchasing the Broncos and moving them to Texas. But Denver businessman Calvin Kunz, Jr., a spirited individual, didn't want that to happen. A community-minded person, Kunz felt that the Broncos should remain in Denver. Kunz worked hard and feverishly toward saving the franchise in Denver; and late in the spring of 1961, he engineered a deal that would preserve professional football in Denver.

Kunz had been a member of the board of directors of Rocky Mountain Sports, Inc., the corporate owners of the franchise which the Howsams controlled. He succeeded in getting three other members of the board to join him in buying the franchise. They were Gerald H. Phipps, a prominent building contractor who was the chairman of the board; Ben F. Stapleton, Jr., an attorney who was the treasurer; and Edward Hirschfield, president of the largest printing company in the area.

Kunz also gathered six new financial supporters. They were Walter C. Emery, president of the Bank of Denver; William Grant, chairman of the board of KOA-Radio and TV; Robert T. Person, president of the Public Service Company of Colorado; Allan Phipps, an attorney who was also Gerald's brother; Charles W. Schoelzel, senior vice president of Van Schaack & Co., a real estate firm; and James E. Stokes, another prominent realtor. On June 1, a week after the deal was consummated with Howsam, Kunz was named president and operating head of the new group that was known as Empire Sports.

It was too late for Kunz to make any significant changes regarding the field operations of the Broncos. While some of the other more affluent AFL teams strengthened themselves, the Broncos acquired little in the way of new player personnel. As a result, Tripucka still led an offense that consisted basically of everyone who was eligible running out for a pass. The Broncos remained as dismal on the field in artistry as well as dress. They finished with a 3-11 record. But the Tripucka to Taylor passing combination was the best in the league. Taylor finished with a record-setting 100 receptions, and he and McFadin were named to the All-AFL team. Still, the fans hadn't been stimulated. Total attendance slumped to 74,508, or an average of only 10,648 a game.

As soon as the season ended Kunz took action. He fired Filchock and replaced him with Jack Faulkner. The highly regarded Faulkner had been an assistant to Sid Gillman for fourteen years. Griffing was also fired, and Faulkner took over the duties of general manager in addition to his coaching responsibilities. It was what Faulkner had demanded, anyway. He had accepted Kunz's offer only with the stipulation that he would have total control of the football program.

Faulkner immediately took appreciable strides toward improving the Bronco situation. Long before the 1962 season began, he added Ray Malavasi, Mac Speedie, Gary Glick, and Jack Martin to the coaching staff. Then Faulkner turned his attention to the Denver uniforms which had been a longstanding joke around the league. He changed the jersey colors from the drab gold and brown to a bright

Owner Gerald Phipps saved the Broncos for Denver in 1965.

orange, blue, and white. Then he gathered all of the hideous brown-and-gold vertical-striped socks and burned them in a public ceremony at Bears Stadium.

Faulkner then turned his attention to producing results on the football field. Before every game, he would give the players a game plan. For Tripucka, this was heaven. Faulkner would prepare his team soundly for every opponent, and the players responded. After losing their first two exhibition games, they then won the next two. One of these victories was significant and seemed to turn the whole operation around. Playing the Dallas Texans in Fort Worth, the Broncos were behind 24-17 with about five minutes to play. The Texans had a fourth and 1 on Denver's 29-yard line. The Broncos rose to the occasion and stopped the powerful Texans. Minutes later, the Broncos scored the tying touchdown and then won the game in overtime, 27-24.

Despite the inspiring win, Denver fans were adopting a wait-and-see attitude. They had suffered through two losing seasons and weren't about to get excited over a pre-season victory no matter how inspired it had been. Season ticket sales did not increase noticeably, but Faulkner was getting it together on the field. The players respected his knowledge and his systematic way of doing things. They had experienced neither during the first two years.

Still, an overflow crowd of 24,928 crowded their way into Denver University Stadium to watch the Broncos upend the San Diego Chargers, 31-21, in the season opener. When the Broncos won six of their first seven games, the fans were excited. One of the triumphs was a 20-10 verdict over the Houston Oilers before 34,496 fans. It was the largest crowd ever to see a sports event in the history of Denver.

But the second half of the season was disastrous. The Broncos were involved in several close games but lost six of the remaining seven to finish the 1962 season with a 7-7 record. Despite the slump, Faulkner was voted the AFL coach of the year for his efforts in guiding the Broncos to the runner-up spot in the Western Division.

The Broncos attracted 175,413 fans that season for an average game attendance of 25,059. Everyone around the league noticed that, but something else was happening to the team. The players felt it, offensive lineman Jerry Sturm, for one.

"Faulkner was loose and easy at the beginning, fun to play for," recalls Sturm. "Then he started changing things, making things more complicated. We had begun the season with forty, maybe fifty, plays on offense and played very basic defense. By the seventh game we were trying to run about 150 different plays. I think that perhaps the pressure of being on top, leading the division, got to him."

Still, optimism permeated the Denver ozone before the 1963 season. In three short years the Broncos had become a .500 club, and that was substantial progress. Then, for the first time in their abbreviated history, the Broncos did well in the draft. Denver signed four of their draft choices: tackle Ron Nomina, a second round pick from Miami of Ohio; halfback Tommy Janik, a third round choice from Texas A & I; quarterback Mickey Slaughter, a seventh round selection from Louisiana Tech; and fullback Billy Joe, an eleventh round pick from Villanova. Faulkner also added two more coaches to his staff, Red Miller on offense and Ed Hughes on defense.

With a bumper crop of rookies plus additions to the coaching staff, Kunz felt that the Broncos might even surpass their 1962 showing; and no one could blame him for his optimistic feelings. However, even with the infusion of new blood, the coaching end began to fall apart. Faulkner became more immersed in his duties as general manager and as a result the practice sessions were not well organized. The players took advantage of the situation and began to loaf. In the first two years, the baseball personnel from the Denver Bears used to help out with the football operation. Now, Faulkner was doing it all. It took too much of his time away from coaching.

"You could go to that Quonset hut at midnight, and Faulkner would be in there making hotel reservations for a trip or allotting tickets or something," Tripucka remembers. "The guy was buried."

But Kunz remained enthusiastic. Every so often he would drop by and attend a quarterback meeting. Sometimes Faulkner would ask him for an opinion, and Kunz would gladly give one. At times Kunz would give fight talks to the players right in the dressing room before a game. But Kunz was in strange surroundings, and the franchise still suffered from the lack of sufficient money that an AFL team needed to operate successfully.

The Broncos tumbled back to the depths in which they had floundered during their first two years in the league. They finished the 1963 season with a dismal 2-11-1 record, and it appeared as if the bottom had fallen out. By now, the Denver fans had grown not only restless but extremely vociferous. Len Dawson, the star quarterback of the Kansas City Chiefs, never will forget playing in Denver that year. In fact, in the opening game of the 1963 season, the Chiefs trounced the Broncos, 59-7; and the Denver fans were raucous.

"We were beating the Broncos badly, and it was late in the game," recalls Dawson. "We had just scored another touchdown, and the fans at the south end started throwing things at us. There was a guy with a bull horn encouraging them. He was getting on the referee, our coach Hank Stram, and finally, me. He really had the fans fired up. The more we scored, the more frustrated the fans became.

"First they threw paper bags, then beer cans, and now that the game was almost over, whiskey bottles. They had a good shot at us, too, because the south stands were only about eight feet from the field. I've never seen such emotional fans. It was no wonder they called the south stands 'the snakepit.'

"After we scored the final touchdown, Stram called the kicking team over. He told them not to kick the ball deep because he was afraid that if our defensive team had to play at that end of the field the fans might kill them. Instead, he ordered an onsides kick in the middle of the field. But of all things, we recover the ball. Now the fans are really mad. They thought we kicked onsides to recover the ball and go for another touchdown.

"The game finally ends, and Stram orders us not to leave the field. We gathered in the middle of the field to wait until the crowd leaves, but nobody left. We then decided to make a run for it, but the fans were ready. I waited until the first group of players took off. As they galloped across the field, debris began flying in all directions. Then, before they could gather more things to throw, I took off and made it into the locker room safely.

"Stram thought he could escape injury by walking off the field with Doak Walker. Everybody in Denver loved Walker. But you know what happened? Walker gets hit in the head with a bottle!

"When we played Denver that season we always felt that we could beat them. But they had a tough defensive tackle named Bud McFadin. He was famous for his left hand flip. Most defensive tackles were generally right handed, but McFadin did his number with his left hand. And tough? I heard a story one time that McFadin got shot in a bar by someone with a .45. He hardly staggered, walked over, took the .45 from the guy's hand, and pistol whipped him. Our tight end, Fred Arbanas, was about the toughest tight end around. In one game, one of the Denver defensive ends got hurt, and McFadin moved over to the outside. Arbanas sees it. He came into the huddle and tells me about it.

" 'Lenny, McFadin is on the outside. I've heard how tough he is all these years. I want to find out. Give me a shot at him.'

"Well, the game was almost over. We had them beat, and we were just running out the clock. So I called a running play to McFadin's

Cookie Gilchrist

Running back Cookie Gilchrist was the first big star the Broncos signed in 1965. He was also the team's most colorful individual. An injury ended his career in 1967.

side. We gained about a yard, and it was McFadin who made the tackle. Arbanas came back into the huddle all excited and said, 'I was really too anxious. I overshot him. I missed him, but he's not so tough. Run the play again.'

"So I did. Then I heard this big thud, and I looked over to see what had happened. Here comes Arbanas staggering back to the huddle. His face mask is cracked, and his headgear is turned around so that he's looking at me through the ear hole.

" 'If you ever listen to me again,' he said, 'I'm going to whip your butt!'

"I remember another time when we were beating Denver quite badly. Our other quarterback, Pete Beathard, went in to replace me. On one play, he took a cheap shot from one of the defensive ends that knocked him cold. I had to go back in. Our offensive line was furious. I asked them what they wanted to do about it, and they all said to run a sweep. I handed the ball to Bert Coan and stepped back out of the way. Everybody went for the defensive end. Back in the huddle the linemen said, 'Let's do that again.' Boom, everybody took another shot at the end. When we came back into the huddle, the linemen want to run the same play for the third time; but Coan spoke up.

" 'Hey fellas, wait a minute. While nine of you guys are chasing *that* guy, the other ten are knocking the hell out of me. Give me a chance!' "

The Denver fans didn't want that kind of a season any more, but in 1964 they had to suffer again. The Broncos repeated their exercise in futility, finishing once more with a 2-11-1 record and their fourth last place finish in five years. Before the season was over, the Broncos were undergoing more changes.

After the Broncos were drubbed quite handily in their first four games in 1964, Kunz fired Faulkner as head coach and replaced him with Mac Speedie; and for one glorious week, Bronco fans knew joy. In Speedie's first game as the new head coach, the Broncos upset the heavily favored Kansas City Chiefs, 33-27, but before only 16,885 fans in Denver. At one point during the game, Speedie was so happy that he led the crowd in cheering.

Speedie was a great believer in fan support.

He didn't hesitate in opening the Denver practice sessions to the public. Also appearing at the workouts was Gerry Phipps. With the dismissal of Faulkner, Phipps acted as the team's interim general manager.

"After we had lost our first four games quite badly, I could see that without a doubt something had to be done," Phipps recalls. "I began going to practice to observe things. It was more of a learning experience than anything else. I felt I needed to know more about the operation from every standpoint before I could offer any help with the solutions to our problems, and we had many."

When the season ended, there were even more problems. Attendance had dropped to

16

Ron Lamb takes a handoff from quarterback Steve Tensi in a 1968 game against the New York Jets.

an average of 16,862 a game. Empire Sports lost still more money. Kunz was now convinced that pro football would never go in Denver. In order to recover the near $2 million Empire had lost, he decided to sell the club to out of town interests. Along with Earl Howsam, James Stokes, Walter Emery, Ben Stapleton, and Edward Hirschfield, Kunz formed a voting trust that controlled 52 per cent of Empire Sports.

There were at least three prospective buyers. One was Arthur Allyn, who owned the Chicago White Sox. Another was Nicholas Troilo, a Philadelphia toy manufacturer who had also looked at Miami as a possible new

franchise. However, the most likely prospect was the Cox Broadcasting Corporation, who reportedly tendered a $4 million bid with the idea of moving the Broncos to Atlanta.

The Kunz group had the majority vote. However, the sale was conditional on one important aspect, the buyer wanted all of the stock. In this regard, the Phipps brothers refused to sell. They were determined to keep the Broncos in Denver. It was an apparent stalemate. Finally, Gerry Phipps made Kunz a $1.5 million offer for the remaining 52 per cent of the stock that he controlled. Kunz agreed. On February 15, 1965 the deal was consummated. Phipps was indeed happy.

Denver's defense tries to get at Oakland's Daryle Lamonica in a 1970 contest.

"We are trying to attract industry to this community," Phipps disclosed shortly after the sale. "Nothing would hurt us more than headlines around the country saying that Denver had lost its football team. I would be cutting my own throat if I did something that would set back the community. If we can sell 20,000 season tickets, we can break even financially."

The day after the contract was signed, things began to happen. It was like a new reawakening in Denver. A one-day record of 143 season tickets were sold. An outdoor advertising company displayed a large sign that read: "Thanks To Gerry And Allan Phipps For Keeping The Broncos In Denver." The Peoples Bank of Aurora proposed a program devised by its vice president, Ron Hermes, that allowed fans to purchase season tickets on an interest-free installment plan. The Hermes method was so successful that other banks and associations followed suit. By April 1, 20,000 season tickets had been sold. Before the season began, the Broncos had more season seats sold than five of the other seven teams in the league. Suddenly they were one of the liveliest franchises in the AFL.

By the end of the 1965 season, Denver led the Western Division in attendance with 219,786, an average of 31,397 per game. But while the Broncos had turned the corner financially, they still were pathetic on the field. Even the acquisition of running backs Cookie Gilchrist from Buffalo and Abner Haynes from Kansas City didn't help appreciably. They finished with a 4-10 record and another last place spot.

Cookie Gilchrist's arrival in Denver prior to the start of the season had its dramatic moments. The first thing he said after disembarking from the plane was that he wouldn't report to training camp because he had been "coerced" into signing his contract and he couldn't play under that kind of situation. Cookie's Buffalo contract was for $28,000. The Broncos had given him $35,000, making him one of the highest paid runners in the league. Nevertheless, Cookie holed up in the Denver Hilton for a week while the rest of the Broncos underwent the rigors of training camp.

Finally, at four o'clock in the morning seven

Running back Floyd Little was Denver's first bona fide star. He was the club's number one draft choice in 1967, the first number one selection to ever sign, and he played for nine years, retiring after the 1975 season. He is the all-time rushing leader with 6,323 yards, including an NFL-leading 1,113 in 1971. His playing number, 44, is the only uniform retired by the Broncos.

days after his arrival, Gilchrist signed a contract for better terms. Later in the morning, he appeared on Starr Yelland's television program. He was scheduled for a ten minute segment, but Cookie was so charming he remained for 40 minutes.

"I wanted to be in the big money centers of the league, in New York or out on the West Coast," Cookie told Denver viewers. "But after being here in this wonderful city for only a week and learning about all the wonderful Bronco fans you have here and the great enthusiasm this city has, I can see I was wrong. I sometimes think too much of money when I really should think of the finer things in life like friendship and loyalty and being in a nice place to live. I realize that I have all this in Denver.

"And I got to thinking about the ball club. It's not a bad team. There's a lot of good, young players on it. What it needs is just an older person like myself who can help the club. I know that there are other older players on the team that are good, and we can all work and make the Broncos into a championship team. That's what I'm dedicated to do now here in Denver, build toward a championship."

One of the clauses in Gilchrist's contract was that he would be paid an additional $5,000 if he gained 900 yards rushing. Gilchrist played well his first season in Denver. He was well on his way toward the 900-yard figure as the Broncos made preparations to travel to Kansas City for their final game of the year. Cookie boarded the plane with the other players, reached his seat, and then got up a few minutes later and began to leave, mumbling that he couldn't fly on a rickety plane like this one, that management was cheap, and that he wasn't going to play in the final game. With that he stormed off the plane.

But it wasn't in Cookie's nature to turn away from $5,000. He boarded a commercial flight and arrived in Kansas City a few hours later. His presence put Speedie on the spot. In essence, Gilchrist should have been suspended. But if the Broncos didn't allow Cookie to play, he could blame them for keeping him out of the game just to save the $5,000; and management was very sensitive about that particular situation. They had a reputation for being

cheap, and there was the undeniable fact that they had never come up with enough money to sign a number one draft choice. So, management allowed Cookie to play, much to the chagrin of Speedie. Gilchrist managed to break a couple of long runs, finished the season with 954 yards, a Bronco record, and got his $5,000.

Gilchrist was popular in Denver. The fans loved him. He was the first genuine hero they had during the early dismal years. Cookie attended quarterback club functions and thrilled the fans with his lore. But by the 1966 season, the romance had ended, at least as far as management was concerned.

Surprisingly enough, Cookie reported to training camp on time; but he had another surprise for Speedie. He was accompanied by Willie Ross, a running back who had been cut by the Buffalo Bills. Cookie made it clear that Ross should be added to the camp roster. Speedie was furious. He told Gilchrist in no uncertain terms that neither he nor anyone else came to training camp unless they had been invited to come, and Speedie sure hadn't invited Ross. Besides, Speedie added, he had better backs than Ross anyway.

Gilchrist was upset by Speedie's attitude. He felt that he had only been trying to help the club by bringing in another player for a trial. He claimed that Speedie was prejudiced and that he always carried a chip on his shoulder toward him. So, Cookie bolted camp and was prepared to sit out the season on principle alone. When Speedie was fired after the second game Cookie talked with management; and they agreed to trade him to Miami for a third and fifth round draft choice. The trade came after the expansion Dolphins won their first game in history by beating Denver, 24-7.

Season ticket sales continued to climb for the 1966 season. Still, the Broncos couldn't match the fan enthusiasm with their playing ability. Once more they were 4-10 and finished at the bottom of the Western Division. The team had looked lost and disinterested. In the opening game of the season against the Houston Oilers, they lost 45-7 without even making a single first down. Then they lost to the Boston Patriots in their home opener, 24-10, and didn't make a first down until the second quarter.

Lou Saban was hired in 1967 to lead the Broncos out of the doldrums. He resigned as coach with five games remaining in the 1971 season.

Kansas City wide receiver Otis Taylor hauls in a pass against the Denver secondary in a 1971 game.

Speedie's fan involvement was unorthodox, to say the least, and it helped lead to his demise. On close fourth down decisions, he would turn to the crowd and ask them what they wanted him to do. Fans, being fans, would always go for the first down rather than punt. When the plays worked, the fans had fun, all the while thinking what a great guy Speedie was. But when the plays backfired, they felt it wasn't their fault; and they began to boo Speedie regularly. Upon his dismissal, an assistant coach, Ray Malavasi, guided the Broncos over the remaining twelve games.

Phipps's determination to improve the club was evident at the end of the 1966 season. In a dramatic move, he signed Lou Saban as coach and general manager for ten years. Saban had been AFL Coach of the Year in 1964 and 1965 when he coached Buffalo. He left the pro ranks after that season and coached the University of Maryland in 1966, but the lure of pro football was too much for him to stay away.

"The challenge of directing the Denver Broncos is the most stimulating assignment I

The optimistic John Ralston was named to replace Lou Saban as coach in 1972. Despite producing the finest year in the club's history, 9-5, in 1976, he was fired after the season.

have undertaken during the years I have been associated with football," Saban said upon his arrival. "Our goals are two-fold. We want to build a solid organization, and we want to win football games. The two go hand in hand. They can be accomplished."

The first thing that Saban accomplished of any significance occurred during the pre-season. The Broncos became the first AFL team to defeat an NFL team, 13-7. The older league still looked upon the AFL, and the Broncos in particular, with ridicule. In fact, before the game, Alex Karras remarked that if the Lions lost to the Broncos, he's walk all the way back to Detroit.

Ironically, before training camp began, Saban re-acquired Cookie Gilchrist from Miami. The two had been together in Buffalo, and Cookie held a great deal of respect for Saban. In fact, so incensed was Cookie about Karras's remark that he challenged Karras to a fight after bumping him into the goal posts after the Detroit game. Sadly, after an outstanding exhibition season, Gilchrist's relationship with Lou Saban and the Broncos

ended in the opening game of the season. Cookie broke his leg in the 26-21 victory over the Patriots, and his career was ended.

But a new career began for another runner, Floyd Little. The highly regarded Little was the club's number one draft choice. His development and that of the Broncos into a first rate football organization went along together, and Lou Saban played a key role in both regards. He designed and had built new training facilities. He insisted on enlarging the seating capacity of the stadium from 32,000 to 50,000. Saban never forgot Cleveland Browns' owner Art Modell's remark that "his team will never play in Denver," once the NFL-AFL merger was fully implemented.

Saban worked long hours; and it can be said that professional football, in its true meaning, arrived in Denver during the Saban era. Visiting teams no longer could complain about the fact that one could stand on a chair in the visitor's dressing room and look over the wall into the Bronco dressing room. Saban made additions to the coaching staff and improvements in scouting techniques. He shuffled

Cornerback Leroy Mitchell defends against Oakland receiver in a 1973 contest.

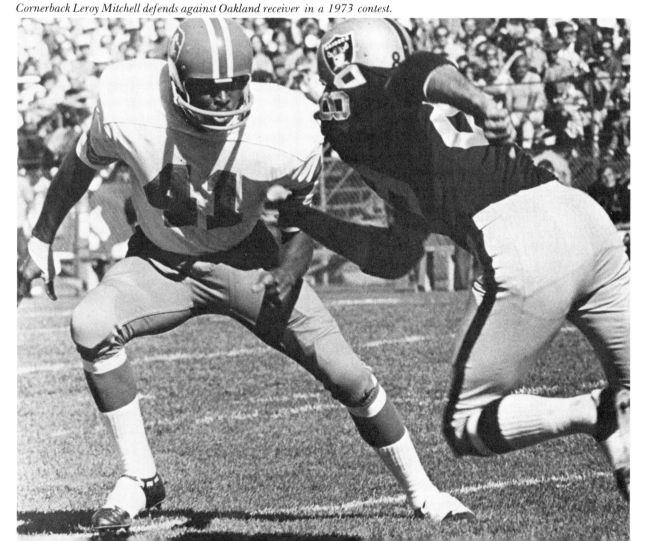

players in and out, week after week, in an effort to upgrade the personnel. His practice sessions were well run and coordinated. He worked his players fairly but hard, always seeking to improve.

Although the Broncos' performance improved on the field, they still weren't winning consistently. Yet, they were no longer considered pushovers. Saban tried hard, maybe too hard, to win. He wanted to make it all happen too quickly. Disappointed at his won-lost record, Saban stepped down as coach after the ninth game of the 1971 season. His record was 20-42-3. He wasn't nearly satisfied. Neither were the fans. Their early love had turned to hate. Saban was booed, hung in effigy, and threatened. He couldn't leave his home unless he was escorted by a member of the Bronco staff. When the 1971 season ended, Saban also resigned as general manager and returned to Buffalo.

Phipps appreciated Saban's efforts. He hated to see him leave.

"When Saban came here in 1966, the organization was in pretty sad shape," Phipps

Floyd Little

would admit at the time. "We looked to him to bring us respectability in all phases of the operation. He has done an absolutely superb job of it."

Now Phipps had to go in search of another coach. This time he turned toward the college scene and selected John Ralston of Stanford University. Ralston joined the Broncos on January 5, 1972, just days after his second consecutive Rose Bowl victory. He would represent still another era of Denver football history.

"We will have a positive approach in everything we do," promised Ralston upon his arrival. "I know I have a lot of learning to do, but I intend to have a flexible program here and to make intelligent decisions. Our goal is winning the Super Bowl. There's no question that we'll make it. The only thing we don't know is how long it will take. My basic philosophy is if you hang in there tough enough, long enough, work hard enough, dedicate yourself with a positive approach, anything can be accomplished."

Ralston took over a team that contained

some highly promising players because Saban had managed to lay a foundation for the Broncos to build on successfully. Through trades and draft choices, the Broncos were not all that lacking in quality players.

One such player was Floyd Little. He was the club's number one choice in 1967, and in 1971 became the first runner in Denver history to gain over 1,000 yards in a single season. He led the NFL in rushing with 1,133 yards after topping the AFC the previous year with 901. In his first five years with the Broncos, Little was not only the star rusher, but also ran back kickoffs and punt returns as well as being utilized as a receiver. Though hampered by injuries his first three years, Little held just about every rushing record imaginable for the Broncos.

Winning the rushing title gave him special satisfaction. Throughout his career he always had to fight the opinions of others that at 5' 10" and 195 pounds, he was too small for professional football.

"When I came up to the pros, everybody said I was too small," Little later remarked. "They still said it after I made it. Every time I went out on the field I had to prove myself again. The same thing happened back in school. People said I'd never get to college. Then they said I'd never graduate. I've always been prejudged. I've had to fight for everything I got."

Even as a rookie with the Broncos in 1967 Little had to overcome frustration and disappointment. He carried the ball less than ten times a game for an average of only 2.9 yards a run. The Broncos were young and inexperienced; and with Little's lack of experience, it was felt that it would be better for the rookie not to play as much.

"You can't learn from carrying the ball one time in a series," explained Little. "You've got to carry the ball three or four times in a row. That's the only way you know what your guards are doing and what the defenses are that we're running against. When you carry the ball four or five times in a row, you can say, 'Well, this guy's playing it this way. If I duck in, I can go outside of him.' You have to set a guy up and whoosh."

But Little had to learn, and he learned well with hard work and discipline. The other

Lyle Alzado didn't always have a beard. He joined the Broncos in 1971, and grew his beard later.

players looked up to him as a leader. He paid the price in learning by getting hit often and hurt almost as much.

"Little couldn't block, catch a pass, or protect himself when he got here," recalled Fred Gehrke, the club's director of personnel. "He ran over his own blockers, and he had to learn to wait for the pulling guards. He was hampered by nagging injuries, which were the results of the beatings he took."

One more than obvious physical characteristic of Floyd Little were his bowlegs. They were more bowed than a cowboy's. As a youngster, Little had tried to straighten his legs by lashing them together at night with belts. Later, he grew to feel that his awkward looking legs were an asset.

"If I have a good stride going and I'm hit from the side, it doesn't knock me down," Little claimed. "My knees won't hit each other because they'll never meet. And if some guy comes in and gives me a pop on the side of the leg, my knee just straightens up into a normal position instead of getting all banged up. Straighten me up, and I'm a good 6'2"."

Steve Ramsey was one of many Denver quarterbacks through the years. In 1977, he was traded to the New York Giants in a deal that brought Craig Morton to Denver.

Defensive end Rich Jackson (87), and linebacker Chip Myrtle discuss strategy on the sidelines.

*Veteran quarterback
Charley Johnson came
to Denver in a 1972
trade. He lasted four
years.*

When Saban announced he was leaving, Little was concerned. He held a deep respect for Saban even though the hard pressed coach pulled him out of a game once for a mistake.

"In leaving, Saban just did something I've been thinking of doing," revealed Little. "I think it's the type of people playing the game now. Every year they've got a different attitude. They don't understand what the game is and what it means. One game I had to almost kill a couple of guys at halftime for their attitude. You can't get them to do anything extra. I don't mind doing it. I want to. It's part of the game. I saw a couple of guys out there who could have done more. It's things like this that make you want to say the hell with it."

In 1975 Little retired after nine years. Denver fans will remember his final game. He ran for 56 yards, scored a touchdown, caught five passes for 94 yards including one for a 66-yard touchdown in a 25-10 victory over the Philadelphia Eagles. Little ended his career as the seventh all-time rusher in NFL history with 6,323 yards. The following year, in ceremonies at Mile High Stadium, the Broncos retired number 44, Little's jersey.

Ralston's first year in 1972 offered promise. Despite another losing season, the Broncos did play much better football, closing out the campaign with two straight victories. Little finished the year with a club record of thirteen touchdowns as the Broncos finished with a 5-9 record.

"We could have had a winning season if we had won the close ones," claimed Ralston. "In some of those losses we weren't mentally prepared, and that was my fault."

In 1973, the Broncos almost put it all together, finishing with their first winning season ever, 7-5-2. What was even more dramatic was the fact that the Broncos could have won the Western Division championship on the final day of the season. Instead, they dropped a heart breaking game to the Oakland Raiders, 21-17. It was a game that many have replayed since.

The Broncos were trailing, 14-10, in the fourth period. They had a fourth and 10 on

As Denver quarterback Charley Johnson looks over the situation, Kansas City linebacker Jim Lynch sets the defense in a 1975 encounter.

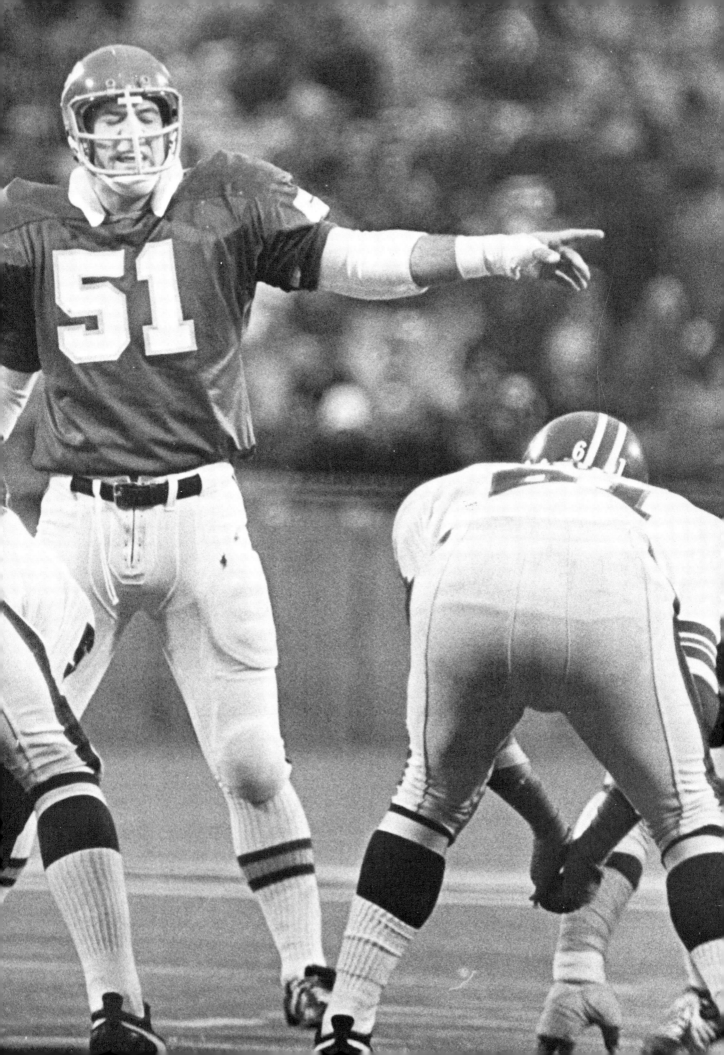

Coach John Ralston congratulates Floyd Little on his last game as a Bronco in 1975.

their own 49. Their defense had been magnificent, holding the Raiders without a second half first down. Instead of punting, Ralston decided on a trick play, one that he had pulled off at Stanford in the 1972 Rose Bowl game against Michigan. But the play was badly mishandled, and rookie Otis Armstrong never got the chance to run with the ball when Joe Dawkins fumbled a bad snap from center. Three plays later, the Raiders scored the winning touchdown.

The 1974 season also ended on a sour note. The Broncos had won three games in a row, scoring 88 points in the process. The final game was against the San Diego Chargers, the worst defensive team in the AFC that year. With a 7-5-1 record, the Broncos were assured of their second straight winning season.

"We want to finish with four in a row and with eight wins for the first time in Bronco history," Ralston said before the game. "That will give us the momentum going into next year, when hopefully we won't let some of those early lapses keep us out of the playoffs."

It never happened. Not only did the Broncos lose, but they failed to score in a mistake filled 17-0 loss.

Still, Ralston's optimism wasn't dulled for the 1975 season. An advocate of the Dale Carnegie School, Ralston had already portrayed himself in Denver as the eternal optimist.

"We learned a lot about playing under the pressures of a contending team," explained Ralston before the 1975 season opened. "We didn't sneak up on anyone in 1974 after our good season the year before. Everyone was pointing for us. We will profit from our mistakes, and we will be better in 1975."

But the Broncos weren't better. They experienced a losing season and finished with a 6-8 record. Injuries contributed a great deal to the team's performance. Most notable was that Armstrong, who led the NFL with 1,407 yards the year before, missed ten games. In all, nineteen starters missed at least one game.

"We developed some problems in 1975 that contributed to our dropping below the .500 mark for the first time since 1972," pointed out Ralston. "Some of them we can correct, but obviously there is little control we have over injuries; and losing the number of players we did was certainly a major factor.

We approached 1975 feeling we were a potential playoff team, and for 1976 we feel even more strongly that way."

But the players were starting to lose confidence. Not in themselves, but in Ralston. They felt that he assigned authority to members of his staff because he was incapable of coaching himself. Before the season began, Ralston called in the players who lived in the Denver area and asked them to voice their complaints. It opened up a Pandora's Box. Players have a habit of mumbling under their breaths to each other. But give them a public forum, and they'll let loose; and that's what the Bronco players did. When Ralston didn't satisfy their complaints, they felt patronized and betrayed. He admitted to the players that quarterback Steve Ramsey wasn't good enough and that he was going to be replaced. However, when training camp opened, Ralston desperately tried to extoll the virtues of Ramsey. By then, the players questioned his integrity.

The players' unrest reached a point where they approached Gehrke about their discontent. Gehrke tried to put out the fire by convincing them that with their easy schedule they could walk into the playoffs. That satisfied them for the moment.

After dropping their opener, the Broncos won the next three games. However, their frustrations became visible in the fifth game of the season against the Houston Oilers. Just before the game, offensive coordinator Max Coley became ill and was taken to the hospital. Without Coley, the team didn't have anyone to turn to. The Broncos could only gain 17 yards in the second half and lost, 17-7.

"That was the turning point," exclaimed Armstrong. "We were very unprepared. John Ralston never took a major role in the offense; and when Max Coley was gone, he didn't know what to do."

But the players knew what to do. Despite the fact that they finished with a 9-5 record, the best record in Denver history, they wanted Ralston removed. Their winning season had occurred, the players claimed, not because of Ralston but in spite of him and because of their pride in themselves. Management was confronted with an explosive situation, a players' mutiny. They couldn't turn their

Injuries cut running back Bobby Anderson's career short with Denver. Anderson played from 1970 through 1973.

backs on it, either. It was too big. On January 31, 1977 Ralston was fired. The next day, February 1, an effervescent redhead, Red Miller, was named coach.

It was only the beginning. . . .

3
ROBERT "RED" MILLER

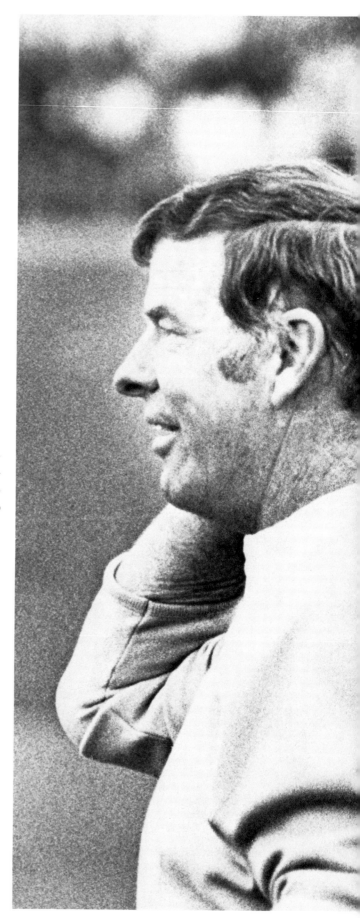

The involvement was there. It was to-tal. It was there right from the be-ginning, in the heat of training camp under a hot July sun. The Bronco players realized from the start that they had a head coach who was part of them. That was the first important thing they noticed about Red Miller, long before they ever played their first game for him, before anyone would ever realize how beautiful the 1977 season would be.

There is a certain drudgery to training camp. The laborious two-a-day workouts, the heat, the exhaustion. For most rookies it is a very serious time. Every bead of perspiration is given with the hope of making the team. It is much like a college training camp, only this time there is no tomorrow. But on the first night at least, there is a time for merriment. It serves as a reminder that tomorrow's dawn will usher in the first of many long, hard days of training.

Actually, it's a ritual that has been part of the training camp scene around the National Football League for years. What it is, basically, is an initiation. The rookie players are in-structed to put on a show for the endearment

Red Miller and quarterback Craig Morton like what's taking place on the field.

41

Miller had the feeling that something good was going to happen in Denver when training camp began in 1978.

of the veteran players. It is somewhat of a theatrical spoof. A rookie will give his name and his alma mater and then proceed to either sing, dance, or recite a poem before the coaching staff and the veterans. It's a "fun thing."

Miller had placed his top two draft choices, guard Steve Schindler from Boston College, and running back Rob Lytle from Michigan, in charge of production. They couldn't refuse the appointments. It was, after all, a way of life; but they did something that perhaps no other rookies had ever done before. They challenged Miller as a way of testing him.

"Shouldn't a rookie head coach be in the rookie show, too?" they asked.

"Get a piano," Miller shot back, "and the rookie head coach will be there."

And he was, too. Miller sat at the piano and pounded out one ragtime number after the other; and with every song, the players cheered. Red Miller was their kind of coach. He had become involved. After the theatricals were over, Miller walked off to a vigorous applause. It was an important moment, and he knew it. They had accepted him; and it was an acceptance that his predecessor, John Ralston, never got. With the cheers ringing in his ears, Miller knew that he had bridged the gap.

Although Miller was new to the Broncos, he wasn't new to Denver although he wasn't exactly a household name. Miller had toiled as the Bronco offensive line coach from 1963 to 1965, when a lot of people were wondering if the Broncos would ever succeed in Denver. But when you don't win, nobody remembers you. The Denver Broncos hadn't won many games those three years. Eight victories will never earn much applause, not for Miller or anyone else.

So, Miller had moved on. Probably nobody ever noticed. Offensive line coaches aren't that recognizable. Moving on was a way of life with Miller. He had begun coaching in the professional ranks in 1960 with the Boston Patriots. Two years later he was in Buffalo and then Denver. Following the 1965 season, Miller moved on again, this time to St. Louis.

But it didn't end there. After St. Louis there was Baltimore. After Baltimore there was Boston again. Miller had gone the full circle. He had started in Boston almost in obscurity in 1960 with a new team in a new league. Thir-

teen years later he was back, this time as line coach and offensive coordinator for the Patriots. It appeared that Miller was destined to be only an assistant throughout his coaching career.

Yet, among his peers he was well respected. He had done some wonderful things. Over the years he had developed about a dozen players who had been named to the Pro Bowl. In his final year at New England in 1976, he made a lot of other people around the NFL take notice. Not only did three of his players make the Pro Bowl, but the Patriots' offense was as explosive as any team in the league. The Patriots scored 376 points which was the second highest total in the NFL. They rushed for 2,957 yards which was the fifth highest total in NFL history. New England topped the league in allowing the fewest quarterback sacks, nineteen. Their quarterback, Steve Grogan, set an NFL record by running for twelve touchdowns.

It was something that Denver's general manager, Fred Gehrke, recognized. Gehrke, too, had been one of the major steps in the Broncos' reorganizational structure. He had been on the Denver staff since 1965 as the player personnel director. In December 1976 Gehrke was elevated to general manager; and the following month, unknown to anybody, Gehrke sent for Miller.

They had a private meeting. All the hopes that Miller had about someday being a head coach dropped as quickly as the snow in Denver. What Gehrke offered Miller was the job as offensive coordinator of the Broncos. Nothing was said about the head coach vacancy that Miller wanted so desperately, the one that he thought Gehrke would offer him. Disappointed, Miller refused. He wouldn't allow himself yet another lateral move.

But Miller wanted the head job, so in a somewhat melancholy mood, he left the meeting in Denver and returned to his home in New England. For two weeks he didn't hear from Gehrke, but Gehrke meanwhile was busy making inquiries about Miller. He talked to Joe Collier, the Broncos' defensive coordinator. Collier had known Miller a long time. They had coached together at Western Illinois for three years, then remained together in the early years of the American Football League, first at Boston and later at Buffalo. When Miller joined the Broncos the first time in 1963, Collier remained at Buffalo. Collier became head coach of the Bills for three years, 1966-1969, before leaving and landing in Denver in 1969. Collier knew the qualities that Miller possessed. He recommended Miller for the head coaching spot. Gehrke respected Collier's recommendation. After all, Collier himself had been a head coach and he, too, could have possibly been a candidate for the job. Things had begun to turn around in Denver, and it was due in a large part to the magnificent work that Collier had accomplished with the defense.

As the days went by with no word from Gehrke, Miller had just about resigned himself to the fact that he would remain with the Patriots. He began to look ahead to the 1977 season after the Patriots had come so close to winning the AFC championship the year before. The idea offered him some consolation. If New England could make it to the Super Bowl in 1977, maybe, just maybe, Miller could get a shot at a head coaching job.

Then one night as he was reviewing some Patriot plays in his play book, the telephone rang.

"I'll bet that's Fred Gehrke," said his wife, Nancy, confidently. "He's going to offer you the Denver job."

"How do you know?" asked Miller. "It could be anybody."

"Just wait and see," she replied, as she got up to answer the phone. It was indeed Gehrke. She smiled as she handed Miller the telephone.

"Since you wouldn't come to Denver as the offensive coordinator, how would you like to come as the head coach?" asked Gehrke.

"You got a deal," answered Miller.

It was that quick. Miller didn't even ask anything about a contract or how much he would be paid. He was that happy. It was also his style. The terms would come later. All he knew was that he was going back to Denver, only this time as the head coach. He had paid his dues. For seventeen years he had been a journeyman assistant coach around the NFL. Now he had a head coaching job of his own.

Yet, it wasn't a normal situation. Miller had replaced a coach who had finished with a 9-5 record the season before. Winning coaches are rarely fired in the NFL. Besides, Ralston had been quite popular with the Bronco fans for at least providing them with three winning seasons during his five years as coach. But the players' rebellion was too much to ignore, too deep and serious not to make a change.

Miller himself called the situation unique, and he went about finding out where it was all at. The first thing he did when he arrived in Denver was to analyze the Broncos' performance during the 1976 season. After studying game films for hours at a time and poring through page after page of statistics, he characterized the season as "peculiar."

"The Broncos were one of the highest scoring teams, but the way they scored a lot of their points was peculiar," he observed. "Four of the touchdowns were scored by the punt return squad, four more by the defense on interceptions, and another two on fumble returns by the defense. That's over 25 per cent of our scoring, and it's not realistic to expect that many points from these sources.

"However, instead of rebuilding from a team that was 1-13 or 2-12 as many head coaches must do, I inherited a team that was coming off the most successful season in the history of the franchise. We had some very talented players. Overall, we had a squad that needed a player here or some improvement there to become a championship team.

"The first trade I made was to get a quarterback. I didn't hesitate in trading Steve Ramsey for Craig Morton. I needed a veteran who had been there to get us there again. We also made some other trades that we felt would help us—Mike Montler, the center, for one, and Bernard Jackson, the safety, for another. Andy Mauer, the tackle, was still another. Then, too, we made a fine draft pick in Rob Lytle.

"But I didn't feel any extra pressure in taking over a winning team. Sure, I felt the fans would expect us to keep right on winning, to possibly improve on a 9-5 record. Still, I knew the best way to approach the challenge would be to take one game at a time, and do the best I could. What else could you do? I wasn't going to create a pressure situation within myself. I was just going to do the best that I could.

"I've been in the league eighteen years and

In his very first season as head coach, Red Miller brought Denver its first American Football Conference championship.

have been coaching twenty-eight, and I have learned one important thing. The winning edge is very small. I have discovered that most games are won or lost in the fourth quarter. So I made up my mind that if I became a head coach, I would go with that philosophy. If we stay close, the fourth quarter belongs to us.

"Things were different in Denver since the time I was last there. In the first place, the owners had come out and said, 'Hey, let's build a winner.' Secondly, the whole city had begun to get behind their Broncos. Third, the organization had expanded. There were more people working in the organization now; and they were better people, too, and more competent. But the players are the team's most important assets. My second job in coaching was as assistant coach to a man named Art Keller at Carthage College in Carthage, Illinois. Keller had been with the college a long time and stayed on as coach when the college moved to Kenosha, Wisconsin. He was a Christian man and, in my book, a great man. Keller could take a bunch of kids that you would swear could never make a football team. He would take them and teach them. In three weeks he would mold them like putty. He won so many games that you wouldn't believe possible. In the three years I spent there, I think we lost only two games.

"But besides football knowledge, he knew how to handle people. He made face to face contact with each player every day. That's one thing I made a promise to do if I ever became a head coach. I don't mean just to say hello to a player but to talk to them, say a few words, and ask How is this? . . . We have to do this today . . . How do you like the way we are going? . . . You're doing a good job . . . Hey, you need to get better. Things like that.

"That's one part to coaching. The other is teaching. A lot of coaches make the mistake of not knowing or not realizing or not caring about the teaching part. When you get right down to it, coaching *is* teaching. If you are not a good teacher, you sure as hell aren't a good coach."

During training camp, the Bronco players saw how intense a teacher Miller was. One afternoon he demonstrated a blocking technique to Claudie Minor, the team's offensive tackle. Minor is 6'4" and 260 pounds. Miller is

not quite six feet and just about 200 pounds. In full pads, Minor looks even bigger. They lined up against each other, charged, and butted heads. Miller sustained a cut over his left eye that began to bleed quite freely.

Instead of walking over to the sidelines, Miller told Minor to line up again. He wanted to make sure that Minor had it right. Minor took a look at Miller's eye.

"Coach, you're bleeding," he exclaimed.

"Don't worry about it," replied Miller.

"Coach, I'm sorry," replied Minor.

"It's okay," said Miller.

"Gee, coach, maybe you ought to see the trainer," pleaded Minor.

Miller wiped the blood away.

"I'm fine," he said. "Now get back down and make sure you have that blocking technique correct."

That's Miller's way. He'll teach and coach football all week; but on Sunday, he'll play it. He is easily recognizable on the sidelines. He's an emotional person who is involved in the game. Miller wants to be in on every play. He does so by means of a head set strapped on his head. At times during a game, he is talking to an offensive coach high up in the press box. Then, he simply flips a button and talks defense to one of his defensive coaches.

Although he is the head coach, Miller is still the team's offensive coordinator. He sends in each play during a game to the quarterback, preferably by alternating his running backs. In play calling, Miller is not the ultimate word. He allows the quarterback the opportunity to change his play. But he brings his point across by saying that if you do change the play, make sure you have the right one. Obviously, Miller's plays aren't changed much at all, if any, during the course of a game.

"It takes a lot of pressure off the quarterback," offers Miller. "I tell him I'm going to send in the plays but that he can rub one off any time and call his own. I tell him he'll never be second-guessed if he rubs it off but to just have a reason in mind for anything he does. So, the quarterback is the boss of the field, the leader of the offense. I'm just helping him out.

"I can see the field better than a quarterback. It's kind of like a big chess game. You have to have kind of an overview of the whole field and what's going on. What I try to visualize is the position of my team in relation to the magic line that runs down the middle of the field—the 50-yard line. After you've studied this game long enough, you learn that there is a definite correlation between field position and winning or losing.

"Field position is best described by pluses and minuses. Your chances of scoring from minus territory, which is beyond the fifty, are far less than they are from plus territory; and they increase tremendously as your position improves. The fifty is the magic line. But there is a gray area in there on the other side of it, and that's the area you have to control.

"Field position can be controlled on both offense and defense. The most successful teams do it with defense. I approach a game with two prevailing ideas. The first is never give the other team possession in our minus territory. The second is to try and take the ball away from them in their minus territory.

"Most mistakes that occur during a football game are made on offense. It is much easier to control field position with defense. In the NFL you start with a strong defense. You study the history of the game, and the most successful teams have always had the strong defenses. Only rarely do you find an exception, like Oakland's team in 1976 which was more of a super offensive team."

That was another problem that Miller had to overcome when he took over as the Broncos' field boss. The team was distinctly split between offense and defense. The defense had established itself as a championship one, and they were easily the favorites of the Denver partisans. Their popularity resulted in the frenzied establishment of the "Orange Crush" defense. When the defense played well as they did throughout most of the 1976 season and still lost, they looked with disdain at the offense for not scoring enough points.

So, Miller had to bring the team back together as one. He acknowledged that the defense played together as a team; but on offense, it was more of an individual effort. He had to convince the offense that by making personal sacrifices they would contribute to the overall success of the team's performance.

Miller truly believed that no player can go all out for sixty minutes, and he wanted his players to go all out whenever they were on

Miller, kneeling, and his championship staff. From left, Myrel Moore, Bob Gambold, Fran Polsfoot, Babe Parilli, Paul Roach, Marv Braden, Joe Collier, Ken Gray, and Stan Jones.

the field. He had a theory that he sold his players on. It involved substituting running backs, wide receivers, and defensive linemen at various times throughout the game. In that way he felt that he would have an edge during the fourth quarter when most games were won or lost.

"I asked the players to alter their egos a little and think about what's good for the Broncos," revealed Miller. "The best kind of football player is one who can tell himself, 'I'm the greatest,' and mean it, and at the same time be a 100 per cent team player. When you have an athlete who has both great confidence in his own ability and a realization that he can't do it alone, you've got a football player.

"Our philosophy is hard, aggressive, error-free football based on running the ball. But I don't believe in banging my head against the wall. If I have to throw on every down, I will. We want everybody going like hell on every down, which is hard to do when you're out there for sixty minutes. We want everybody playing because this is a team game. Every guy should feel he's a part of things. My approach to this game is team unity. I don't care much for individual records. What we want are team results.

"We don't go down much in quality when we substitute. We make up for it by confusing the other team with different pass rushers. Of all the people on a football team, the offensive backs take the most shots. We alternate four backs, first to keep fresh people on the field, and second because football is a game in which you want to come on in the fourth quarter. You want to have something left.

"I'm not on an ego trip. Unfortunately, a great many other coaches are. Players make this game. That's where it's at. I think of myself as a players' coach. I'm just here to help them perform better.

"One thing, though, we play with a lot of emotion; we play as hard as we can all of the time, through the fourth quarter, and make it ours. We want to make things happen in the fourth quarter. The winning edge is somewhere. Where? It's usually in the mind of the individual player. If I can get to that mind and tell him the fourth quarter belongs to us and have him legitimately believe that, then I've got something going for us."

What Denver has going for them is Red Miller. He is a fighter, a feisty alley cat who wouldn't back down from a challenge no matter what the odds. He told his players what he wanted, and showed them how he wanted it done. No fancy frills. That isn't his style. He is as subtle as a punch in the mouth.

Miller is refreshingly human. In a sport in which some coaches are unapproachable and other possess large egos, Miller is as unassuming as a bale of hay under a hot August sun. Take the time he was returning to his office after a practice session and was approached by a man who gave him a rather large turquoise ring. It was shaped like a football and had Miller's name engraved on the side.

"Thank you very much," said the surprised Miller.

There were others waiting for him that day. There were two women and a man who was holding a small black and white dog on a leash.

"Whatta you have there?" inquired Miller, looking down and smiling at the dog.

"We would like you to see our dog," remarked one of the ladies. "He can hike a football."

"He can what?" exclaimed Miller. "This I gotta see."

Unpretentiously, Miller led the two women and the man through the locker room, much to the surprise of the players, some of whom were half undressed.

"Don't look, ladies," ordered Miller. "Just follow me."

The group marched through the locker room and onto the practice field. As Miller looked on, the man set the dog down; and one of the ladies removed a miniature football from her purse. Unhesitantly, the little dog approached the football, put his front paws on top of it, and hiked it through his hind legs.

"That's the damnedest thing I ever saw," laughed Miller.

The dog went through the routine a couple of more times. Each time Miller shook his head, smiling at each snap the dog performed. Then with a twinkle in his eye he said, "Sorry, I don't think we can use him. He doesn't get enough height on the ball. Besides, how could I tell our regular center he is being replaced by a dog?"

It is this kind of human warmth that Miller transmitted to his players. As much time as he spent at the blackboard dwelling on X's and O's, he always felt that the players should enjoy football. Often during practice sessions he would add a trick play, like a double reverse, to startle the defense as most of the squad bent over with laughter. That's Red Miller.

"Every week I'd toss two or three special plays of that kind into the game plan," disclosed Miller. "I've always kept a book of gimmick plays, and I thumb through it occasionally. They're partly to make football more fun for the players. They take a little extra time to practice, but you have to have some fun in this game."

Miller's idea of fun was to drink a few beers with his players during the time he bounced around the country as an assistant coach. Most owners frowned on this sort of fraternization and it probably cost Miller a head coaching job along the way. Naturally, such antics have a way of being blown up out of proportion. But Miller felt that by having a beer with his players it afforded him an opportunity to establish a closer relationship with them; and as long as he got results, then who was anyone to render criticism.

"I was a free spirit," admitted Miller. "I operated on a different wave length than most coaches. I was highly excitable, and I'd get down on the line with the players. I think some owners felt that I was too exuberant. Too many coaches believe that you only play the game with your head. I happen to feel the opposite way. I believe you play the game with emotion as well as your head. Other owners and coaches couldn't identify with this."

But somehow Gehrke did. He felt that Miller's chemistry would be just what the Broncos needed. It was also a chemistry that Miller exuded to the Bronco fans. Before the 1977 season ever began, Miller publicly implored the Denver fans to support the Broncos in no uncertain terms.

"I want you to turn Mile High Stadium into a snake pit," he demanded. "I want you to yell and scream your heads off. I want opponents to remember what it is like to play in Denver. I want them to be afraid to come here to meet the Broncos."

It was the start of "Broncomania." It probably had always been there, in the bosoms of the Denver faithful, but Miller intensified it. The Bronco faithful had waited a long time to be heard, and suddenly Miller was their clarion. He not only was a players' coach but a fans' coach, too. One that they could relate to.

Through it all, Miller hasn't changed. Maybe he doesn't have time to lift a few beers with his players, but that's only because he is working longer hours. There isn't much time for even a beer after you have put in sixteen or eighteen hours. That's what head coaching is all about. Time and detail.

"I don't think I've changed too much over the years," conceded Miller. "I feel good that I can say I've paid my dues, and I feel right about behing a head coach.

"The challenge was to convince the Broncos that the way to win was not as individuals or as an individual group but as a team. They needed a commitment to the idea of sacrificing personal glory for the good of the team. Broncomania was a great part of what happened to us in 1977. And I mean all of us. I've got an orange telephone, an orange radio, orange shower curtains, even an orange toilet seat. I'm putting together a collection of the stuff in my basement."

The one thing Red Miller wanted to collect was the Vince Lombardi Trophy. In Super Bowl XII, he missed. But if he ever does win a Super Bowl in the years ahead, don't be surprised if he paints the coveted trophy orange.

4
CRAIG MORTON

There were many before him. In the eighteen years that the franchise had existed, the Denver Broncos had twenty-five quarterbacks. It's unheard of. In fact, it reached a point where it became a trivia joke around the National Football League, like, "Name at least ten quarterbacks who played for Denver." Most older teams don't have that many quarterbacks in the entire history of their franchise. But in all the years the Denver Broncos were searching for an identity, they were also looking for an established quarterback. It is ironical that finding one would be achieved with finding the other. Before the Broncos ever reported to training camp for the 1977 season, they had their 26th quarterback. Only this time it was different. They were on the verge of gaining the recognition they had vainly sought all those years. They were hoping Craig Morton would finally succeed in getting it for them.

It was a strange parallel. At the seasoned age of thirty-four, Morton himself was seeking recognition. It had escaped him throughout his twelve years in the league. He had some good years at Dallas and some strange ones

The first trade that Miller completed after he joined the Broncos was for quarterback Craig Morton from the New York Giants.

with the New York Giants. His somewhat checkered career made him an enigma. He had the size, 6'4", the arm, and the intelligence; yet he somehow never managed to earn the recognition as an outstanding quarterback. Personally, it pained him. Professionally, maybe he tried too hard to win his place in the sun. Whatever the reason, Morton was easily identified as the Broncos' 26th quarterback. There were cynics who chided that he wouldn't be the last even before the regular season ended.

Morton has learned to take the raps, and there had been many in those twelve years. Morton deserved better. Perhaps it was his good looks and free spirit that incensed his detractors. A charmer, Morton had once been quite a ladies' man. At times his performance on the field was often measured to his lifestyle off it. He had an apartment in Dallas, another in New York, and a ski place in Aspen, Colorado. If he sounded like a member of the jet set, he really was. Morton enjoyed the best of two worlds: The football season and what life offered after the season was over. He was intelligent enough to make a distinction between the two.

As an All-American at the University of California in 1964, Craig Morton was considered a prime pro prospect. In football jargon, a blue chip. The Dallas Cowboys had no doubts about Morton's abilities. Through computers and first hand reports and confidential files, the Cowboys' organization is known for thoroughly researching its prospective athletes. Morton easily fulfilled their high standards. In the 1965 college draft, the Cowboys made Morton their Number 1 selection. coach Tom Landry. The only coach in the eighteen year history of the franchise, the taciturn Landry believes that it takes five years to develop as an NFL quarterback. So, when Morton joined the Cowboys for the 1965 season, he began a strange association. Don Meredith was the Cowboys' established quarterback. But Jerry Rhome was also there, and Morton was looked upon as the third quarterback. It was obvious that Morton wouldn't get a chance to play much, and he didn't. In his first two years with the Cowboys, he appeared in only ten games and threw sixty-one passes.

In the next two years, Landry employed his quarterbacks on a game to game basis, although it was conceded that Meredith still ranked as number one. But Meredith wasn't without his share of detractors. In a wide open game of "who's the quarterback," there were many arguments for all three, Meredith, Rhome, and Morton. Finally, when the 1968 season ended, it filtered down to a choice between Meredith and Morton. If each felt insecure, it was quite understandable.

Before the 1969 season began, Meredith had had enough. Although Rhome was long gone, Roger Staubach, whom the Cowboys had drafted as a future in 1964, was released from the Navy and reported to training camp. The thought of another quarterback version of musical chairs was too much for Meredith. At the still young age of thirty-one, he retired, even though he had helped the Cowboys reach the playoffs in two of the last three years of his career.

So, Landry handed the ball to Morton. After all, Morton was ready to start his fifth year in the league. The timing was perfect, and for a while, so was Morton. In his first three games, he amazed everyone by leading the NFL in passing, hitting on over 70 percent of his attempts. However, in the fourth game of the season, Morton injured his right shoulder. Despite the painful injury, one which affected his throwing, Morton continued at quarterback for the remainder of the 1969 season. As soon as the season was over, he underwent surgery.

Shoulder operations to a passer are very serious ones indeed. When Morton returned for the 1970 campaign, he had trouble throwing the ball. He also had a new worry. Staubach had taken a crash course in becoming an NFL quarterback and loomed as a threat to his job. When the season opened, Landry decided to go with Staubach as his number one quarterback. The genuine feeling was that he was doing so in order to give Morton time to fully recover.

In the third game of the season, Staubach threw two interceptions against the St. Louis Cardinals. Landry pulled the erratic Staubach and inserted Morton. It turned out to be the right move, whether by actual design or Landry's luck. Morton took a staggering Cowboy team and led them right to Super Bowl V,

despite playing all year with a painful right elbow which he injured earlier in the season. In an error-filled game, the Baltimore Colts defeated the Cowboys, 16-13, on a last second field goal. The winning kick was made possible by an interception by linebacker Mike Curtis. Morton had attempted to hit running back Dan Reeves with a pass. Reeves leaped, and the ball went through his hands and into those of Curtis. Later, Reeves admitted that he should have caught the ball.

Five weeks after the Super Bowl mishap, Morton wrote a guest column for the *Dallas Times Herald*. It displayed a deep sensitivity:

Coming from the University of California at Berkeley in 1965 and being the number one draft pick of the Dallas Cowboys seemed to fulfill many goals of a young man.

Thinking that it would be a short time before I was the Cowboys' starting quarterback, I approached the season with as much enthusiasm as a hungry dog at mealtime.

I was, of course, told that it would take five years to be an effective quarterback in the NFL. But I was there to disprove the theory which I later came to realize fully under Mr. Landry.

In my first season I got to play quite a bit when Don Meredith was benched in favor of a shuttle system involving Jerry Rhome and myself. The system wasn't particularly effective so Coach Landry decided to show his confidence in one man for the remainder of the year—Meredith.

For the first time we became a winning team and ended up in Miami for the Playoff Bowl.

My second through fourth years were devoted to learning and waiting out some very, very frustrating moments.

In my fourth year an unusual but persistent creature arose from the stands of the Cotton Bowl. His name was "Boobird." He started in small numbers, but as time passed he multiplied into thousands. From within these Boobirds came the birth of the Morton supporters. These seemingly increased—as did the Meredith Boobirds.

How times have changed. The Meredith Boobirds have switched their allegiance to Morton, and many of the Morton supporters now have chosen another.

I have come to realize the deep hurt and frustration that Don once felt and which may have put an early end to a great career. At first I felt all the personal things that booing represents. I accepted them and made this rejection a personal challenge.

Despite my personal commitment, injuries greatly affected my throwing. First came the dislocated shoulder with which I played eleven games in 1969 and became the fifth-ranked quarterback in the NFL. Then, in 1970, I played some eight games with a bruised and infected elbow and again wound up the Number 5 quarterback in pro football.

I could never really accept being called the worst quarterback in football and receiving much of the criticism and blame for losses which in my mind weren't all my fault.

I do not write to complain, but to relay to the fans the absurdity that surrounds the personal life of a celebrity.

Many people consider me aloof and carefree. Some say I need a wife to settle me down, still more consider me a playboy. Others had voiced added opinions.

Perhaps in others' eyes I do touch some part of these typecastings. But when I look at myself I see a sensitive, quiet, dedicated person who enjoys people and has always given as he has received.

I probably have become more withdrawn the last two years because of many unpleasant moments in public. I know all this goes with being an athlete, and I accept it as such. I have accepted criticism and blame without comment, and I have been the first to praise others where praise is due. I have always done these things and will continue to do so as it is a part of my real self.

The past year was without question one of great frustration. First, being benched was a blow. But it was one from which I had seen Don come back. I was booed soundly, but accepted it for I had seen Don fight against it.

I heard and received unbelievable words and letters, but learned to accept them because another— Don—had come before me. You see, those who criticized forgot that they weren't original. I had studied under the best and was prepared for their unknowledgeable forecasts, bits of "inside information," and "real scoop of victory and defeat."

I did achieve something with the help of a great football team that only a handful of quarterbacks have accomplished: a trip to the Super Bowl. I am extremely proud to have been a part of this, and it will be the highlight of my career until the day of victory in this game.

I love Dallas and its people, but I will not change my beliefs or goals for those who scorn and criticize me. You see, I enjoy my own company. Although I do have many faults, as all of us do, I try to understand

them and correct them just as the birds who hover above and about the Cotton Bowl.

In conclusion, I have one prediction that will shock some, be laughed at by others, and perhaps agreed upon by a few. But it will not elude me.

Craig Morton will be the best quarterback in football.

Morton underwent surgery again. This time on his right elbow. But when he reported to training camp for the 1971 season, he wasn't given the number one job back. Landry said the job was open, and it was up to either Morton or Staubach to take it. After a few sleepless nights, Landry awarded the starting spot to Staubach. If he hadn't, Staubach revealed that he would have asked to be traded. So, he stayed and led Dallas to a 24-3 triumph over the Miami Dolphins in Super Bowl VI.

Naturally, Staubach was now entrenched as the team's regular quarterback. But in a 1972 pre-season game against the Los Angeles Rams, Staubach injured his right shoulder and immediately was operated on. He wasn't expected back for at least three months, and Morton was asked to lead the Cowboys again. He got them into the playoffs as a NFC wild card team. But in the opening playoff game against the San Francisco 49ers, the Cowboys were in trouble. Trailing 28-16 in the fourth quarter, Morton threw a bomb to wide receiver Bob Hayes. It looked like a certain touchdown until Hayes dropped the ball. In the next series of downs, Landry sent Staubach into the game, and he miraculously pulled out a 30-28 victory. However, in the NFC title game the following week against the Washington Redskins, the Cowboys were dismal in a 26-3 loss.

Reverting to form, Landry threw open the quarterback job once again during the 1973 pre-season. The competition was extremely close. In the final exhibition game against Miami, Morton played well and felt he had won the job again. But when the season started, Landry turned to Staubach. Like Meredith before him, Morton had had it. He asked the Cowboys to trade him, preferably to Denver. After six games of the 1974 season, the Cowboys did trade Morton; only instead of Denver, they sent him to the New York Giants.

Morton welcomed the trade. He finally felt that he had a team of his own. As soon as he joined the Giants, he took over as the club's starting quarterback. In the next two years, Morton learned that New York was not Dallas. The Giants were a losing team. They had a new coach, Bill Arnsparger, who had been the brilliant defensive coordinator for the world champion Miami Dolphins in 1973. But Arnsparger's defensive genius couldn't help the offense. The team appeared to be lost and floundering. Just after the midway point of the 1976 season, Arnsparger was fired.

During his two and a half years with the Giants, the team experienced one losing season after the other. When a team loses, the quarterback is the first one who is pointed at. The boobirds that Morton heard in Dallas were now flying around New York. It wasn't justified. The Giants lacked many quality players on offense. Neither Morton nor even a Ken Stabler could overcome it on his own. Once again, Morton was victimized by a situation. And once more, he hoped for a trade, hopefully to a contending team.

Red Miller made it possible. The first trade he made about a month after he took over in Denver was to obtain Craig Morton. All he had to yield in return was quarterback Steve Ramsey, who had been equally booed in Denver, and a future draft choice. Miller didn't hesitate. He didn't exactly excite everybody in Denver with the trade, but he knew what he was getting in Morton. Miller had been around as an offensive coordinator too long not to recognize a quality quarterback like Morton.

"I knew that Craig had experience, which was what we needed at the position," explained Miller. "But I also knew that he had a great throwing arm. I didn't believe all the criticism. Why, he's a quality player and always has been. You just had to understand the circumstances he was involved in. I was pleased as punch to get him.

"When he came to meet me for the first time, I approached him one on one. I sat down with him privately and laid it on the table to him. I told him we were going to do it together. I stressed that it was an exciting thing for him, because he rarely would get this kind of opportunity this late in his career. But I emphasized the first thing he had to do was win the job because I wasn't going to hand it to

Morton rolls out to pass in opening AFC Playoff Game against the Pittsburgh Steelers.

Oakland's David Rowe tries to make matters uncomfortable for Morton.

him. The second thing I told him was the team desperately needed leadership offensively. They had it defensively, but the offense didn't know how to win as a team. Craig looked at me and said, 'Coach, this has been a great meeting.'

"Craig had met Chuck Fairbanks about a month or two before he sat down with me. They had dinner together, and Chuck told him all about me. So he was somewhat prepared. Craig was somewhat in a turmoil after being traded to another club, but he was more at ease with himself after our meeting. And, he adopted a Christian-like attitude about life; and I think that has helped him, too. He definitely has a better outlook about everything."

He certainly approached his responsibilities with more vigor and zeal. When training camp arrived, Morton was ready mentally. He had turned his back on the past and was looking toward a new future—Denver, its surroundings, a new team. There were three other quarterback candidates waiting to challenge him, and he won out over all three. After he was with his new teammates for only six weeks, he was elected their offensive captain. That's quite unusual, but that's the impact Morton made on the rest of the team. They felt that in Morton they had someone who could lead them to the Super Bowl. It was somewhat of the same feeling the club had felt during the 1976 season, but there wasn't anyone around then to lead them.

"When we got Morton, we thought it could be a repeat of the incredible Y.A. Tittle story," said general manager Fred Gehrke. He was referring to the time in 1961 when the New York Giants obtained the aging Tittle from the San Francisco Giants. Tittle went on to lead the Giants to three conference championships.

"We had Morton rated very highly," Gehrke recalls, "and we also felt he had the supporting cast that he needed—better runners, better receivers, a better offensive line, a better defensive unit, and a better field goal kicker. Mostly, we thought of him as a leader; and from the first day he arrived, he has been the leader of our offensive unit. It wasn't long before he was voted our offensive captain."

Steelers' Dwight White (78) and Joe Greene (75) put pressure on Morton.

The Broncos held Morton in higher regard than Giant teammates had. Even the Giant fans were disenchanted, booing Morton unmercifully when he actually didn't deserve it. He alone couldn't carry a weak offense. Until John McVay took over as head coach, Morton had been working with an offense devised by Arnsparger.

"It was very frustrating for Craig," disclosed a close friend of Morton's. "He was the victim of a front office that didn't bring in any experienced wide receivers, and the victim of a coach who had no real offensive system or philosophy. Arnsparger was trying to use the Miami Dolphins' offense without the personnel that made it work. The more Craig was unable to produce big plays, the more frustrated he became. This plus the fact that the Giants were so used to losing, they didn't know how to win."

The New York experience was hard on Morton. Fans cursed him and threw garbage at him. The city that he loved, the night spots, the good restaurants, the Broadway plays, the plush apartment he lived in, suddenly turned into a nightmare. He became somewhat of a loner. He kept out of the bright lights and moved around only in the company of close friends. The Giants couldn't win, and he couldn't make them win. He took the blame for all their deficiencies and it weighed heavily on his shoulders.

"The time I spent in New York I learned a lot and enjoyed a lot, but playing football there was not one of the high points of my career," Morton confesses. "It was two and one half years of total frustration. We all tried hard, but we never could get any stability. On offense, we were very predictable. We also had a lot of injuries and a lot of people who came from nowhere and played first string for us. I realize now I tried to do too much with the Giants. One guy can't turn a team around. The New York Giants wouldn't have won the last few years no matter who was playing quarterback. To win, you have to be surrounded by good people."

That's what Morton found at Denver. In 1976, the Broncos finished with a 9-5 record. Their defense was established, but they needed an experienced quarterback to make their offense click. That's the opportunity that

Morton had. He made it happen. He finished the 1977 season as the second best quarterback in the AFC behind Bob Griese of the Dolphins. Stretching it further, he was ranked fourth in the entire NFL. One can't get much better than that, especially if one winds up in the Super Bowl.

"I think I needed vindication," reflected Morton after the season. "I am the same player I was before, and I have no regrets about what's happened along the line. But people don't realize that just when I was going great in Dallas, I hurt my right shoulder on a play where Atlanta's Tommy Nobis tore up his knee. That was in 1969; and the doctors transplanted about twelve inches of tendon from my toe, foot, and leg into my shoulder. They did a great job, but it took three years before I was right again. Then after I had a big year in 1972 with 185 completions for 2,396 yards and fifteen touchdowns, I hurt my elbow. I had a good year in New York in 1974; but when your team averages three years of pro experience, it's hard to win in a division with St. Louis, Dallas, and Washington. I remember when the trade was made. My dad called me and said Coach John McVay was trying to get hold of me. I called McVay, and he said that they had just traded me to Denver. I said 'Great,' and that was it. I was disappointed I didn't accomplish what I wanted to in New York."

But he did in Denver in his first year with the team. It was quite an accomplishment simply because there is a certain amount of pressure involved in improving on a 9-5 record. But that's what Morton and Miller did together, the two new kids in town.

"The first time Morton came into a huddle he was in total charge," remembers wide receiver Jack Dolbin. "He called the plays with complete confidence. It was that way all season. We were third and 3 at Oakland once, and he called a run. Normally, that might be a pass play. He just looked at the right side linemen and said, 'Fellas, it's up to you. You've got to come off the ball.' We made it. He throws a very catchable ball with a lot of smoke on it. You can really feel it hitting your hands. He has another ability a receiver likes. He throws an 'on time' ball. That's a great feeling for receivers."

Denver was a spa for Morton. He found new life. He always knew how to win. Now he made it happen. Football was fun again. When you win, it's always that way.

"I think I'm a little more patient now than I once was," Morton says. "I feel that here I've got a great defense and great special teams, and I'm not going to take any chances. Let the defense play until we get better field position. This is more or less what Red Miller has instituted in me. Don't make mistakes. Be patient. Let's play defense; and when we get an opportunity, let's put the ball in there.

"If it's between getting sacked and trying to force the ball in there, I'll take the sack. I think that's probably been responsible for a lot of the traps that I had before.

"I've also developed a closeness to the Lord. It was through my wife, Susan, really. It happened when we were going together, before we got married. You know, people accept the Lord for different reasons. I certainly didn't accept Him in order to be the number one quarterback. That wasn't my purpose at all. I accepted Him because I believe. There were no conditions at all."

There are a lot of people who believe in Craig Morton now.

Speedy Rick Upchurch is a double threat either as a wide receiver or as a kick return specialist.

5
THE OFFENSE

I t was a new and totally different approach. It had never been tried before. In a very real sense it was the beginning of another era. Red Miller was a new coach with a new philosophy, and he had to convince the players that it would work. What he wanted the players to do was to pull back on their separate egos and play team ball. Individual goals would no longer matter. Everyone had to contribute. The word "regular" would practically be removed from Miller's vocabulary. What he wanted each player to do was to step back and decide what was best, not for him but for the entire team. Miller's concept wouldn't be an easy one or a very popular one to relate to.

He realized that the defense felt that way, but the offense was something else again. That's where most of the headline-making statistics are kept. Individual performances are measured in yards, but Miller wasn't concerned about 1,000-yard seasons or 100-yard games. He was much more concerned with the bottom line. If two backs could produce 100 yards in a game, it would be just as effective as if only one had done it. Miller wanted to inject more versatility into the Denver offense by alternating his running backs. He strongly believed that four or five or even six fresh backs would be more productive than the standard two or three employed by other teams.

But to make it work, to get the players to believe in his approach, Miller had to have a leader on offense. Up to that time the Broncos never had one. Without a leader on offense, one who would take charge on the field during a game, there was no unifying factor. Miller had to have a leader, someone the players would respond to. Miller had gotten his leader when he traded quarterback Steve Ramsey for quarterback Craig Morton of the New York Giants. It was a strange union. Miller, after being around the NFL for seventeen years, was getting his first chance at a head coaching job nearing the age of fifty. Morton, at the advancing age of thirty-four, was being reborn high up in the Rockies.

"I appreciate the opportunity, and I'll work my butt off," was how Morton greeted the trade. "Nobody ever hands you anything on a platter in the NFL. I know the Broncos have two fine young quarterbacks in Craig Penrose and Norris Weese. They'll be competing for my job, and that's the way it should be. I think my knowledge will help bring them along to where one of them will eventually replace me. My attitude is that I can do a lot for the Broncos, and they can do a lot for me."

Miller had decided that he would send in the plays. Morton didn't disagree with him. Perhaps the more difficult part was to impress the rest of the offense with his belief that the team, not individual players, was the core of the offense. The key would be in convincing Otis Armstrong, a speedy running back who had experienced and enjoyed two 1,000-yard seasons his first four years with the Broncos.

Armstrong was considered one of the premier runners in the NFL. He was drafted by the Broncos on the first round of the 1973 college draft. In his rookie year, he watched and learned as Floyd Little did most of the running. In the fourteen games in which he appeared during his rookie season, he only carried the ball twenty-six times for 90 yards. He hardly broke a sweat.

But in 1974, he took over. He was the leading runner in the NHL as he established a Denver single season rushing record with 1,407

Running back Otis Armstrong joined the Broncos in 1973 as the club's number one draft choice. However, he hardly played that year. In 1974, he led the NFL in rushing with 1,407 yards to establish a Denver record. In 1976 he again ran for a thousand yards—1,007.

yards. He was the new hero in Denver. And all the while, Little, whom he displaced, offered him advice and comfort. It was quite an inspirational setting, the new star and the one who was about to retire.

Armstrong particularly remembers the Sunday that the Broncos were playing the Houston Oilers in Houston during the memorable 1974 season. It was the next to last week of the season, and Armstrong was having a big day; and he was doing it against a defense that was designed to stop him. Houston linebacker Greg Bingham had been assigned to key on Armstrong. It was an ironical confrontation because Armstrong and Bingham had been rivals in high school and teammates at Purdue.

Late in the contest, Armstrong trotted wearily over to the Denver bench. He approached Little.

"Hey, I'm dead tired," he said. "Why don't you come in and give me a rest the next time we get the ball?"

"Are you hurt?" asked Little.

"No, just tired," sighed Armstrong.

"Then get back out there," snapped Little. "When you get tired, you go as far as you can. Tell yourself that you're better than ever. Give it all you got."

When the Broncos went on offense, Armstrong went back on the field. And he ran and ran until he finished the game with 183 yards. He broke Little's single game rushing mark against a rugged Oiler defense. Little had shown the youthful Armstrong how to catch his breath and at the same time learn how to get the tough yards on a second effort.

"Floyd helped me more when he wasn't playing," remembers Armstrong. "He used to tell me to rest when I came off the field. I think he was looking after me because I was just beginning to understand what it was to be number one and have to go through a lot of punishment. I'd tell him, 'Man, those guys are really hitting out there,' and he'd say, 'Go over there and sit down. Take care of yourself.'

"I watched Floyd and learned from him. I didn't copy his style because no one can be another Floyd Little. He was very inspirational to me. He knew the system and helped me to get it right."

The following year, Armstrong didn't play

Riley Odoms, who was a number one selection in 1972, is considered one of the premier tight ends in the National Football League.

much because he was hurt, hobbled by a severely pulled hamstring muscle. As a result, he only appeared in four games. Still, he managed to gain 155 yards, averaging 5.0 yards a run. Armstrong worked hard during the off season to offset his injury. When the 1976 season began, Armstrong was ready. He finished the year with 1,008 yards, his second 1,000-yard season.

Armstrong is considered one of the best draw runners in the league. He has tremendous leg strength and acceleration. His great speed and balance enable him to change directions in a wink.

"That unfortunate experience in 1975 taught me something," Armstrong claims. "I learned that as a running back you must stay in prime running shape. When I hurt myself in the second game of the season, I missed almost two weeks of running. When I came back, I discovered that the body says 'no' when you're not in the condition you're supposed to be in. It was a shock to me."

A shock of another kind came when Miller first talked to Armstrong about his new offensive philosophy. Miller felt the best way to approach Armstrong on the subject was to tell him straight out that he wasn't going to carry the running load all by himself. Armstrong learned about Miller's thoughts the day of the 1977 college draft when the Broncos were certain of making running back Rob Lytle of Michigan their number one choice.

"I just shrugged my shoulders," disclosed Armstrong. "Hey, I didn't understand what he was talking about; and at that point, I didn't like it. John Ralston made me what I am. He built the offense around me. But with Red, I started off as just another guy.

"It was hard at the beginning; but every time we registered a win, it got easier and easier. I think I started to accept it when we were all in the locker room, hugging and kissing and jumping up and down. I'd never been in a situation of winning every week. The old days I'd get 140 yards and we'd lose.

"I don't think it's impossible to platoon and still get 1,000 yards. As for not starting me in games and switching me with Rob, I understand that. Sure, I used to want to play the whole game; but Red explained that he doesn't believe in personal achievement. Hey,

Wide receiver Haven Moses came to Denver from Buffalo in a 1972 trade.

72

Rick Upchurch

In another good trade, the Broncos got big running back Jon Keyworth from the Washington Redskins in 1974.

when we were losing I only cared about myself, about being up there with the rushing leaders. Winning as a team, I dig it. I've never had a team feeling before. And, believe me, Red didn't ask me if this system would be okay with me. He said it's the way it was going to be, and I accepted that. Red is probably the most knowledgeable coach I've been around. There's something about the guy. He gives you a winning attitude. It carries over from week to week and builds into confidence. I haven't had this feeling since high school.

Riley Odoms, the 6'4", 230-pound, talented tight end, also liked the way Miller did things. Miller's offensive philosophy was particularly pleasing to Odoms, who is regarded as one of the best tight ends in the NFL because of his size and speed. Odoms was Denver's number one draft pick in 1972 and was named to the All-Pro squad in three of his first four seasons. However, last year he didn't catch too many passes simply because in Denver's offensive scheme, he wasn't thrown to very often, although he was hampered by a broken hand.

"Miller uses every receiver," exclaimed Odoms. "Last year most of our passing involved dumping the ball off to the backs. Now we go to the wide receivers and tight ends more. Knowing that, you try harder on every play. Many times I'm the second or third receiver, but I fight to get open knowing there's a good chance the quarterback will come back to me."

In the 1977 pre-season, Odoms led the Bronco pass receivers. He knew it would be a better year for him, not only because of Miller's more vitalized offense but also because of a new league rule that affected receivers. Defensive players could now only make contact with a receiver in a three-yard area at the line of scrimmage. If contact wasn't made at that point, they were allowed a bump, but only one, no more.

"The new rule has got to help," observed Odoms. "In previous years, it really was tough getting loose. Those guys would beat up on you at the line and then grab everything from your face mask to your jersey to keep you from running your pass route. Fortunately, I

Veteran kicker Jim Turner, who came to Denver in 1971 from the New York Jets, is the Broncos' leading all-time scorer.

Jim Turner

Mike Montler

was used to it after working against our guys in practice. Our linebackers are tougher on tight ends than most. They make you work hard just getting off the line. When I got into game situations, I was ready for anything.

"I've always taken pride in my blocking. But I'm a better blocker now because the coaches put so much emphasis on technique. A lot of blocking is desire. If you have that and add the right techniques to it, you've got to show improvement."

Wide receiver Haven Moses knows about desire. For years, he labored in virtual obscurity, victimized by losing seasons in Buffalo and also in Denver. Moses was a wide-eyed youngster from San Diego State College who was drafted by the Bills on the first round of the 1968 draft. But winning in San Diego and losing in Buffalo were two different worlds.

"With a loser, you have to keep from going through the motions," Moses admits. "It's so easy to say, 'Protect yourself. Don't get hurt. Play the last game, get packed, and get out of town before the next storm.' But the fans who pay the money deserve more than that, and I can honestly say I always gave my best. I don't get a lot of publicity. Other receivers are more spectacular than I am. Still, I've always been

an optimist. I always knew I was good and that someday I'd be on a team that was a winner."

It was the same feeling for center Mike Montler. He, too, had endured losing seasons with New England and Buffalo. The 6'4", 240 pound Montler joined the Broncos before the 1977 season began and helped solidify the offensive line which was an area Miller knew needed strengthening. In a sense, Montler was returning home. He had played at the University of Colorado where he was an All-American tackle. The Patriots made him a second round draft choice in 1969, and Montler started every game for four straight years before he was traded to the Bills. Near the end of the 1973 season, Montler was switched to center. There was some speculation that Montler might be moved back to tackle when he arrived at the Broncos' training camp.

"I really wasn't too interested in that," he disclosed later. "But I've done other things that I didn't think I would do. I really enjoy playing center. It's tailor made for me. I'm not really big, and I'm not very fast; and center is a position where you just kind of stay in one spot and muscle. You want your tackles quick and about 260 pounds."

What was the opinion of Red Miller? "No

78

offense is going to move a lick without a good coach," Montler says. "I've had six different coaches my first nine years, and I've never seen anything like this before. You can't dismiss Miller's enthusiasm, either."

Veteran kicker Jim Turner was impressed. Miller put his arm around Turner and told him right from the beginning that he would be his kicker. Turner appreciated the confidence. Overlooking the fact that Turner was thirty-six years old, Miller was also aware that Turner was one of the few players who had openly supported Ralston. It was understandable since Ralston had coached Turner at Utah State where he had been quarterback.

Turner came to Denver in 1971 from the New York Jets. It didn't take him long to become Denver's all time leading scorer. In fact, Turner is now the fifth ranked scorer in NFL history. He is only one of three players who has kicked 250 or more field goals. His thirty-four field goals in 1968 are still a NFL single season record. Turner's string of 221 points after touchdown, that was broken in 1974, is the second longest on record.

"I'd like to keep going another five years," beams Turner with new found enthusiasm.

Miller's infectious verve will probably make it possible. The buoyant Miller stabilized the offense and finally brought it some well-deserved recognition.

6
LYLE ALZADO

He was a street kid, mean and tough. He had to be to survive. The streets of New York's run-down neighborhoods aren't exactly something out of Camelot. Far from it. They are dark and dirty and overflowing with trouble. Being poor and hungry was a way of life. It wasn't any place for a weakling. Anybody who was, stayed inside at night. As bad as it was during the day, it was a veritable asphalt jungle at night. That's when most of the fights took place, when most of the crimes were committed. Even the sunrise brought little hope. One day was the same as the next. The same hunger. The same poverty. The same crime. The same bloody fights. All there was to do was survive.

Lyle Alzado managed to survive. Perhaps he more than anyone else epitomizes what the Denver Broncos are all about. Like Alzado, the Broncos, too, had to survive their youth. But Alzado could relate to it even more. He was trying to survive when nobody cared, at a time when there wasn't anyone to offer hope. Just to go on living from day to day was hard. Nobody but Alzado knows just how hard it really was. He's been there. He earned his right to survive against the odds.

Alzado was born in Spanish Harlem. Anybody who has been there knows what it's like. His father was part Spanish and part Italian. His mother was Jewish. She wanted a better neighborhood to raise her children, and they moved to Brooklyn. The part of Brooklyn they moved to wasn't much better. Later during his youth, the family moved to Inwood, Long Island. That, too, wasn't much better. By now, Alzado's parents had separated. His mother was determined to raise her five children on her own. She had no other choice.

"We were always hungry," remembers Alzado. "The apartment we had in Inwood was a filthy mess. I can remember coming home at night and seeing the roaches running around the kitchen table near the loaf of bread I'd have to eat for breakfast the next morning. My mom worked real hard in a flower shop. She made about $60 a week. There were five of us. What can you do with that?"

That's when Alzado learned to fight and steal. That's what survival was to Alzado, and he was very good at it. He never lost a fight. By the time he was only fifteen years old. Alzado was a bouncer in a bar his father owned. But his father lost the bar shortly afterwards, and then a paint store, too.

"He was a drinker and a street fighter," Alzado recalls. "He was trying to succeed in a world that wouldn't let him. The frustrations began to build up. He was a good man, I'm sure. But he just never took care of the family. Maybe he just didn't know how."

If there was any one thing that Alzado's father taught him, it was how to fight. His father had also been a boxer at one time. So, learning how to fight enabled Alzado to survive his environment.

"I've never been beaten up," admits Alzado. "I learned how not to be, how to use my hands and my feet. I learned my back-alley fighting when I was a bouncer. I thought you got attention by being the toughest kid in school, beating up everybody. I was color blind. I beat up blacks, whites, greens, whatever. I hated them all."

One night Alzado was at a dance. About an hour after the dance started, a young man came in with his face bloodied. Alzado asked what had happened. " 'Two guys beat me up,' " he said. "We went outside, and then all of a sudden this guy whistles," Alzado recalls. "Ten guys pile out of a truck with tire irons and chains. Things happen quick in a fight. I kicked a guy with a tire iron in a leg and knocked him down. Then I picked up the tire iron and beat him on his legs. By the time I was a junior in high school, my reputation was terrible. I remember going to parties and girls coming up to me saying. 'What's your name? Alzado? You beat up my boyfriend a couple of weeks ago.' "

Alzado's activities often got him in trouble with the police. His police record was probably much more impressive than his scholastic one at Lawrence High School. He was thrown in jail often enough. The last time he was in jail convinced him there must be a better way.

"I'd thought I'd be a smart guy; so I took off all my clothes and started doing push ups, jumping jacks, whatever. I yelled, 'Hey, you creeps. Let me outta here.' All of a sudden a guy in the next cell said, 'Yeah, you're just like me. You're nothing but a bum.' No one had ever called me a bum before, and he was right."

Perhaps the one person who influenced him most to change his violent ways was Marc Lyons. They were classmates and close friends.

"I met Lyle when we were in junior high, and we became like brothers," said Lyons, who is the head football coach at Stamford High School in Connecticut. "When things were bad at home, he'd come live with us. The trouble we got into mostly was fights. Lyle was a tough guy with a tough reputation. I would tag along. We weren't really bad guys, but we were always underdogs because we were poor. Poverty gives you an inferiority complex. We'd break some kid's nose in a fight. Then, when we'd get home, there would be the cops on our doorstep because the kid's father was a lawyer or an important doctor; and he'd have complained, and the police chief would hop right on it. I finally told Lyle that the only way we could get out of this mess was to believe in ourselves and do something right."

So, Alzado was encouraged to play football. He was 6'3" and weighed 190 pounds and was considered a prime athlete. Now Alzado, Lyons, and two other friends, Richie Mollo and Sal Ciampi, began to work out. Mollo and

Denver's loyal fans made themselves known around the NFL.

Left: *Kicker Jim Turner shows the form that has made him the Bronco's all-time leading scorer.*

Below: *Running back Otis Armstrong runs to daylight.*

Overleaf: *Barney Chavous and Rubin Carter combine to stop San Diego's Bo Matthews.*

Left: *Jon Keyworth gets ready to throw a block.* Below: *Armstrong is stopped in a 1974 game against the Detroit Lions.*

Below: *Bronco defenders bring down Oakland's Clarence Davis in AFC championship game.* Right: *Running back Rob Lytle looks for running room.*

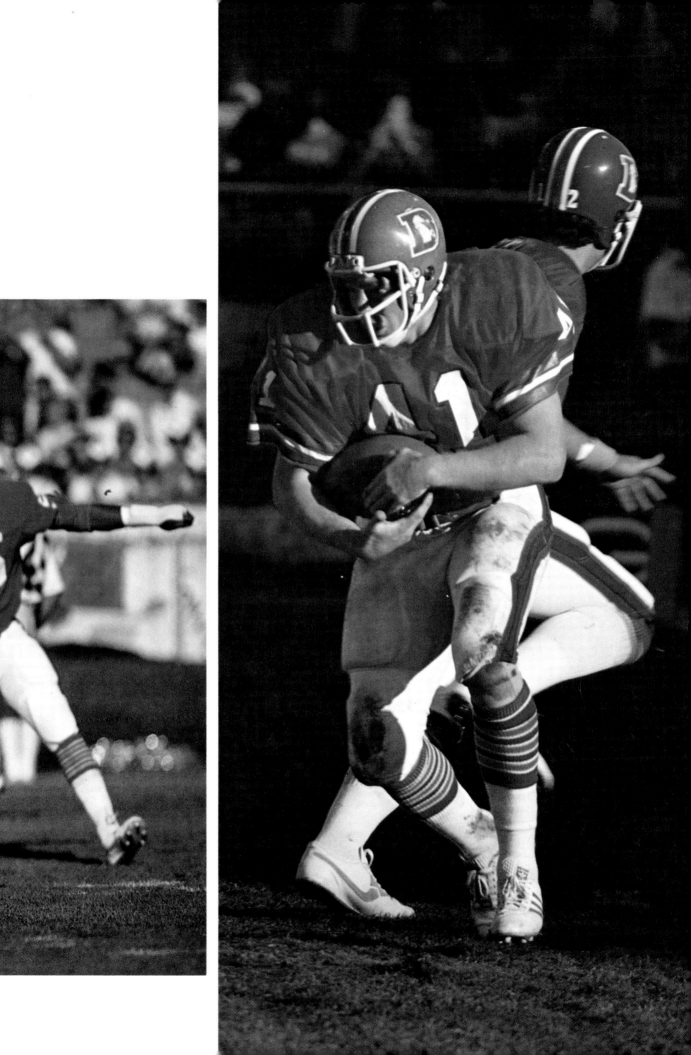

Happy Bronco players lift coach Red Miller on their shoulders immediately following Denver's dramatic 21-17 victory over Oakland for the AFC championship.
Right: Craig Morton drops back to pass. He ranked second among AFC quarterbacks as he led the Broncos to their first Super Bowl.

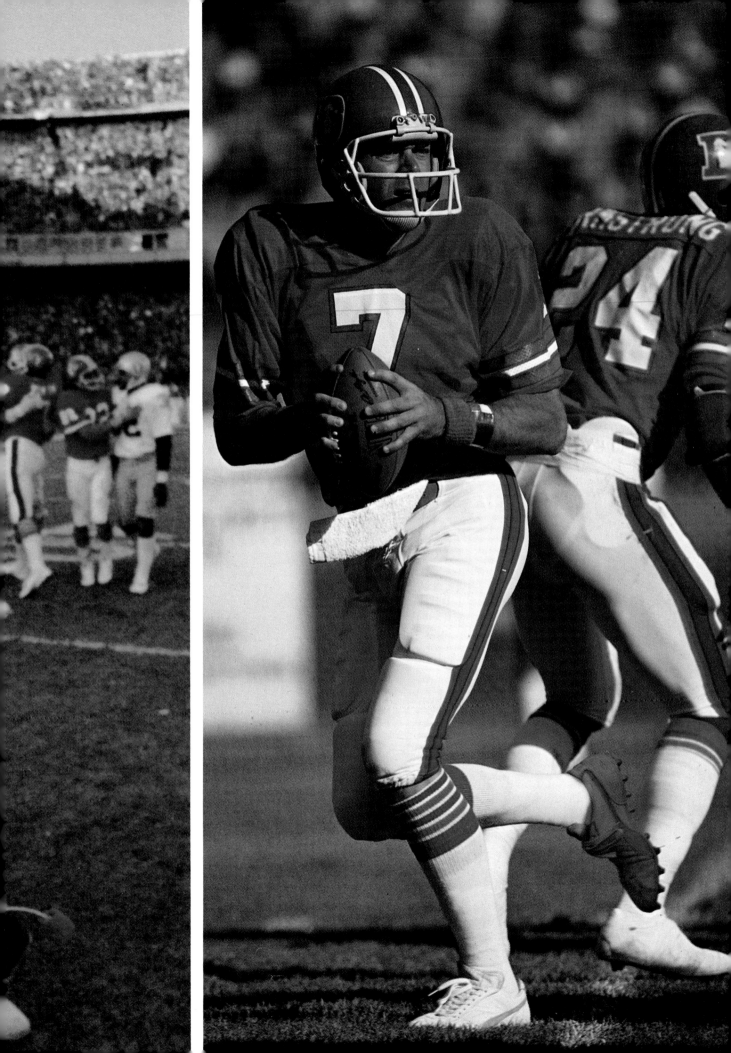

The spirit of the Broncos that prevailed throughout the 1977 season reached its peak before Super Bowl XII.

Rob Lytle was Denver's top rusher against the Dallas Cowboys in Superbowl XII.

Coach Red Miller gives vocal support on sidelines.

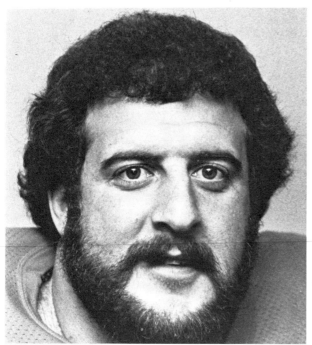

Lyle Alzado

Ciampi were already playing football. They worked out in Mollo's father's garage, a little place where the weight records were written on the wall. Every time a weight record was broken, they'd have a ceremony.

"They were succeeding in the same environment that I was in, and they wanted me to succeed," said Alzado. "I guess you could say I love those guys, even though we're far apart and I see them maybe only once a year now."

Alzado still had a long way to go. During his junior year in high school, he was practically thrown out of every game for fighting. He at least managed to harness his fighting instincts by participating in an amateur boxing program. He participated in the Police Athletic League program and won twenty-seven straight fights. By his senior year, Alzado had taken football seriously. He controlled his temper and had an outstanding season. Alzado also excelled in the ring. He appeared in Madison Square Garden and made his way to the Golden Gloves semi-finals at Omaha, Nebraska before he lost, quite an accomplishment.

Still, Alzado was far from encouraged. He felt that everything good that was happening to him was happening too late. Although he developed into a good football player when he finished high school, he didn't know where to turn.

"I wanted to go somewhere, but my grades weren't good. I had several offers for a scholarship; but when they saw my grades, I was quickly turned down. I had decided to join the service. But my high school coach, Jack Martilotta, said to give it one more try. New Mexico State had offered me a partial scholarship, and I was all set to go. But two weeks before I was scheduled to arrive in Las Cruces, I received a letter saying that the scholarship was not available. They didn't say why, but I think it was because they had gotten hold of my police record."

Then Alzado decided to give Kilgore Junior College in Kilgore, Texas a try. He got down there, and they made Alzado try out as a split end because of his speed. But nobody ever said that Alzado had good hands, so he didn't make it. He hitchhiked all the way from Kilgore to New Orleans. Once there, Alzado called Martilotta for help. Martilotta wired him the money to get home.

Alzado was truly discouraged, but Martilotta wasn't. He looked through the many letters that he had received regarding Alzado and decided to call the first small school they came to, which turned out to be Yankton College, a small private school in Yankton, South Dakota. Martilotta made a telephone call. Surprisingly enough, they were still interested even though the school year had begun. Alzado was put on a bus and began a long journey into the midlands of America.

It was a strange feeling for Alzado, leaving the asphalt of the city jungle for the tranquil environs of Yankton, South Dakota. He was met at the bus station and taken first to lunch.

"The coach took me off the bus and bought me two hamburgers," smiled Alzado. "I didn't have any money to pay for it. The coach told me not to worry, he would take care of it. I decided right then and there that I was never going to leave that place."

Alzado started on a weight lifting program that was designed to add weight to his tall frame. He went from 190 pounds to 230 pounds. He also played three positions on the football team. He started as a fullback, switched to linebacker, and finished his college career as a defensive end.

He also continued his boxing, and he did well. He reached the finals of the Golden Gloves tournament in Omaha before losing to

Defensive end Lyle Alzado, who arrived in Denver in 1971 from little Yankton College, is the soul of the Denver defense.

Ron Stander, a current heavyweight contender. The fight was a close one, and just about everyone felt that Alzado had won. One judge voted 60-59, another 59-60, while a third called it even at 59-59. However, the decision was awarded to Stander on aggressiveness, a verdict that was booed by many in attendance.

Alzado earned several honors in football. He was All Tri-State Conference twice, was the most valuable player in the Copper Bowl against Montana Tech, and earned a spot on the College All-Star team. He had his heart set on a professional career, but what pro scout would hold his exploits at Yankton College in high regard?

Yet, at Yankton, Alzado found himself. He developed an awareness of what life was really all about. It was important to him as a person because every summer he returned to his ghetto neighborhood and worked with his friend Marc Lyons on the back of a garbage truck.

"It was tough working behind a rotten, smelly garbage truck," Lyons says. "Lyle and I wore twenty-pound vests and ankle weights, and we'd run along behind the truck which was going about six miles an hour. We'd get in five miles of roadwork that day. After the garbage route, we'd go to Mollo's father's garage and lift weights for another three hours. Then I'd play baseball, and Lyle would go box. By the end of the summer we'd be in great shape and so sick of lifting weights that we couldn't wait to go back to school."

Alzado first began to major in physical education, but he changed that after a short while to special education.

"One day the wife of the athletic director asked me to come over to the grammar school to move some chairs," Alzado recalls. "While I was there I saw some little kids playing kickball. A little girl who was retarded, only I didn't know it, asked me to play. I said, 'I can't play your game.' She looked at me and said, 'It's not my game, it's everybody's game.' Can you imagine a little kid saying that?

"Then another time I walked into a class, and there were a lot of kids just sitting there. I asked one if he wanted to play, and he paid no attention to me. They told me the kids were retarded. I didn't even know what a retarded child was, but I figured it must be bad and maybe I could do something about it."

He still pined to play pro football. He figured it would happen naturally. That's how naive he was.

"If I was good enough, I felt they would find me," reasoned Alzado. "I thought that if you played well, you could go to East Cupcake U and still make the pros."

However, it wasn't that simple. In fact, it took a twist of fate for Alzado to even be recognized. Stan Jones, an assistant coach with the Broncos, was on a scouting trip to Montana in the winter of 1971. When he reached Butte, he experienced car trouble.

"I got the car to a mechanic, and he told me it would take all day to fix," Jones remembers. "I asked if there was a college nearby, and I was given a ride to Montana Tech. I figured I might as well make use of my time by looking at game films. The coach at Montana Tech said I should keep an eye on a kid named Alzado, who had played against him in the 1970 Copper Bowl. He kept popping up on every play, and I got interested. He wasn't very tall, but he was quick. We went into the college draft that year convinced the kid could play defensive line for us. He had that kind of strength and quickness; and he was a good, tough kid. I liked everything I heard about him, and I was relieved when we got him."

The Broncos made Alzado their number four selection in the 1971 college draft. Their announcement of Alzado raised numerous eyebrows around the league. In fact, one Denver newspaper wondered how the Broncos could possibly waste such a high pick on Alzado. Hardly anybody ever heard of Yankton College, and nobody from the school had ever made the pros.

Denver appeared solid enough on the defensive line. At least six veterans were ranked ahead of Alzado, but fate was on Alzado's side. Pete Duranko, a former All-American at Notre Dame, injured his leg during a preseason game. Jones gave Alzado a chance. "It's your job if you can handle it," Jones said.

There was only one game remaining in the exhibition season when Alzado got his chance. Naturally, he was excited.

"Lyle was like a kid when he first came to us," admitted owner Gerald Phipps. "He would lose his temper, get upset, and not play

as well as he was capable of playing. When Duranko hurt his knee, Lyle became a starter right off the bat. That's a very tough thing to do. His first game was against the Chicago Bears, the dirtiest team around."

When the game was over, one in which the Bears won, 33-17, Alzado wore the price on his face. He finished the day with four stitches on his nose and two more on his forehead. That was his indoctrination into professional football, but he hung tough and has been a starter in the line ever since that game.

As the Broncos were growing, so was Alzado. He played in twelve games for his rookie season and played in every game for the next four years. But in 1976, Alzado was cut down. It happened in the opening game of the 1976 season against the Cincinnati Bengals. In one play, he was sidelined for the entire season.

"I felt nauseous," remembers Alzado. "But I said, what the hell, I'm probably just nervous."

He stayed in the game for another play and then realized he couldn't go on any more. He knew he was hurt, but how badly he couldn't be sure. He hobbled over to the bench, and soon got the bad news. The diagnosis was torn ligaments. He had to have surgery. He was finished for the season.

It was a tough season on Alzado in more ways than one. His injury made him moody. It also enabled him to do a great deal of thinking. He had an opportunity to observe his teammates play, and he didn't like what he saw.

"I tried to watch," he discloses. "I went to one of the games, the Jets game, sat on the sidelines one half, and left. I'm very emotional, and the frustration I felt was enormous. I knew I would be playing if it wasn't for the damn knee, so I decided to stay home and watch the game on television. I felt very distant from the team, sitting there and watching everybody playing hard and working hard."

One day he erupted. After their opening loss to Cincinnati, the Broncos had won three games in a row. During the fifth week of the season, they were playing the Houston Oilers in Houston. He was at home watching the

Lyle Alzado brings Dallas' Butch Johnson to the ground.

game with friends. In the third quarter of the closely contested game, the Denver offense bogged down. Alzado couldn't hold back his frustration any longer. He picked up one of his crutches and flung it at the television set. His accurate throw resulted in the complete destruction of a 27-inch color screen.

"To be coming off my best training camp and exhibition season and then not be able to play while the defense was having its greatest year was the hardest thing I have ever had to take," Alzado declares.

Others experienced Alzado's anguish. His wife, for one. "If it happens again, I'm packing my bags," confides Sharon. Alzado's friend and road roommate for the last seven years, defensive end Paul Smith, admitted that "It tore him up a bit."

It was Alzado's fierce pride. How else can it be explained. The Broncos' assistant trainer, Steve Antonopulos, experienced Alzado's torment each day. He readily understood what Alzado was going through.

"He didn't want anybody to look at his leg," disclosed Antonopulos. "He always wanted to work when nobody was around. He'd say, 'Meet me at eight in the morning,' and then he'd work an hour and a half before anyone else showed up. He's the hardest working guy I've ever seen. Before he got hurt, he was the third or fourth strongest guy on the team after Rubin Carter, Otis Armstrong, and Paul Howard. Now he's first."

Although he didn't play after the opening game of the 1976 season, Alzado was a very important part of its outcome. The Broncos finished with the best record in their history, 9-5. Yet, the players had an empty feeling. They felt they should have done better. In private meetings, they expressed their sentiments to Alzado. They asked him to be their spokesman with management in asking for the dismissal of John Ralston as head coach. It was a bold decision. If anything, Ralston was popular with the Bronco fans. But the players had to overlook that in their quest for a championship.

Alzado's efforts on behalf of the disgruntled group earned them the title of "The Dirty Dozen." Yet, despite the shock they created and the nasty telephone calls they received, they remained undaunted. They sincerely believed

they were doing what was best for the team and for the city of Denver. They wanted to give the city a championship.

When the season ended, the players, led by Alzado, laid their careers on the line. They were emphatic in wanting Ralston removed. Management listened; and the first step they took was to make Fred Gehrke, who had served as the club's assistant general manager since 1973, as general manager. A month later, Ralston resigned.

"It's hard for me to express how I felt that year," Alzado explains. "I wasn't playing, so it was difficult for me to be on top of what was happening. But things weren't right. I hated seeing us lose games we should have won. Against New England, the quarterback, who was Steve Ramsey, threw an interception and came off the field smiling. You can't win with that kind of an attitude; and dammit, I wanted to make winning possible. By coming out against Ralston, I took a big chance. If he had stayed, my career, in Denver anyway, was over.

Alzado is very active in the Denver community, spending much of his time working with underprivileged kids.

"It wasn't a personal thing with Ralston for any of us. Let's face it, he was a good man but not, in my opinion, a good coach. I took a stand I had to take. I have no regrets."

The only regret that he possibly did harbor was the fact that he was never truly recognized for his playing ability until the 1977 season.

"It's easier to gain fame when you're playing on a championship team," acknowledges Alzado. "But I'm going to play this game a long time—fifteen years is what I'm shooting for—and I'm not going to worry over publicity. I'm concerned by only three things. First, I want the respect of my coach, Stan Jones. Then, I want the respect of the people I play with, my teammates. Third, I want to be respected by those players looking at me from across the line. If I have those three things, you can have the rest. I don't have to prove anything to people out there."

The people out there who really love him are the kids in Denver, and the ones Alzado touches most are the afflicted youngsters. When it comes to sick children, Alzado is a softie. He is also actively involved with the police department with work on their drug-control program and athletic activities.

"It takes an awful lot of my time," admits Alzado. "But I need to help kids. I wake up in a sweat sometimes after a nightmare that puts me back in the hole I crawled out of in Brooklyn. I talk to kids every chance I have. I tell them, 'You've got to do it for yourself. If you don't, you'll stay in the hole you're in your entire life.' "

Early in 1977 Alzado received a letter informing him that his high school graduating class was holding a reunion.

"I asked my wife if I should go back," said Alzado. "She told me, 'Lyle, do whatever you feel is right.' I didn't go. I didn't want to be remembered for what I once was. I want to be remembered for what I've become."

Everybody in Denver will agree with him.

7
THE DEFENSE

They are a very proud bunch, which says something about their character, and they have a lot of it, too. They were put together without a lot of build up. Their backgrounds varied. One was an All-American at Ohio State. Another came from the tough streets of New York. Still another came from the poverty of the south. Others were signed as free agents when no one else wanted them. It is no wonder that they clung together and made it work better than most teams did. So much better that the Denver defense is perhaps the best in pro football; and that's saying a lot.

The defense was really the first good thing that happened in Denver. They began to get recognition in 1976. That season only three teams scored more than seventeen points against the Broncos in a single game. In 1977 it was even better. Only one team scored more than fourteen points against the Broncos in a single game. It was a defense that was aggressive, and had a relentless swarming pursuit. They captured the imagination of the Bronco

The famed Orange Crush defense.

fans and were fondly called the Orange Crunch and later the Orange Crush. Whatever the nickname, they were a defense best known for desire.

The architect was Joe Collier, a low profile, quiet spoken student of defense. An indefatigable worker, Collier spends hours watching game film, grading players, and studying techniques. A long time associate of Red Miller, Collier was one of the coaches that was retained after the dismissal of John Ralston following the 1976 season and with good reason. Collier is an expert in coordinating the entire defensive involvement.

"This is the third year that this unit has played together, and that's a big plus," emphasized Collier about the team's 1977 success. "They might get burned once on a big play but not twice. They help each other out, and they have confidence to go with their ability. There are so many excellent players on this unit that they have a hell of a time picking a captain. That says something. It is perhaps the most proficient defensive platoon I have ever coached."

Yet, before the 1977 season began, Collier was concerned about the performance of three players who were coming off injuries the year before. All were defensive ends, Lyle Alzado, Paul Smith, and Brison Manor. Although Manor was only a rookie, the coaches felt he had a great future. All three were out for the entire 1976 campaign.

It is Alzado who personifies the soul of the Broncos' defense. "Everybody on the team studies so much more than we used to," he says. "Collier is so sophisticated, he moves us around so much from week to week that it's difficult for scouts to type us, to be able to say, 'Well, in this situation, they'll be in a four man front.' "

Like Alzado, defensive tackle Rubin Carter absorbs a great deal of pounding during a game. Perhaps more so. In the Broncos' three-man front, Carter is the nose tackle. Being double-teamed by the opposing center and guard is a way of life, but Carter is perhaps one of the best in the league at doing his job.

"A nose tackle has to be able to endure the pounding," Carter easily acknowledges. "On most plays, a 250-pound center and a 260-

Joe Collier, Denver's defensive coordinator.

Lyle Alzado applies the crunch to Dallas quarterback Roger Staubach.

pound guard hit me. That's 510 pounds each play."

Carter knows what it is to endure. When he was a teenager his mother was dying of cancer; Carter and his brother supported the family. His father had died when Carter was only nine. So, while still in high school in Miami, Carter would attend classes from 7 A.M. until noon, practice football until 4 P.M., and work from 4:30 P.M. until 11 P.M. at anything he could find in order to help support his ailing mother and the rest of the family. His mother died during his freshman year at the University of Miami.

Because of his size, Carter didn't impress many pro scouts. He was only six feet tall, and no scout could imagine a lineman being that small. Yet, he was the all-time leading defensive lineman in Miami's history, despite having missed the final five games of his senior year with a fractured leg. But that didn't stop Carter from playing in the Hula Bowl, a showcase for pro scouts. Despite the condition of his leg, Carter played an outstanding game and was voted the top defensive lineman.

Overlooked by the rest of the pro teams, Denver nevertheless picked Carter on the fifth round of the 1975 college draft. It was one of the best selections in Denver history. Carter led the linemen in tackles in 1976 with 107, a statistic that underscores Carter's great strength and quickness. Thickly muscled at 252 pounds, Carter can bench press 525 pounds.

"I really feel this team can't be stopped," Carter says. "I've never been part of anything like this. It's the best defense in the NFL. And there's no one standout. It's an entire team."

Because of his size, Carter does have certain advantages. At the snap of the ball, he can dive underneath the center and get leverage against the anticipated blocks. His strength and quickness force opposing teams to double up on Carter.

"If just a center can handle our nose tackle, we have no advantage with the 3-4," Collier explains. "But if the nose man can force a double team, then we have a free linebacker to track down the ball. Rubin's strength lies in his ability to get away from blocks and that means the opposition has to double-team him. The 3-4 is very difficult for linemen. They can't be

Randy Gradishar is considered one of the NFL's most active linebackers.

free-wheeling or creative because there aren't enough other linemen to cover up for them if they make a mistake. Most defensive linemen don't like the 3-4 because they don't get the sacks. The linebackers get them."

It is the Denver linebackers that are the pursuers, and the Broncos are acknowledged to have the best group of linebackers in the NFL. They are also a heady bunch. All four of them have to diagnose a play accurately and react quickly.

"By moving in and out of the line, an opponent is never sure where our defenders will be; and that confuses the blockers," Collier points out. "The growth of the linebackers was a basic reason for the growth of our success, that and the fact that we began to draft defensive players high. Randy Gradishar was our first number one pick for defense, and cornerback Louis Wright was our second. We hit on a couple of free agents, such as linebackers Bob Swenson and Joe Rizzo. With Gradishar and Tommy Jackson, a number four draft pick, it solidified that unit and allowed us to go into the 3-4 effectively.

"We haven't made many changes the past two years, and that's a plus no matter what style you play. We rely on being able to pursue. We have quickness and speed, in contrast to a Pittsburgh defense, for example, that just overpowers you. Our biggest lineman goes about 250. None of our linebackers are exceptionally big. Gradishar is the biggest, and he isn't 230."

Gradishar was the first number one draft choice the Broncos ever took on defense since the pro football merger enabled a common draft in 1967. That's how much they thought of the former Ohio State All-American. Woody Hayes, the venerable Ohio State coach, considered Gradishar the best linebacker he ever coached.

Although he began as a middle linebacker with the Broncos in 1974, Gradishar shifted to the inside slot when the defense went to the 3-4 in 1976. It didn't affect Gradishar in the least. He led the defense in tackles with 198.

Gradishar is the acknowledged leader of the defense. During a game, he looks over at the sidelines to get the defensive alignment from Collier. Once he gets the signal he takes over. "All the plays come from Collier," Gradishar

Tom Jackson, another active linebacker, is the defense's holler guy.

96

says. "He signals them to me, and my job is to get the huddle organized and relay the coverage to the rest of the guys within the 30 seconds we're allowed. We have some audibles. If the offense shows us something different by a shift, for example, it's my responsibility to check off. Most of the audibles are planned in advance, and we really don't have a lot of checkoffs. We all know what to expect of each other. Somebody might make a mistake, and nine times out of ten the guy next to him will cover for it."

On linebacking, Gradishar says, "I've always enjoyed tackling; but I think it takes some natural ability, too. You have to have a sense for the ball. Linebacker is the perfect position for that because it's such a free position. You get to be involved in every play, and you're free to freelance. Speed and quickness, that's the whole defense."

And something else—emotion. Linebacker Tommy Jackson has it, and it becomes infectious during a game. He is the most vocal Bronco on the field and can quickly give his teammates a lift. At 5'11", Jackson wasn't rated

Cornerback Louis Wright was the Broncos' number one draft choice in 1975.

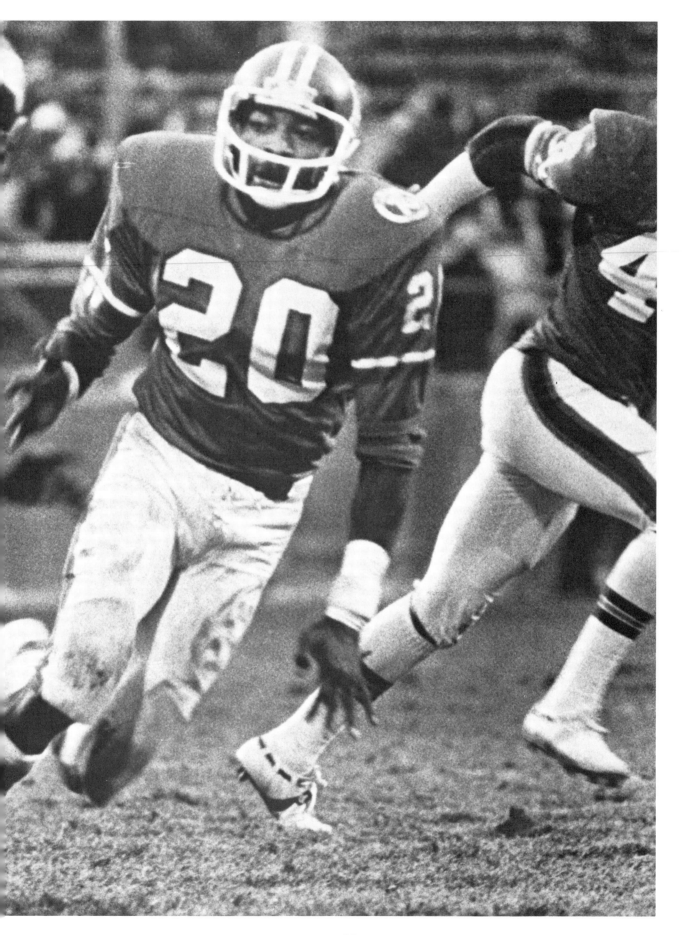

too highly by the pro scouts; but he has made it big with the Broncos as the weakside linebacker. In 1976, he led the team and all other AFC linebackers in interceptions with seven. Because of his speed, Jackson is excellent on pass coverage. So much so that he has become recognized as Denver's big play man.

"I see my role as making the play that makes the opponents change their philosophy of offense," explains Jackson. "Because of our speed, it's tough for a team to get outside on us, and it's tough for a team to beat us deep. So that means they have to pretty much go to short passes or, when they run, get four or five yards up in the middle. What I try to do is make that play that forces them into a third and long situation by stopping somebody in the backfield for a two- or three-yard loss or pressuring the quarterback. Just something to disrupt their offensive flow so they have to do something they didn't want to do."

As to emotion, Jackson says: "Some teams are afraid to show their emotion. They think it's uncool to feel that excited about a football game. Our team is not afraid to show emotion. I'm a hyper person, and sometimes it looks as though I'm out of control on the field. But I'm really not. The linebackers are the heart of our defense, and I feel it's our job to do the extra things it takes to get the team psyched up."

Bob Swenson and Joe Rizzo, the two remaining linebackers, were bargain basement discoveries. Both were signed as free agents, Rizzo in 1974 and Swenson the following year. Rizzo, 6'1", 220, was originally drafted by Buffalo out of the Merchant Marine Academy but was released while still recovering from knee surgery. A solid hitter, Rizzo plays the strong side. Swenson, 6'3", 215, was signed out of the University of California, where he played defensive end. Because of his range and quickness, Swenson plays on the outside.

The linebackers were under the tutelage of linebacker coach Myrel Moore. Like some others on the staff, he is a holdover from the Ralston era. His defensive system has drawn raves from other coaches around the league.

"It's a system that is unlike any other in the world of football," explains Moore. "I think we've helped overcome some of the old-fashioned theories about linebackers. The 3-4

Bill Thompson is one of the top safeties in the NFL.

100

Bill Thompson

defense is not new, but the way we play it is. Most teams just take a fourth lineman and stand him up to confuse the offense as to where he'll be rushing from. Then on third down they may bring in another man for pass drops. When they asked me to take over the linebackers in 1974, I wanted to go for the good athlete who had speed and quickness and some height but maybe wasn't as big as a defenseman usually is. A Dick Butkus probably wouldn't fit in with our style. By going with these people, we have the speed to get a 10-yard drop rather than the normal 8-yard drops most teams use; and we don't do it back-pedaling. We're flexible and versatile enough to protect against the run, but yet we have the personnel to defend against the pass. It confuses teams. For example, an offensive tackle may line up against a defensive end one play. Then, on the next play he may be lined

sive linemen. In this system our linebackers may be smaller, but they're protected from constant beating because they are not getting head-on shots on most plays. Swenson has to take a lot because teams usually run to the strong side, but he's a tough player. Jackson, meanwhile, can play loose and follow the flow of the play. We were fortunate because these types of players were not high on the lists of most other teams because they didn't fit the normal linebacker mold. Now other teams are changing their philosophies about what a linebacker should be like, and it makes it tougher for us to get them. We've got the nucelus now that would be together for years, and I think a lot of people are coming over to our way of thinking."

The Oakland Raiders, for one, did. After the Super Bowl they lured Moore away from the Broncos to not only coach their linebackers but to become their defensive coordinator. It was high tribute indeed.

While the linebackers attempted most of the attention, Collier pointed out the importance of the secondary. He felt that its versatility was exceptional although sometimes it went overlooked.

"In our secondary, some guys can play all four of the positions if necessary," Collier says with a smile. "Steve Foley and Bernard Jackson are familiar with assignments at either corner or safety. Louis Wright is another number one draft choice who has made marked progress as a corner, and Billy Thompson is one of the most dedicated athletes I have ever been around. He knows nothing but 100 percent, whether in practice or in a game."

Thompson, along with defensive end Paul Smith, are the senior ranking members of the Broncos. Smith joined the club in 1968, and Thompson arrived the following year. Thompson is regarded as one of the league's finest strong safeties.

"I've slowed down a little over the years, but experience and positioning have made up for it," says Thompson. "There's not a tight end in the league that I can't keep up with, plus I have a better overall awareness of the field."

By now, everyone in the National Football League has become aware of the Orange Crush.

up against a linebacker. You're blowing the guy's mind, and it begins to affect him.

"What helped us was that we were looking for the kind of athlete that didn't fit into the style of other teams. Five or six years ago a Tom Jackson, who is a super player, might not have stuck in the league because no one would have known what to do with him. They might have put him at inside linebacker, and he would have gotten pounded to death by offen-

8
THE 1977 SEASON

It was a different kind of training camp. The Bronco players noticed it right away. When you take their candy and soda away from them, you're really making a point. That's the first thing that caught Red Miller's eye on the opening day of training camp. He noticed that the players had a special attraction for the candy and soda machines in the corridors outside the meeting rooms the team utilized at Colorado State University. Early that evening, Miller called a general meeting. It was the first time that he had assembled his squad together since he became coach five months earlier. It was, in essence, his first team meeting. Lyle Alzado recalled it well.

"I remember it like it was yesterday," smiled Alzado. "He called in everyone, trainers, doctors, ball boys, coaches, and players. He opened the meeting by saying, 'Good evening. I'm Red Miller, your new coach.

"'I've noticed that when you go to meetings you stop by the soda pop and candy machines

For the victors, champagne. Linebacker Bob Swenson pours champagne over the heads of coach Myrel Moore and Billy Thompson as head coach Red Miller applauds following title clinching win over the Oilers.

105

to bring something to sip and chew in the meeting. I don't want you to do that anymore. When you go to a meeting, I want you to concentrate on football.'

"Miller then turned away as if he was finished. He suddenly turned back and pointed a finger at us and said loudly, 'And I mean it!' He definitely had our attention."

That particular moment also impressed a lot of other players, particularly the veterans. It was Miller's first real contact with the club, a team that had become deeply divided when the 1976 season, the most successful in the club's history, had ended. It was Alzado and a number of others who were in the vanguard demanding the dismissal of John Ralston as coach. Alzado, for one, had stared hard at Miller during that first meeting. Indirectly, he and the others were responsible for Miller becoming head coach of the Broncos. That's why the 1977 training camp was such an important time in formulating the ground work for whatever success the team would enjoy in the season ahead. They knew everybody would be watching, measuring their achievements against the 9-5 record the team had produced in 1976.

What the players had disapproved of was the way Ralston had run the team. He had acted more like the chairman of the board of a company, delegating serious responsibilities for the offense and the defense to other members of the coaching staff. The players wanted a head coach who would be more involved during a game. Ralston just hadn't shown the right kind of leadership, and the Broncos had no one else who did.

Among the players, the new quarterback, Craig Morton, was the one who was looked upon for leadership. Like Miller, he was unknown to the Bronco players; but also like Miller, he was a veteran. Morton had been an NFL quarterback for twelve years and was successful in leading the Dallas Cowboys to Super Bowl V in 1971. Morton approached his challenge with a fresh attitude.

"All the quarterbacks that were here before did not concern me," stressed Morton. "I knew what I could do. I didn't know what had gone on in 1976, but in the short time I was there I could see that Miller had found a way to blend in with the players. He doesn't sub-scribe to the theory that a coach can't be close to the players. He keeps his distance when he should, but he's not afraid of personal contact; and the players like that."

Billy Thompson, the star strong safety, also liked Miller's approach. He was convinced that the new coach could bring the mutinous Broncos together. He liked the way Miller did things. He knew Miller had the solution.

"I could feel the difference after just three days of training camp," exclaimed Thompson, who, like Alzado, was deeply involved in the movement to oust Ralston. "There was just something about this man, the way he talked, what he said, and how he made you work. He had us all working harder than we'd ever worked. And no one was complaining.

"You have to start with a plan, and Red Miller had one. It was the most organized training camp I've ever been in. It was five minutes here . . . fifteen minutes there . . . then back over here. Everything was moving. Nobody was standing around.

"The team began to take on a lot of character. Before, it was a team that was indecisive, kind of wandering and unsure of itself. Red Miller came, and that all changed.

"When I heard that Miller got the Denver job, I was with Sugar Bear Hamilton, the Patriots' middle guard. You know what he said to me? He said, 'Bill, you SOB, you stole our coach. Wait till you meet this guy. You've got a treat in store for you.' "

Even before regular training camp opened, Miller knew that it would be a different kind of year, that something good would happen. He felt it that spring when he brought his players in for a mini-camp. The first group he brought together were the rookies, then the veterans, and finally, all of them together.

"Through those camps I think we got our message across," Miller recalls. "We ran the living hell out of them. We worked them hard, and the players knew they were in for something. But it was the first day they reported for training camp that I realized it was going to come together. I was so excited that I even told Fred Gehrke about it. The players' attitude showed it. They were the best conditioned athletes I had ever seen. They were lean and had great team speed, the best team speed I had ever seen. They were ready to go.

Fred Gehrke

Naturally, you couldn't tell how well they were ultimately going to do. But they had trained. They had run and lifted and stretched. They believed in the entire program that I had initiated. So I thought to myself, 'We've got something going here.'"

But Miller needed more input before the regular season opened. He conferred with Mac Speedie, one of the club's top scouts. Speedie felt that the club was lacking enough quality players on offense to really be considered a championship one. So, after first securing Morton, Miller was determined to strengthen an area that seemed weak, the offensive line. Shrewdly, he obtained Mike Montler, who could play either guard or center, from Buffalo and tackle Andy Mauer from San Francisco. In trading for safety Bernard Jackson from Cincinnati, Miller also strengthened his defensive secondary. All the while Miller practiced his cardinal rule of maintaining daily contact with the players.

"Miller had us respecting one another," admitted Alzado. "Don't get me wrong. Everybody isn't in love with everybody else on this team. That's an impossible situation. But we found that Miller was somebody you could relate to. He's a down-dirt right guy, and he's also a brawling guy. He'll take on guys at wrestling right in the locker room—and he won't lose, either."

One such time Miller was jostling with a free agent center, Kenny Brown, who was 6'3" and weighed 240 pounds. They got to mixing it up pretty good and wound up in a wrestling match.

"Red picked Kenny up, threw him down, and tied him into a pretzel in the space of about thirty seconds," remembered wide receiver Jack Dolbin.

"You see him rolling around on the floor like that, and it's kinda like a father down on the floor with one of his kids," added running back Jim Jensen. "But he's also the last person in the world anyone would want to pick a fight with."

That was one of Miller's ways of overcoming the doubts and dissension that hovered over the Broncos. He had to make it happen fast, before the season opened. Three months isn't much time.

"Frankly, I was skeptical," conceded kicker Jim Turner. "Me and Jack Dolbin were the only guys who had stood up for John Ralston. I had played for John in college. It was a sick situation on this club. But Miller impressed me two ways. One, he met with each guy and laid it on the line to him, told him what to expect, told him what we could achieve. Okay, a lot of coaches do that; and a lot of them BS you, too. But everything that this guy said was true. I also had to like the fact that he didn't bring another kicker to camp. He told me, 'You're my kicker, period.' I liked that. Not that anyone else was going to take my job away, but coaches sometimes like to harass you by bringing other kickers into camp."

Finally, to remove any inner frustrations the team might harbor, Miller appointed a bitch coach from among the players. Recognizing that linebacker Randy Gradishar did the most complaining he named him the "Bitch Coach" for the 1977 season.

"There has always been the usual amount of little gripes about this and that on any football team I've been with," said Miller. "If no one is bitching, that usually means that something is very wrong. But you have to keep the bitching down to a proper level, and so I appointed Gradishar the bitch coach. He was the team's main bitcher anyway, and I did it mainly to shut him up. And by God, it worked."

So, down deep, Miller was optimistic when the regular 1977 season drew nearer. He had unified the club, established offensive leadership in Morton, strengthened his offensive line, and sold the players on his philosophy. He had them ready. All he had to do now was turn them loose.

"Predictions?" Miller was asked just before the season started. "I don't make predictions. I just want to win one game at a time."

Game One: ST. LOUIS
September 18, 1977

The first game was against the St. Louis Cardinals. It was also the Broncos' home opener, and a record crowd of 75,002 fans turned out to see what Miller had put together. During the pre-season schedule, the Broncos distinguished themselves with a 5-1 record, the best in the club's history; and it gave the Denver faithful reason for optimism. But the Cardinals were a stern test. They were a highly explosive team that were looked upon as solid contenders for the Eastern Division championship of the National Football Conference. On paper it was an ideal match, the Cardinals strong offense against the Broncos solid defense.

Except for the opening series of downs, the Broncos were kept pinned deep in their own territory during the first quarter. The first time they had the ball after the kickoff, they

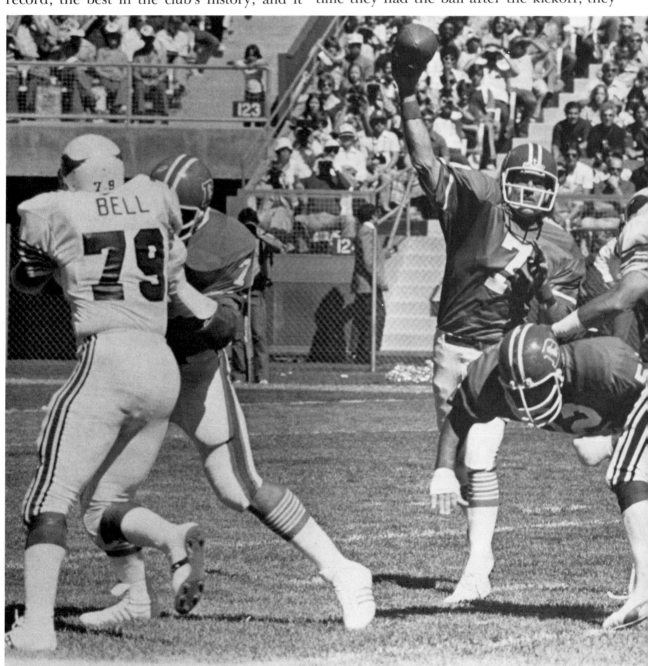

Behind a fine block by center Mike Montler (52), quarterback Craig Morton cuts pass loose against St. Louis Cardinals.

110

almost got something going. On second down, Morton hit Rick Upchurch with a pass at midfield. However, Upchurch fumbled; and the Cardinals' Roger Werhil recovered on the St. Louis 38.

Neither team could generate much in the way of an offensive drive. But with under six minutes left to play in the quarter, quarterback Jim Hart hit speedy Mel Gray with a 48-yard pass that carried to Denver's 13-yard line. Then, with a fourth and 1 play on the Denver 4-yard line, the Cardinals decided to go

for the touchdown. Running back Jim Otis tried to go straight up the middle but was repulsed by Brison Manor and Gradishar. Minutes later, with the ball back in their possession, the Cardinals' Jim Bakken missed a field goal from 32 yards away.

The second quarter was also scoreless, with the Cardinals again mounting the only threat. With just over a minute left, Bakken's 37-yard field goal attempt was deflected by Manor. Then, as time ran out, Thompson intercepted Hart's pass on the 9-yard line to frustrate the Cardinals once again.

After receiving the second half kickoff, the Cardinals moved for a first down before they were forced to punt. But punter Terry Joyce mishandled the attempt, and the Broncos took over on the St. Louis 34. After Armstrong gained four yards, Morton passed to Dolbin for six more. However, the Cardinals were penalized 15 yards on the play for roughing the passer; and Denver had the ball on the St. Louis 12-yard line. Keyworth got two yards to the 10. Then, quickly, Armstrong burst over the right side for the touchdown. As the game progressed the Bronco's knew they had to make a 7-0 lead hold up. Two more times Bakken was futile on field goal tries. His first attempt from 33 yards was wide. Then Alzado tipped his kick from 24 yards out.

With two minutes remaining in the game, the Cardinals came close to scoring the tying touchdown. They had a third down and 6 on the Broncos' 7-yard line, but Hart's last two passes were knocked away by defenders. Led by Gradishar's ten tackles, four assists, and a sack, the Broncos' defense had asserted themselves. It was a portend of things to come. The Orange Crush was real.

"We've been saying all along that our defense has to take another step up, and today we did that," said Miller. "We beat a good team today, and we had to hold them scoreless to do it."

ST. LOUIS	0	0	0	0	0
DENVER	0	0	7	0	7

SCORING

Denver: 4:02 Third Period—Armstrong 10 yard run (Turner kick).

Game Two: BUFFALO
September 25, 1977

Anytime O. J. Simpson is on the field, it is trouble. He has established himself as perhaps the game's greatest runner. Only Jim Brown, who played with the great Cleveland Brown teams, has gained more yards than O.J. has. The difference was that the Buffalo Bills were nowhere near the champion team the Browns were. Yet in any given Sunday afternoon, O. J. can beat a team single-handedly with his explosive running. This was what the Broncos had to prepare for. If they could stifle Simpson, they could smother the Bills' otherwise weak offense.

The Broncos' second game of the young season was also at home; and the first time they got their hands on the ball, they scored. Upchurch had put Denver in business by returning a Buffalo punt 28 yards to the Bills' 37-yard line. On the first play, Morton connected with Odoms for a 17-yard advance to the 20. Armstrong tried an off-tackle slant that didn't get anything, and Morton's second down pass was knocked down by linebacker John Skorupan. Then, when Morton was sacked for an 11-yard loss, it appeared as though Denver might be out of field goal range. However, Miller showed Turner how much confidence he had in him by sending the thirty-six-year-old veteran on to the field to try a 48-yard field goal attempt. Turner came through for a 3-0 lead.

Denver carried that edge into the second period, but a Bronco mistake enabled the Bills to score a touchdown. On a third down play on his own 17-yard line, running back Lonnie Perrin fumbled the ball. Buffalo linebacker Bo Cornell picked it up and ran in for a touchdown. Buffalo's conversion try had missed, but they had a 6-3 lead.

After Denver punted on the next series of downs, Billy Thompson set the Broncos up for a touchdown. On a third and 5 play, he intercepted quarterback Joe Ferguson's pass on the Bills' 39-yard line and scrambled all the way down to the 1 before he was stopped. After Perrin was stopped and Armstrong lost four yards, Morton made the Denver crowd stand up and cheer. He rolled out around right end and seeing clear sailing ahead went in for the touchdown that put the Broncos on top, 10-6. That's the way the score remained as the first half ended.

A poor Buffalo punt early in the third period got the Broncos on the scoreboard again. Marv Bateman shanked a kick that only carried 11 yards to the Buffalo 36. Armstrong almost made it all on one play. He shook loose around the left side before safety Tony Greene nailed him on the 1-yard line. On the next play, Armstrong leaped over for the touchdown that gave the Broncos a 16-6 edge. Turner couldn't add to the margin as his conversion attempt hit the left upright.

Later, with some four minutes left in the quarter, Morton led the Broncos on their longest drive of the embryonic season. Beginning on his own 18-yard line, Morton mixed his plays well and drove his team 82 yards on twelve plays. He artfully secured the touchdown with a 1-yard pass to Odoms and a 23-6 lead.

Early in the fourth period, Turner drilled a 26-yard field goal to clinch the victory, 26-6. It was all left to the Bronco defense. With Alzado leading the way, eight tackles, one assist, and a 10-yard sack, the Orange Crush didn't yield a point. And they had held Simpson to just 43 yards in fifteen attempts.

"I don't want to categorize our team as anything now because we won two games," Miller emphasized to a reporter after the game. "It's wrong to talk about the playoffs now. After eight or nine games, maybe."

BUFFALO	0	6	0	0	6
DENVER	3	7	13	3	26

SCORING

Denver: 11:27 First Period—Turner 48 yard field goal.

Buffalo: 13:21 Second Period—Cornell 22 yard fumble recovery. (Kick failed).

Denver: 8:22 Second Period—Morton 1 yard run (Turner kick).

Denver: 11:11 Third Period—Armstrong 1 yard run (Kick failed).

Denver: 3:41 Third Period—Odoms 1 yard pass from Morton (Turner kick).

Denver: 14:02 Fourth Period—Turner 26 yard field goal.

O.J. Simpson of the Buffalo Bills gets squeezed by linebacker Tom Jackson and cornerback Louis Wright.

Game Three: SEATTLE
October 2, 1977

In two weeks, the Orange Crush hadn't yielded a touchdown, but the defense was facing a challenge in their next game. Although the Seattle Seahawks were a young expansion team, they had an offense that could score points. Unfortunately, their defense wasn't as proficient; and as a result the Seahawks were involved in many high-scoring games. Seattle's quarterback Jim Zorn wasn't shy about throwing the ball, and the Broncos expected as much in their first appearance ever in Seattle's Kingdome.

However, Zorn had suffered an injury the week before and wasn't able to play. Rather than risk him against the Broncos, Coach Jack Patera felt it was more prudent to start Steve Myer instead. Even then, Denver couldn't afford to take the Seahawks lightly.

Myer came out throwing. His first pass went for 12 yards and a first down. However, on a third and 13 play, he got in trouble. Scrambling around to avoid being tackled, he was finally sacked by Alzado on the 20. As he was hit, the ball flew out of his hand and was picked up by Paul Smith who ran to the 2-yard line before he was downed.

Morton, staring at a touchdown, almost lost the ball on the snap from Mike Montler. He quickly covered the ball on the 3-yard line. Perrin got 2 yards back, but on third down Armstrong was stopped for no gain. Miller didn't want to settle for a field goal. On fourth down he called a running play, and Perrin took it in. Turner's conversion made it 7-0.

Otis Armstrong goes airborne in an attempt to score against the Seattle Seahawks. He was stopped on the 1-yard line by Terry Beeson (58) and Charles McShane (59).

Seattle, however, didn't bend. They came right back after the kickoff. Myer took his team 68 yards on nine plays for the tying touchdown with the help of a Denver mistake. On a 54-yard field goal try by John Leypoldt, the Broncos were detected off sides. The Seahawks kept possession and continued their drive to the end zone.

But when the Broncos got the ball back, they scored. Just when their drive stalled on the Seattle 18, Turner delivered a 36-yard field goal as the first quarter was coming to its conclusion.

Although there wasn't any scoring in the second period, there was plenty of movement up and down the field. Leypoldt tried to tie the game with a 52-yard field goal midway through the period that fell short. When the half concluded, the score remained 10-7.

Morton didn't wait long to increase the Broncos' lead when the second half began. On a first down play, he tossed a pass to Lytle in the flat, and the rookie running back broke loose down the sideline for a touchdown. Turner's extra point gave the Broncos breathing room, 17-7.

However, a fancy maneuver by Seattle running back David Sims brought the Seahawks close again. After faking a run, he threw a 43-yard pass to Steve Largent, who made a diving catch in the end zone. The touchdown narrowed the Broncos' margin to four points, 17-13. John Grant kept it that way by reaching up and blocking Leypoldt's extra point try.

Just before the quarter ended, Morton got Denver out of danger. He took the Broncos 72 yards in ten plays, going over for the touchdown himself on a 1-yard sneak. Turner's conversion gave Denver an 11-point advantage, 24-13.

Early in the final period Upchurch's fumble on a punt gave Seattle an excellent opportunity to score from the 15-yard line, but the Bronco defense turned the Seahawks back after they reached the 10. That was the closest they came to scoring the remainder of the period as Denver achieved its third straight win, 24-13.

"Enough is whatever it takes to win, and that's all I'm interested in," summed up Miller. "Seattle never gave up. They kept coming back. We would have liked to put more pressure on the passer. Our offensive line play is improving. This was a team victory, not a one unit victory."

DENVER	10	0	14	0	24
SEATTLE	7	0	6	0	13

SCORING

Denver: 11:49 First Period—Perrin 1 yard run (Turner kick).

Seattle: 8:32 First Period—Howard 7 yard pass from Myer (Leypoldt kick).

Denver: :19 First Period—Turner 36 yard field goal.

Denver: 12:09 Third Period—Lytle 47 yard pass from Morton (Turner Kick).

Seattle: 4:57 Third Period—Largent 43 yard pass from Sims (Kick blocked).

Denver: :27 Third Period—Morton 1 yard run (Turner kick).

Game Four: KANSAS CITY
October 9, 1977

Following their first road win, the Broncos returned to Mile High Stadium to face the Kansas City Chiefs. In their long standing rivalry with the Chiefs, the Broncos didn't fare well. In thirty-four meetings between the two teams Denver had only won ssven times. But this was another season, and the Broncos were off to a fine start.

It was a perfect day for football. The day was sunny; the temperature was 68 degrees, and the wind was hardly noticeable at four miles per hour. The only thing that could be better would be another Denver victory. The Denver fans expected as much. Kansas City was a struggling team.

After six minutes had gone by, the Denver defense made its presence felt. On a first down play on the Chiefs' 15-yard line, Mark Bailey was jolted by Paul Smith who stripped him of the ball. John Grant quickly recovered on the 16.

Keyworth moved forward for four yards to the 12. Then Armstrong picked up five more to the 7. On third down and 1, Morton tried to beat the bunched up Chief defense with a touchdown pass to John Schultz but missed. However, Turner calmly booted a 25-yard field goal to get the Broncos on the board, 3-0.

The next time Kansas City got the ball, the Denver defense turned it around again. Quarterback Mike Livingston tried to throw a bomb from the Chiefs' 42-yard line. Louie Wright played the ball all the way and succeeded in pulling it down on Denver's 9-yard line. Wright started up field and almost shook loose for a touchdown. He ran 51 yards before Livingston, the last player between him and the goal line, tripped him up on the Chiefs' 40. When the Chiefs were slapped with a 15-yard penalty on the play, Denver had the ball on the 25-yard line.

On a delay up the middle Keyworth bolted for 11 yards to the 14. Then Keyworth tried the right side and got six more yards to the 8. After Keyworth was stopped, Armstrong could only get a yard. Now the Broncos had a fourth down and 3 on the 7. Mil-

ler decided to go for it. Morton took the snap, kept the ball, and ran a bootleg around the right side for a touchdown. When the quarter ended, the Broncos were on top, 10-0.

Denver threatened again as the second period began. In the closing seconds of the first quarter, Billy Thompson intercepted a Livingston pass on the Denver 43-yard line, and brought it back to the Chiefs' 32. However, after one first down the Bronco offense stalled. Still, Turner put more points on the board with a 33-yard field goal and a 13-0 lead. The next time the Broncos got the ball, Turner came through again. This time he kicked a 33-yard field goal to give Denver a 16-0 bulge which was how the first half ended.

In the third period, the Bronco defense set up another score. Tommy Jackson intercepted Tony Adams's pass to give the

Broncos possession on the Chiefs' 46-yard line. On a first down play from the 35, Morton was dropped for a 10-yard loss. However, he came right back with a beautiful 44-yard pass to Upchurch on the 1-yard line. Armstrong took it over from there as Denver put the game out of reach, 23-0.

A 2-yard run by Ed Podolak with eight minutes left in the game averted a Kansas City shutout as Denver prevailed, 23-7. The Broncos had won their fourth straight game. Linebacker Bob Swenson led the defensive heroics with ten tackles, one assist, and a pass deflection.

In a jubilant locker room after the game, Miller, with justifiable pride, summed it up. "This was the first time in a long time, maybe ever, that the Broncos ever went out and dominated a game against the Chiefs."

KANSAS CITY	0	0	0	7	7
DENVER	10	6	7	0	23

SCORING

Denver: 7:31 First Period—Turner 25 yard field goal.

Denver: 1:32 First Period—Morton 7 yard run (Turner Kick).

Denver: 12:32 Second Period—Turner 33 yard field goal.

Denver: 5:06 Second Period—Turner 33 yard field goal.

Denver: 9:17 Third Period—Armstrong 1 yard run (Turner kick).

Kansas City: 7:25 Fourth Period—Podolak 2 yard run (Stenerud kick).

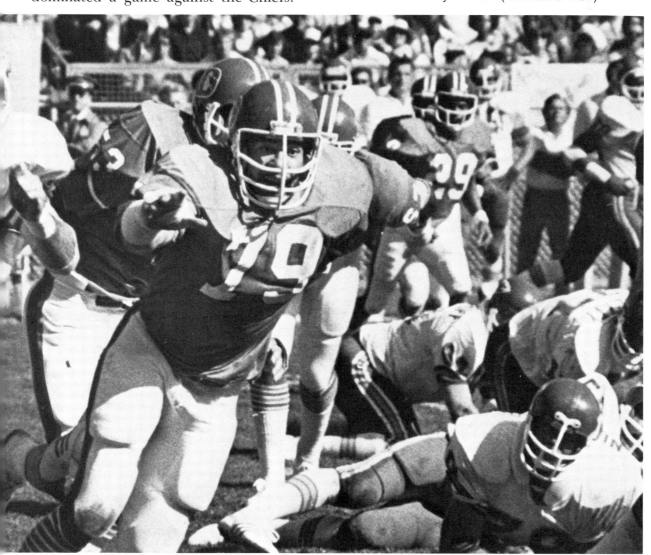

Ed Podolak of the Kansas City Chiefs tries to get past defensive end Barney Chavous.

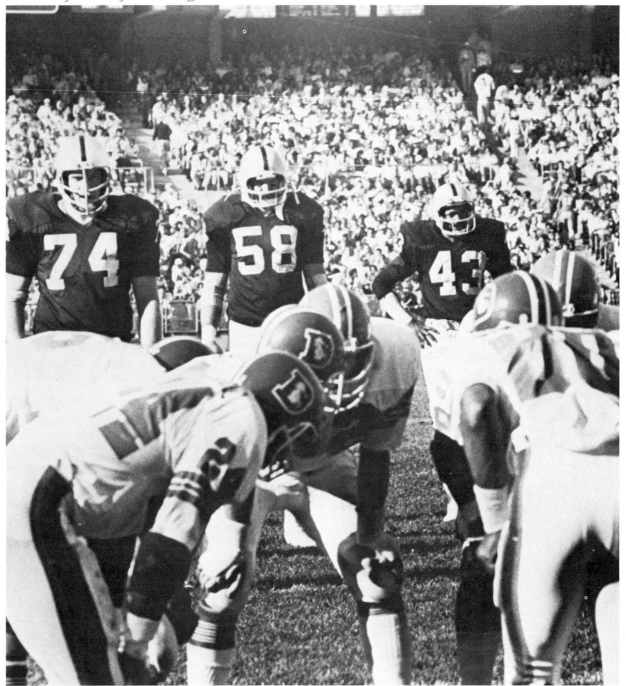

Game Five: OAKLAND
October 16, 1977

The fact that the Broncos had gotten off to their best start in history wasn't cause for undo celebrating. Although unbeaten through four games, the Broncos had to place their early season success against the also unbeaten Oakland Raiders in Oakland. The Raiders, the defending world champions, had an undefeated string of seventeen regular season and playoff games. In their own backyard, the Alameda County Stadium, they were virtually unbeatable. The contest would most definitely serve as a barometer in judging just how good the Broncos really were.

It was no surprise that the Raiders were favored, and they started according to form. Taking the opening kickoff, quarterback Ken Stabler took the Raiders straight down field, 70 yards in just ten plays for a touchdown on a 9-yard pass to his tight end, Dave Casper.

Defensive end Brison Manor crashes through to dump Oakland quarterback Ken Stabler for an 8-yard loss.

Safety Bill Thompson tries to elude Oakland guard George Buehler in an attempt to get running back Clarence Davis.

The second time the Raiders got the ball, Stabler had them moving again. After two first downs, they had a second and 8 on the Denver 41. Stabler looked to throw. Linebacker Joe Rizzo was ready. He picked off Stabler's pass and carried the ball 38 yards before being caught on the Oakland 29-yard line.

Denver came alive after that play. It didn't take Morton long to tie the contest. He got the Broncos in the end zone in six plays, hitting Odoms on a third down pass from the 10-yard line. When the first period action subsided two minutes later, Oakland and Denver were deadlocked at 7-7.

In the early moments of the second period, Denver's defense kept Oakland in poor field position. They began one series on the 14 and had to punt. Then they began on the 1-yard line and were forced to kick again as the Orange Crush pressured Stabler.

The Broncos had the ball on the Raiders' 42. After two first downs, they had reached Oakland's 16. Then Lonnie Perrin broke loose around right end and scored standing up. Morton had moved the Broncos 42 yards in just six plays for a 14-7 lead.

Now the Bronco defense was fired up. Rizzo again intercepted a Stabler pass on the Denver 49-yard line, but the Broncos couldn't turn it into points. But only minutes later, Rizzo plucked off another Stabler pass, his third of the game. Again the Broncos came up empty as Turner missed a 45-yard field goal attempt.

However, three plays later the Broncos got the ball again. This time Gradishar intercepted Stabler and gave Denver possession on the Oakland 32. After three plays, the Broncos had a fourth and 3 on the Oakland 25. Turner was sent in to try a 33-yard field goal. Reserve quarterback Norris Weese knelt to hold the ball for Turner. He took the snap, rose to his feet, waited for Turner to run down field, and then calmly threw him the ball. The heavy-legged Turner caught it all

alone and went in for a touchdown that catapulted the Broncos into a 21-7 lead just before first half play ended.

In the third period, the Bronco defense continued to pressure Stabler. With just four minutes left, Stabler tried to hit his speedy wide receiver Cliff Branch on his own 18-yard line. But cornerback Louie Wright moved in front of Branch, intercepted the ball, and ran for a touchdown. The Broncos' edge remained at 27-7 as Turner's conversion try was wide to the left.

It was obvious that the Raiders were in deep trouble when the fourth quarter began, and Stabler couldn't contend with the Bronco defense. He was intercepted twice more before he left the game. After the second time, Turner kicked a 32-yard field goal with seven minutes left in the game to put the game away, 30-7. Incredibly, the Denver defense had intercepted seven Stabler passes. The Broncos' convincing victory left the Raiders in shock.

"This team has been around the fringes too long," said Miller after the game. "People will start looking up now. All we want is the respect from other teams."

DENVER	7	14	6	3	30
OAKLAND	7	0	0	0	7

SCORING

Oakland: 9:27 First Period—Casper 9 yard pass from Stabler (Mann kick).

Denver: 2:19 First Period—Odoms 10 yard pass from Morton (Turner kick).

Denver: 6:36 Second Period—Perrin 16 yard run (Turner kick).

Denver: :59 Second Period—Turner 25 yard pass from Weese (Turner kick).

Denver: 3:45 Third Period—Wright 18 yard interception (Kick failed).

Denver: 7:07 Fourth Period—Turner 32 yard field goal.

Game Six: CINCINNATI
October 23, 1977

Following their inspiring victory over the Raiders that left them on top of the Western Division with a 5-0 record, the Broncos faced another tough road opponent. On the sixth week of the season, they went against the Cin-cinnati Bengals who had championship visions of their own.

The Bengals scored first after they took the opening kickoff. Capped by a 65-yard gallop by Pete Johnson, the Bengals scored on the next play when the big rookie plowed in from a yard out.

With some five minutes left in the quarter, the Broncos struck back. Reserve linebacker Larry Evans recovered a fumbled punt on the

Bengals' 40-yard line. In four plays, all on the ground, the Broncos scored. Armstrong ran for 14 yards, and then Keyworth broke open for 16 to the 10-yard line. Keyworth carried again for a yard. Morton called his number again, and Keyworth crashed into the end zone for the tying touchdown.

In the opening minutes of the second period, kicker Chris Bahr sent the Bengals in front again with a 19-yard field goal. After the Bengals got the ball back, Evans made his presence known once again. This time he intercepted quarterback Ken Anderson's pass on the Bengals' 45-yard line.

Morton managed to produce two first downs as he got the Broncos as far as the Bengals' 24-yard line. But his third down pass to Moses went incomplete, and Miller sent in the field goal team. Turner connected on a 41-yard kick that evened the game at 10-10.

Linebacker Larry Evans picks up a loose ball against the Cincinnati Bengals.

Then, with less than two minutes remaining, the surprising Broncos stunned the Bengals. With the ball on their own 20, Armstrong was stopped for a yard loss. There was only 1:15 showing on the clock when Morton faded back to pass. Insofar as Red Miller's offensive philosophy was concerned he was throwing from a minus field position. But Morton was on target. He fired the ball to wide receiver Jack Dolbin who sped all the way for a touchdown. The pass covered 81 yards, the longest play of the year. The Broncos left the field at half time with a 17-10 advantage.

In a hard fought third quarter, no scoring took place. In fact, neither the Broncos or the Bengals even got close enough to attempt a field goal.

However, in the opening minutes of the last quarter, the Bengals attempted a comeback. They got as far as the Broncos' 7-yard line before they had to settle for a field goal. Bahr's 24-yard kick brought the Bengals to within 17-13. Still, Cincinnati had an uphill struggle. Anderson, who had been hurt near the end of the third quarter, was finished for the afternoon.

The Broncos were also left without Morton for the remainder of the game. He, too, had been injured in the third period and was replaced by Craig Penrose. The final outcome of the game still hung in the balance. Miller encouraged his offense to keep things going, and they did.

There was 8:20 left to play in the game when the Broncos got the ball on their own 37-yard line. Carefully, Penrose moved the Broncos on the ground. He threw only one pass, but it set up the Broncos' final touchdown. On first down from the Bengals' 24-yard line, Penrose hit rookie running back Rob Lytle with a swing pass that gained 22 yards to the 2-yard line. Three plays later, Jim Jensen went over from the 1 to insure the win, 24-13. The Broncos had won six games in succession. To many it was unreal, but not to Red Miller.

"Our team grew up quite a bit today," Miller said. "You have to build from the bottom up. The guys on the bench have to play up to the caliber of the starters. Our guys came in and did that today. It was the key to the victory."

DENVER	7	10	0	7	24
CINCINNATI	7	3	0	3	13

SCORING

Cincinnati: 12:32 First Period—Johnson 1 yard run (Bahr kick).

Denver: 3:36 First Period—Keyworth 9 yard run (Turner kick).

Cincinnati: 11:42 Second Period—Bahr 19 yard field goal.

Denver: 4:10 Second Period—Turner 41 yard field goal.

Denver: 1:01 Second Period—Dolbin 81 yard pass from Morton (Turner kick).

Cincinnati: 11:20 Fourth Period—Bahr 24 yard field goal.

Denver: 2:21 Fourth Period—Jensen 1 yard run (Turner kick).

Game Seven: OAKLAND
October 30, 1977

There was more excitement in Denver than there would have been if a gold strike had been announced. The amazing success of the Broncos had turned the entire town on. They were the only team in the AFC to remain unbeaten. There was a championship atmosphere in town. So excited were Bronco fans that the return engagement against the angry Oakland Raiders was designated as "Orange Sunday." Almost every one of the 75,007 fans who attended the game was ablaze with some manner of orange clothing. Tickets were being scalped as high as $150 apiece.

As play commenced, the defense which had yielded a paltry 46 points in the first six games of the season, was still generating the applause. The first two times the Raiders had the ball, they were repulsed. However, a short punt gave the Raiders excellent field position on their own 45-yard line; and it took quarterback Ken Stabler only eight plays to get the Raiders in front, 7-0. The touchdown was a picture play. On a third down and 6 from the Denver 21, Stabler read a blitz. Nevertheless, he stood in the pocket long enough to wait for wide receiver Cliff Branch to run his pattern. Just before getting hit, Stabler released the ball. Branch caught it on the 6-yard line and scored untouched.

The first time Oakland got the ball in the second period, they scored again. Stabler marched the Raiders all the way from his 17-yard line. He appeared moving toward another touchdown when the Bronco defense stiffened. On a third and 2 play from the 24, running back Mark van Eeghen was dropped for a yard loss by Brison Manor. Errol Mann then proceeded to kick a 42-yard field goal that stretched Oakland's lead to 10-0.

After the kickoff, the Raiders got the ball right back and scored again. On a first down play from the 20-yard line, Jim Jensen fumbled. Oakland linebacker Monte Johnson picked up the ball and ran to the 15 before he was stopped. Two plays later Clarence David moved quickly around the left side and scored from the 8-yard line. The Raiders were

Jack Dolbin

now on top, 17-0. Denver had not penetrated further than Oakland's 41-yard line.

With five minutes remaining in the third quarter, the Raiders struck again. Once again they turned another Denver mistake into a touchdown. On a first down play from his own 20-yard line, Morton tried to pass. But the ball was intercepted by linebacker Floyd Rice on the 45, and he picked up 3 yards before being stopped on the 42. Stabler got them in on ten plays, only one of them being a pass. Van Eeghen ran the ball the last five plays in a row, finally going over from the 1-yard line. The big crowd was numb as the Raiders extended their margin to 24-0.

Throughout the entire third period, the Broncos were unable to get past their own 30-yard line. It wasn't very encouraging. However, Morton got them moving in the early minutes of the last quarter. He sparked the Broncos on a ten play, 80-yard drive and produced the Broncos' first touchdown on an 11-yard pass to Jack Dolbin.

Even though Oakland's margin seemed too much to overcome, the Broncos tried. On their next drive, they reached the Raider 36 before Morton was sacked for 14 yards while attempting to pass on fourth down. The next time he got the ball, Morton, connecting on

five of seven passes, took the Broncos 70 yards on nine plays. Armstrong raced in from the 7-yard line to cut the Raiders' lead to 24-14. However, only three minutes were left in the game; and there just wasn't enough time. The Broncos had lost their first game of the season. More importantly, they fell into a tie with Oakland for first place in the AFC with a 6-1 record.

"The one thing we didn't want to give the Broncos was life," Oakland coach John Madden said after the game. "We wanted to keep their backs to the wall and have them staring at eighty yards each time they got the ball."

Miller was disappointed. "We wanted to win so badly for our fans, the city, and ourselves," he lamented, "but we didn't do it. I'm disappointed but not downhearted. Being 6-1 is a helluva record in my opinion."

OAKLAND	7	10	7	0	24
DENVER	0	0	0	14	14

SCORING

Oakland: 5:50 First Period—Branch 21 yard pass from Stabler (Mann kick).

Oakland: 8:05 Second Period—Mann 42 yard field goal.

Oakland: 6:32 Second Period—Davis 8 yard run (Mann kick).

Oakland: 4:28 Third Period—Van Eeghen 1 yard run (Mann kick).

Denver: 12:18 Fourth Period—Dolbin 11 yard pass from Morton (Turner kick).

Denver: 2:51 Fourth Period—Armstrong 7 yard run (Turner kick).

Oakland quarterback Ken Stabler just gets the pass off over the arm of tackle John Grant.

Game Eight: PITTSBURGH
November 6, 1977

The loss to the Raiders the week before put the Broncos' chances for the 1977 season into another perspective. As the campaign was entering its second half of the schedule, the question that was raised around the league was whether the Broncos could bounce back. Many critics felt that Denver's bubble had burst. The telling blow, they claimed, would come against the Pittsburgh Steelers at Mile High Stadium. They believed that the Broncos would be emotionally and mentally down for the game.

Although not appearing as awesome as in their two Super Bowl years, the Steelers were still talented and very physical. They had a 4-3 record after struggling through the first half of the season, one that was filled with an unusual amount of penalties and mistakes. Yet, they were in the thick of battle for the Central Division crown along with Cincinnati, Houston, and Cleveland.

The Broncos were quick to quiet their critics. The second time they received the ball, they scored. Beginning on their own 35-yard line, Morton marched them 65 yards in eleven plays. Three key plays enabled the Broncos to keep moving. The first was a third down pass that Morton threw to Riley Odoms that gained 24 yards. Another was a first down pass to Rob Lytle that picked up another 14. The last came two plays later when Armstrong ripped through the left side for 17 yards to the 3. On third down from the one, Lytle punched it across. Turner's conversion put the Broncos ahead, 7-0.

With about a minute left in the quarter, Rick Upchurch brought the crowd to its feet with an electrifying run. After the Steelers had failed to move the ball, Bobby Walden was sent in to punt from midfield. He got off a kick that Upchurch caught on his own 13. He quickly started upfield, and before the Steelers could realize it, broke it for an 87-yard touchdown. It was the first time since 1969 that anyone had run a punt back for a touchdown against the Steelers. However, of more immediate value, Upchurch had

The Orange Crush applies their muscle to Franco Harris of the Pittsburgh Steelers. From left, Lyle Alzado (77), Bernard Jackson (29), Randy Gradishar (53) and Barney Chavous on the bottom.

stretched Denver's advantage to 14-0.

Midway through the second period, the Steelers still couldn't penetrate Denver's defense. They had a modest drive going when they were abruptly halted. Trying to run up the middle, Rocky Bleier was jolted by Randy Gradishar. In bringing him to the ground, Gradishar stripped the ball from Bleier's arm. Billy Thompson swooped in and recovered the ball on the Denver 47-yard line.

It didn't take Morton long to cash in. On first down he passed to Jim Jensen down the middle for 34 yards to the Pittsburgh 19. After Armstrong lost a yard, Morton went back to his passing game. He found Moses open on the 1-yard line. Moses made a fine catch and fell into the end zone for a touchdown. In three plays, Morton had gained 53 yards. Turner's kick had given the Broncos a surprising 21-0 bulge.

The Steelers tried to come back. Following the kickoff, they reached the Broncos 7-yard line; but Tommy Jackson led the defense in disposing of the threat. He stopped Franco Harris for no gain and then sacked quarterback Terry Bradshaw for a 12-yard loss as the first half came to a close.

The Bronco defense didn't give the Steelers any decent field position the entire third period. The furthest Pittsburgh advance was to their own 40-yard line. When the fourth period began, the Denver fans were hoping for a shutout. Certainly the defense was play-ing hard enough to achieve it.

There were only eight minutes left in the game when the Steelers got the ball for the last time. They were on their own 26-yard line. Aided by two Denver penalties for 25 yards, Bradshaw took the Steelers 74 yards in eight plays for their only touchdown. It came on a 4-yard pass to John Stallworth about four minutes from the end. Led by Jackson, who had six tackles, an assist, and two sacks, the Broncos had indeed bounced back.

Upchurch played a big part in the victory with his kick returns. He carried five of them for 187 yards, a fine afternoon's work. "It seemed like the Steelers weren't getting to the ball," he said after it was all over. "They weren't swarming like they used to."

One thing for certain, the Broncos were!

PITTSBURGH	0	0	0	7	7
DENVER	14	7	0	0	21

SCORING

Denver: 5:12 First Period—Lytle 1 yard run (Turner kick).

Denver: :57 First Period—Upchurch 87 yard punt return (Turner kick).

Denver: 4:59 Second Period—Moses 20 yard pass from Morton (Turner kick).

Pittsburgh: 4:12 Fourth Period—Stallworth 4 yard pass from Bradshaw (Gerela kick).

Game Nine: SAN DIEGO November 13, 1977

The triumph over the Steelers left the Broncos and the Raiders still deadlocked for the Western Division lead with 7-1 records. Miller was satisfied with the resiliency his squad had displayed in convincingly beating Pittsburgh. If they had lost to the Steelers after their initial defeat the week earlier to Oakland, the Broncos could have easily gone into a spin.

In facing the San Diego Chargers on the coast for the first time in the season, the Broncos couldn't take them lightly. Although they were only 4-4, the Chargers were a pesky bunch. Their coach, Tommy Prothro, is an advocate of wide open football. He not only likes the passing game but also improvises trick plays as well.

Yet, neither team appeared to have much of an offense in the early minutes of the game. The first two times the Chargers were in control, they failed to produce a first down. Then, when they got the ball the second time, they gave it away. Starting on the Bronco 35-yard line, Armstrong picked up two yards. Then Lonnie Perrin tried to find running room around left end. He was smacked for a 5-yard loss and fumbled the ball. Defensive end Fred Dean picked up the loose ball on the 11-yard line and rambled in for a touchdown. Quickly, the Chargers had jumped into a 7-0 lead.

Following the kickoff, the Broncos started play on their own 15-yard line. They had a long way to go. Morton almost got them all the way but had to be satisfied with a field goal. He moved the Broncos 67 yards on twelve plays as Turner booted a 35-yard field goal to reduce San Diego's margin to 7-3.

The Chargers came back quickly. When the first period ended, they were on the Broncos' 8-yard line. On the first play of the second quarter, Rickey Young lost three yards when Jackson nailed him on the 11. A penalty set the Chargers back five yards more. When James Harris's pass to Young only gained two yards, Rolf Benirschke attempted a 31-yard field goal. However, Barny Chavous broke through and blocked it.

Still, San Diego came back the next time they got the ball. After Harris threw a 15-yard screen pass to Don Woods, Joe Washington got three yards to the Denver 32. On second down, Harris handed the ball to Washington, who suddenly stopped and threw a 32-yard touchdown pass to wide receiver Charlie Joiner. San Diego went in front by 14-3. That's what the score remained when the first half ended.

When the third period opened, Denver still couldn't get anything going. When Benirschke missed a 51-yard field goal attempt, the Broncos took over on their own 34. After five consecutive running plays, Morton hit Odoms with a quick 7-yard pass on the Chargers' 35-yard line. Three plays later, Morton delivered a 33-yard touchdown pass to Haven Moses. It culminated a nine-play 66-yard drive that narrowed San Diego's lead to 14-10 with eight minutes still left in the period.

Neither team could mount any scoring drives the remainder of the quarter. The game was now a defensive struggle, and it remained that way well into the final period. Time was running out for the Broncos. When they got the ball on their own 46-yard line, there was only 2:37 showing on the clock.

A pass interference penalty and Morton's 12-yard pass to Armstrong got the Broncos to the Chargers' 13-yard line as the two minute warning was given. However, a first-down

Barney Chavous

holding penalty pushed the Broncos back to the 23. Morton then tried to hit Dolbin but missed. On second down, he found Odoms for a 10-yard gain to the 13. He then tried to sneak Lonnie Perrin around right end, but he was stopped on the 8. Now it was fourth down and 5. The outcome of the entire game came down to the one last play for the Broncos. Morton had to pass. He looked over the field and fired an 8-yard touchdown pass to Moses. The Broncos pulled out a 17-14 victory with only 1:36 left in the game.

"We always find some way to win, one way or the other," smiled Miller after the gun had sounded, "and this was the other."

DENVER	3	0	7	7	17
SAN DIEGO	7	7	0	0	14

SCORING

San Diego: 9:27 First Period—Dean 11 yard fumble return (Benirschke kick).

Denver: 4:54 First Period—Turner 35 yard field goal.

San Diego: 11:12 Second Period—Joiner 32 yard pass from J. Washington (Benirschke kick).

Denver: 8:10 Third Period—Moses 33 yard pass from Morton (Turner kick).

Denver: 1:36 Fourth Period—Moses 8 yard pass from Morton (Turner kick).

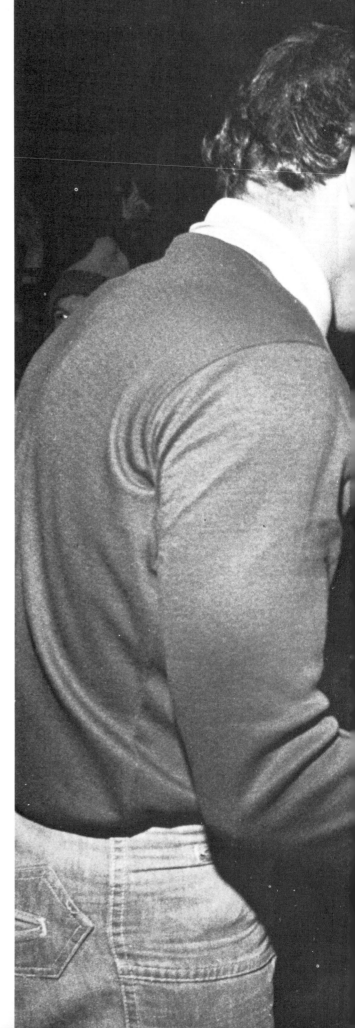

Craig Morton, who threw two touchdown passes against San Diego to give the Broncos a come-from-behind victory, is greeted at the airport by jubilent Bronco fans.

Game Ten: KANSAS CITY November 20, 1977

Although the Broncos had easily defeated the Kansas City Chiefs, 23-7, earlier in the season, Coach Red Miller cautioned his squad not to be complacent. He also didn't want them to look past the Chiefs to the following week's game against the Baltimore Colts. Like the Broncos, the Colts were also 8-1.

The Broncos have never been even mildly successful playing in Kansas City. In their last fourteen appearances there, they had only won a single time. The sole victory occurred in 1974 when Denver edged Kansas City, 17-14. Miller reminded his players about that, too.

There were only 54,050 fans who turned out in Arrowhead Stadium on a mild November afternoon. The temperature was 52 degrees, and the humidity was 60 percent. It was a nice day to watch a football game; but because the Chiefs could only manage a 2-7 record, Arrowhead was well below its capacity of 80,000 fans.

There were just 6:53 left in the first quarter when the Broncos got the ball on the Chiefs' 41-yard line. Armstrong, who had earlier success running on Denver's first series, swept around right end for 12 yards to the 29. After managing only a yard, he broke loose for 11 more before he was brought down on the 17. The Broncos had something going. They got down to the 8-yard line before being faced with a fourth and 1. Miller decided to go for a field goal and sent Turner in. However, the Chiefs had lined up offside and were penalized half the distance to the goal line. The Broncos had a first down on the 4-yard line. Armstrong picked up a yard. Then Keyworth carried up the middle and fumbled. Linebacker Willie Lanier pounced on the ball and killed Denver's chances for a score.

However, as the first period came to a close, the Broncos had another drive working. They began on the Chiefs' 47-yard line as Jerrel Wilson was forced to punt from his end zone following Keyworth's fumble. When the second quarter started, the Broncos had a second and 1 on Kansas City's 20-yard line. Just when it appeared that the Broncos were stalled,

Morton got them going. On a third and 15 from the 22, he connected for a 17-yard pass with Odoms on the 5-yard line. Two plays later, Perrin went over from the 2 as the Broncos earned a 7-0 lead.

It appeared that would be the only scoring of the first half. However, with just 1:43 left, the Chiefs came to life. Quarterback Mike Livingston went to work on his own 38-yard line. He threw eight straight passes, completing seven, to reach the Broncos' 19. Three plays later, with just 17 seconds remaining, Livingston hit Henry Marshall with a 15-yard touchdown pass to tie the game at 7-7.

Again, the defenses dominated play in the third period. Neither team got close enough for a touchdown. However, they did work their way into field goal range. Linebacker Bob Swenson gave the Broncos a chance when he intercepted a Livingston pass on the Chiefs' 33. Morton then surprised the Chiefs on a keeper play, running to the 15-yard line before he was tackled. When the Broncos came

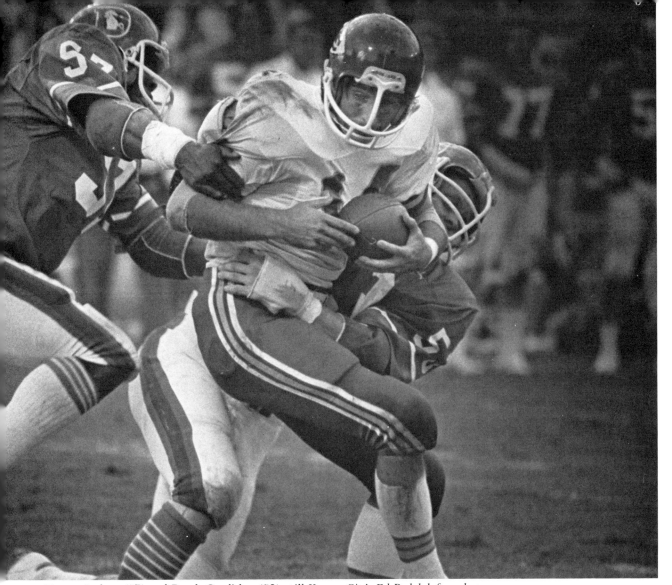

Tommy Jackson (57) and Randy Gradishar (53) spill Kansas City's Ed Podolak for a loss.

up a yard short on the 9-yard line, Turner was given the opportunity to put Denver in front; but his attempt from the 26-yard line was wide to the left. His counterpart on the Chiefs, Jan Stenerud, had the same opportunity from the 36-yard line. His kick missed when it hit the upright.

In the early moments of the fourth period Turner was called upon again. This time he was wide to the left from the 39-yard line. The clock was now becoming a factor. Morton realized it when he took over on his own 48-yard line with 6:08 left. After three running plays advanced the ball to the Kansas City 23, Morton and Moses worked their magic again as they combined on a 23-yard touchdown play.

But the Chiefs weren't finished. On a fake punt, Raymond Burks ran 51 yards before Louie Wright made a touchdown-saving tackle on the 1-yard line. It appeared as if the Chiefs would tie the score. However, the Bronco defense reared up. Two running plays gained nothing. Then Tommy Jackson made the big play when he dumped tight end Walter White for a 6-yard loss back to the 7. Livingston's last resort was a pass that failed. The Orange Crush had preserved the victory.

"First and goal, I thought we were going into overtime," sighed Morton in relief. "Our defense was just unbelievably incredible."

DENVER	0	7	0	7	14
KANSAS CITY	0	7	0	0	7

SCORING

Denver: 11:55 Second Period—Perrin 2 yard run (Turner kick).

Kansas City: :12 Second Period—Marshall 15 yard pass from Livingston (Stenerud kick).

Denver: 4:29 Fourth Period—Moses 23 yard pass from Morton (Turner kick).

135

Game Eleven: BALTIMORE
November 27, 1977

The inspiring goal line stand against Kansas City enabled the Broncos to grow overnight into a serious championship contender. It gave them momentum for the remaining month of the regular season. While they were beating the Chiefs, Oakland was upended by San Diego, 21-7. Denver led the Western Division with a 9-1 record, while Oakland dropped behind with an 8-2 mark.

Threatening their first place existence were the Baltimore Colts. Like the Broncos, they were 9-1 and led the Eastern Division. They also were a strong playoff contender, and many experts picked them to make it to the Super Bowl. Led by quarterback Bert Jones and running back Lydell Mitchell, the Colts had an explosive offense ready for Mile High Stadium.

With five minutes left in the first period, Jones had the ball on the Denver 40. He tried to go deep to his wide receiver Glenn Doughty. However, Billy Thompson intercepted the pass on the 23 and almost got away for a touchdown before Jones pulled him down on the Colts' 47. After Lytle got six yards, Morton struck quickly. On second down he tossed a 41-yard touchdown pass to Upchurch. The crowd roared its delight as Denver went into a 7-0 lead.

Baltimore couldn't do anything the first two times they had the ball in the second quarter. With 9:40 left, the Broncos regained possession on their own 15-yard line. Two running plays gained a first down on the 28. Then Morton took over. He surprised the Colts with a 35-yard pass to Moses on the Colts' 37. Then he hit Dolbin with a 16-yard pass to the 21. Morton wasn't finished. After Perrin picked up two yards, he dropped back to pass for a third time. He looked for Dolbin and found him in the end zone for a 19-yard touchdown. The Broncos jumped into a 14-0 lead.

By now the Bronco fans were as excited as the Colts were anxious. They knew they had to

Craig Morton finds matters crowded, trying to pass against the Baltimore Colts, as tackle Mike Barnes grabs his ankle and guard Paul Howard holds off tackle Joe Ehrmann.

136

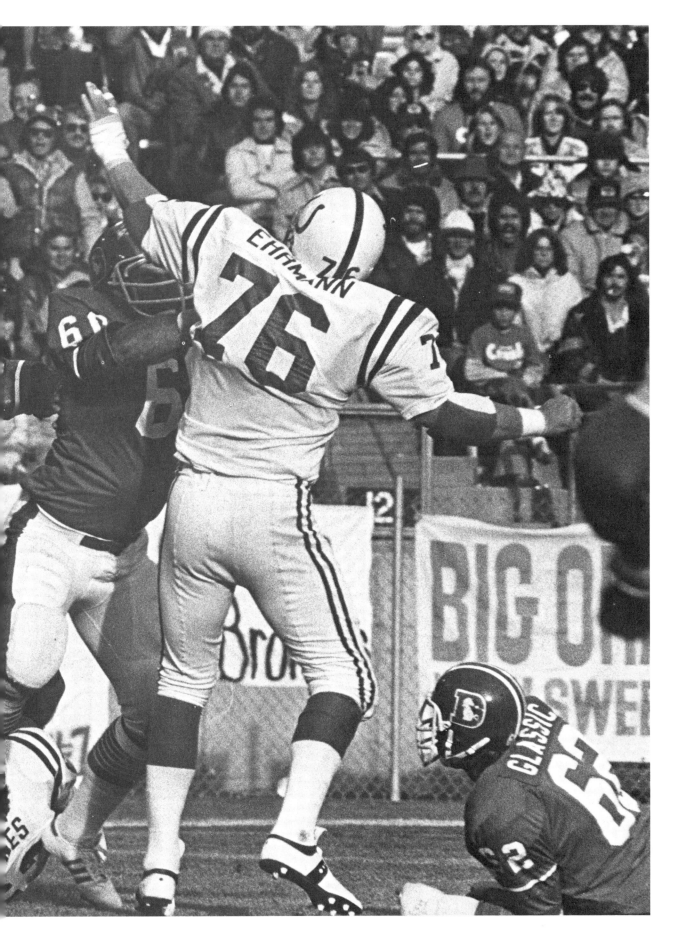

score before the first half finished. After a long drive that carried 57 yards in fifteen plays, Toni Linhart booted a 40-yard field goal to get the Colts on the board. When the first half action subsided, the Broncos were on top, 14-3.

The field goal gave the Colts a halftime lift. In the third period, they dominated the play and began to build momentum. They cut Denver's lead to 14-6 when Linhart kicked a 43-yard field goal. The next time they controlled the ball, they scored a touchdown. Jones carried them 68 yards in eleven plays, passing to Mitchell for a final 11 yards, trimming Denver's edge to 14-13.

The outcome of the game would be determined in the final quarter. The Broncos had to stop the Colts' momentum and turn the game around, but the Colts were driving once again. They had a third down and 7 on the Denver 29. Jones decided to pass for the first down. Tommy Jackson was reading pass all the way. He cut in front of running back Don McCauley, who was waiting for the flare pass, intercepted the ball without breaking stride, and sped 73 yards down the sidelines for a touchdown. The home crowd went wild as Jackson's teammates practically carried him off the sidelines. That one play seemed to break the Colts' back. Suddenly, the Broncos were in command again, 21-13.

But Jones didn't give up. With his talented arm, he can score touchdowns quickly. With only 1:45 left in the game, he was trying. Although deep in his own territory, Jones passed from his own end zone. He threw a long one that was intended for his tight end, Raymond Chester. Louie Wright alertly picked off the pass and ran 59 yards to Baltimore's 9-yard line before he was stopped. On second down

from the 6, Morton rolled around right end for a touchdown. Denver had won its tenth game of the campaign, 27-13. Baltimore left Denver in a state of shock, and the rest of the football world was now beginning to take the Broncos very seriously indeed.

No one was happier than Tommy Jackson. His big interception, the longest in the 18-year history of the Broncos, crushed the Colts' momentum and completely turned the game around.

"Jones was gaining confidence in the flat pass," a happy Jackson explained. "I just decided to come underneath. I don't think Bert ever saw me."

What everyone else around the league did see was that the Broncos, with ten wins and one loss, had the best record in the NFL.

BALTIMORE	0	3	10	0	13
DENVER	7	7	0	13	27

SCORING

Denver: 3:19 First Period—Upchurch 47 yard pass from Morton (Turner kick).

Denver: 6:11 Second Period—Dolbin 19 yard pass from Morton (Turner kick).

Baltimore: 1:10 Second Period—Linhart 40 yard field goal.

Baltimore: 10:38 Third Period—Linhart 43 yard field goal.

Baltimore: 3:36 Third Period—Mitchell 15 yard pass from Jones (Linhart kick).

Denver: 7:20 Fourth Period—T. Jackson 73 yard interception (Turner kick).

Denver: 1:14 Fourth Period—Morton 6 yard run (Kick failed).

Game Twelve: HOUSTON
December 4, 1977

While nobody was actually talking playoffs yet with three games remaining in the regular season, it was not unthinkable that the Denver fans, and even the players, were looking ahead to them. The Broncos maintained a one-game lead over the Raiders. All they needed was another win and an Oakland loss to clinch the Western Division title for the first time in their history.

Although he didn't say so, Red Miller had it figured that way. Without the players knowing it, he had cases of champagne placed on the plane that was taking the Broncos to Houston. The Oilers, too, were thinking playoffs. Even though they were 6-5, they were only one game out of first place in the tight Central Division race. And with quarterback Don Pastorini and swift wide receiver Ken Burrough, they could score quickly from anywhere on the field. The Oilers also had another quick-strike weapon, Billy "White Shoes" Johnson, who was a dangerous kick return runner.

In a tightly played, scoreless first quarter, both teams resorted to conservative football. Pastorini threw only three passes and Morton just one. But Pastorini's last pass on the final play of the quarter woke the crowd up. He collaborated with Burrough on a 51-yard bomb that reached the Broncos' 16-yard line.

When the second period opened, the Oilers were threatening. After a running play gained a yard, Pastorini went to the pass. He tossed his fourth straight completion, a 13-yard pick up to his running back Ronnie Coleman. On the next play, Coleman scored from the 2-yard line to give Houston a 7-0 lead.

Following the kickoff, Morton brought the Broncos right back. He led Denver on a 79-yard drive that consumed fourteen plays. Eight of the plays were passes, Morton completing four of them. The final one was to Odoms, a 13-yard touchdown that tied the game. Morton was moving the club again the next time he got the ball. However, when he reached the Oiler 35-yard line, he was stopped momentarily. Zeke Moore intercepted his pass but fumbled the ball on the Houston 46.

Craig Penrose

Norris Weese

Moses recovered, and Morton got another chance. He threw five passes, completing four. The last completion, with only 46 seconds left, was a 13-yard touchdown to Upchurch. When the half ended, Denver was on top, 14-7.

The Broncos took the second half kickoff, and this time reserve quarterback Craig Penrose kept the team moving. He took the Broncos from their own 35-yard line to the Oilers' 28, at which point Turner kicked a 42-yard field goal, stretching Denver's lead to 17-7.

Pastorini got the Oilers right back in the game after the Broncos had piled up 17 straight points. He drove the Oilers 56 yards in five plays, ending the drive with a 29-yard touchdown pass to Burrough that brought Houston close at 17-14.

Strong safety Bill Thompson (36) tries unsuccessfully to prevent Houston running back Ronnie Coleman from scoring.

Denver fans were a bit uneasy watching the game on television. They knew that the Raiders were trailing in their game against the Los Angeles Rams, but they were still worried as the Broncos and Oilers began their final period of play. However, midway through the quarter they breathed a lot easier. The Broncos charged 54 yards in seven plays to score the clinching touchdown. Quarterback Norris Weese went in from five yards out to send the Broncos into a 24-14 lead with less than five minutes left. The key play in the drive was a third down Morton pass to Odoms that covered 33 yards. With the victory, Bronco fans began to celebrate.

The players didn't celebrate until the plane that was returning them to Denver was over Amarillo, Texas. The pilot informed Miller that the Rams had defeated the Raiders. The Broncos were officially in. They were the champions of the Western Division for the first time in the 18-year existence of the franchise. Miller ordered the champagne to be passed out.

"I thought the players were going to tear the plane apart," beamed Miller. "They were stomping and throwing champagne in the air. We were in the playoffs; and for the first time that season, I was ready to talk about them. When I took the job, my first objective was to win the respect of the other teams."

And if they hadn't by now, they certainly would when the playoffs were over.

DENVER	0	14	3	7	24
HOUSTON	0	7	7	0	14

SCORING

Houston: 14:14 Second Period—Coleman 2 yard run (Fritsch kick).

Denver: 8:04 Second Period—Odoms 13 yard pass from Morton (Turner kick).

Denver: 5:53 Second Period—Upchurch 13 yard pass from Morton (Turner kick).

Denver: 9:57 Third Period—Turner 42 yard field goal.

Houston: 7:21 Third Period—Burrough 24 yard pass from Pastorini (Fritsch kick).

Denver: 4:58 Fourth Period—Weese 5 yard run (Turner kick).

Game Thirteen: SAN DIEGO
December 11, 1977

Their first divisional title assured, the Broncos returned to Mile High Stadium for their last home game of the regular season. But it would certainly not be the last football game of the year in Denver. By winning the previous week while the other playoff contenders in the remaining divisions were losing, the Broncos were guaranteed that they would host the opening playoff round game against the win-

Lonnie Perrin looks for running room against the San Diego Chargers.

ner of the Central Division race, which was still undecided. Looking even further ahead, which Miller did now that he was involved in the playoffs, the Broncos would be the home team, if they got by their opening playoff game, for the AFC Championship game the following week.

So, everything was looking good in Denver as they prepared to take on the San Diego Chargers for the second time. Miller still had his team thinking in positive terms and didn't want to concede anything even though his team was definitely in the playoffs. While some coaches might deem it necessary to rest their regulars in preparations for the playoffs, Miller employed his regular lineup against the Chargers. The only missing member was Armstrong, who was still nursing a leg injury.

Denver obtained the opening kickoff and showed that they were going all out for another victory which would be number twelve. Morton came out throwing. On first down from the 26, he hit Dolbin for 15 yards and a first down on the 41. Three minutes later, Morton produced a touchdown. He blended with Perrin for a pass behind the line of scrimmage that went 41 yards for a touchdown. Denver quickly went out in front, 7-0.

San Diego didn't exactly fold. They took the kickoff on their own 13 and put together a 10-play, 49-yard drive that resulted in a 46-yard field goal by Rolf Benirschke. However, that was the extent of the scoring by both teams in the first quarter which ended with the Broncos in front, 7-3.

When Denver got the ball for the first time early in the second period, Morton was shaken up when he was sacked for a 12-yard loss by Gary Johnson. Craig Penrose took over but was stymied by penalties. Then, when Gradishar intercepted a pass by Dan Fouts, Penrose tried to drive for a touchdown. He reached the San Diego 28 before his third down pass was intercepted in the end zone by safety Hal Stringert. Later, Penrose was at the San Diego 27 when his first down pass was picked off by linebacker Woodrow Lowe to stop still another Denver threat. Just before the half ended, San Diego managed to add another field goal. Benirschke kicked one from 32 yards out to slice Denver's halftime edge to 7-6.

The halftime respite helped Morton. When the second half action began, Morton returned to the field. In his first series, he wasn't productive. Then the Chargers took Bucky Dilts's punt and started a drive on their own 38-yard line. They went all the way down to the Denver 9-yard line before they were stopped. However, Benirschke was accurate with a 27-yard field goal attempt that sent the Chargers in front for the first time, 9-7. That was the score when the third period ended.

The Broncos finally got something going in the final quarter after being blanked for two periods. Their 58-yard drive stalled on the San Diego 19. Yet, it was close enough for Turner to kick a 36-yard field goal that sent Denver in front once again, 10-9

San Diego tried to snap back after the kickoff. After getting a first down, Fouts went back to pass on his own 41. He was sacked by Paul Smith and fumbled. Rizzo covered the free ball on the Chargers' 46. However, in three plays the Broncos only reached the 41. Then, from punt formation, Norris Weese, on a fake, ran for 21 yards and a first down on the Chargers' 20-yard line. After Lytle gained a yard, Upchurch got the ball on an end around and sprinted 19 yards into the end zone. Turner's conversion gave the Broncos a 17-9 lead with less than two minutes to play. The point after clinched the victory as the Broncos won their twelfth game, more than anyone else in the NFL.

"We keep saying we have to win in the fourth quarter," said Tom Jackson. "It was our ability to hang together that did it."

SAN DIEGO	3	3	3	0	9
DENVER	7	0	0	10	17

Denver: 11:32 First Period—Perrin 41 yard pass from Morton (Turner kick).
San Diego: 6:50 First Period—Benirschke 46 yard field goal.
San Diego: :18 Second Period—Benirschke 32 yard field goal.
San Diego: 4:23 Third Period—Benirschke 27 yard field goal.
Denver: 6:39 Fourth Period—Turner 36 yard field goal.
Denver: 1:54 Fourth Period—Upchurch 19 yard run (Turner kick).

Game Fourteen: DALLAS
December 18, 1977

Denver's final regular season game against the Dallas Cowboys had all the ingredients of a classic match up. While the Broncos had won twelve games, the Cowboys had won eleven. Some experts touted the confrontation in Dallas as a possible Super Bowl preview. Miller tried not to make too much of the game inasmuch as he was concerned about the playoffs that would begin the following week.

However, the game did hold a great deal of significance for Craig Morton. He was returning to Dallas for the first time with a winning team, one in which he had directed to the Western Division championship of the AFC. That was the rewarding part. The emotional phase was that Morton was also returning to the city where he had spent his first ten years in the NFL and where he had left under a cloud of doubt and criticism.

The one sad part was that Morton was ailing. His right hip was troubling him, and he probably shouldn't have attempted to even play. But he gave it a try, nevertheless. Unknown to the fans that once booed him, Morton was playing with a great deal of pain. Yet, he never complained or made mention of it.

Dallas grabbed the opening kickoff and didn't stop until they scored a touchdown. They went 62 yards in just seven plays. The touchdown was a result of Roger Staubach's second down pass that traveled 22 yards to running back Preston Pearson.

When the Broncos got the ball for the first time, Morton was at quarterback. But he couldn't move effectively, and neither could the Broncos. Morton lasted just three downs before he left. Penrose took over on the next series of downs without any success. The only threatening gestures were made by the Cowboys before the quarter ended. But Efren Herrara missed two field goal attempts, one from 38 yards out and the other from 45.

The second period was scoreless. Herrara again figured in the only attempt to get points on the scoreboard. However, he missed his third field goal attempt from the 28-yard line. The furthest advance the Broncos made was

Dallas safety Randy Hughes gets through to drop an immobile Craig Morton in the final regular game of the season.

Dallas rookie sensation Tony Dorsett is stopped after a short gain by safety Bill Thompson.

reaching the Cowboys' 36-yard line, the first time they got into Dallas territory in the entire first half.

When the Cowboys got the ball in the third quarter, they scored again. Staubach moved them 60 yards in nine plays with the touchdown being a seven-yard flip to running back Bob Newhouse as the Cowboys stretched their margin to 14-0.

When the Broncos got the ball again, Norris Weese took over at quarterback. He was successful in getting the Broncos moving, positioning Turner's 22-yard field goal with a 67-yard, 14-play drive. At least Denver was on the scoreboard when the period was over.

Weese still had them moving as the fourth quarter began. This time he took the Broncos 38 yards in five plays as Turner booted a 37-yard field goal. It was the final points of the game as the Cowboys won, 14-6, and like the Broncos, finished with a 12-2 record.

The playoffs were next. It was apparent the Broncos were looking forward to them, more so than meeting Dallas in a game that really hadn't meant anything.

"It wasn't because we didn't try, but because we were looking ahead to that first playoff game," Alzado said afterward. "They just beat us. Red teaches us to concentrate on one game at a time, and this is the first time all year we looked ahead."

Cornerback Steve Foley agreed with Alzado. "The team was looking to next week against Pittsburgh," he said. "I'm not saying that's why

146

we lost. But emotionally, I guess this wasn't a big game."

"Losing Morton had some adverse effect," Miller admitted in the locker room. "Craig is a good player, but we didn't want to subject him to any more injury because he had had a tough season. He had been hurting all week. His hip was very, very sore going in. But now our season begins anew. We start the dash for cash. We're going to play the Pittsburgh Steelers, and that's all our mind is tuned in to now. We've had such a good season. I'm sure our players are going to be up for the playoffs."

The Pittsburgh Steelers and the playoffs were only six days away. It would be a new experience for the Broncos and for the Denver fans, too.

DENVER	0	0	3	3	6
DALLAS	7	0	7	0	14

SCORING

Dallas: 10:58 First Period—P. Pearson 22 yard pass from Staubach (Herrera kick).

Dallas: 7:48 Third Period—Newhouse 7 yard pass from Staubach (Herrera kick).

Denver: :33 Third Period—Turner 22 yard field goal.

Denver: 13:24 Fourth Period—Turner 37 yard field goal.

9

THE AFC PLAYOFF

I f Santa Claus was disguised as Red Miller, everybody in Bronco land would have believed it. It was just that the rest of the pro football world couldn't believe the Broncos had reached the playoffs. This was understandable. In seventeen years, Denver never got close. Now that they had finally reached the plateau that separated pretenders from contenders, nobody around America believed that the Broncos could advance past the opening playoff game against the rugged Pittsburgh Steelers on Christmas Eve. Despite the fact that Denver had beaten Pittsburgh quite easily, 21-7, earlier in the season, the Las Vegas bet parlors established the Steelers as 2½-point favorites. And, they were getting plenty of Pittsburgh action, too.

So was the song John Keyworth had written and recorded. It was titled, appropriately, "You've Got To Make Those Miracles Happen." The Broncos were doing just that. This and the concurrence of the Christmas season made Keyworth's record a best seller in Denver. And why not? The Broncos had finished

Steeler linebacker Robin Cole (56), and safety Glen Edwards close in on tight end Riley Odoms after he caught a pass.

the regular season as champions of the Western Division with a 12-2 record. It was as if every week was another miracle. There had never been a Christmas like it before in Denver. All during Christmas week the talk was about Christmas Eve in Mile High Stadium. Who would have ever believed that? Who would have believed orange Christmas trees? There were some who dyed their hair orange. Others wore orange wigs. Joggers were seen brightly attired in orange sweat suits. One diehard bought an old station wagon for $25, painted it orange, drove it to the game, and steadfastly refused a $500 offer for the relic right outside the stadium. It was all happening in Denver. And with all due respects to Bing Crosby's eternal "White Christmas," Bronco fans were warbling about an "Orange Christmas."

Miller approached the playoff game as he did every other game during the season. He treated it as if it was just another game. It was the Broncos' first appearance in a post season contest, and he didn't want to overtly try to make anything special over it. In that sense, he was wise. He kept the pre-game preparations low keyed so as not to create tension among his players. It was simply another week and another game. All that really concerned him were the injuries to two of his players. He was resigned to the fact that running back Lonnie Perrin wouldn't play because of a leg injury; and he wasn't sure whether linebacker Randy Gradishar could make it either. The scrappy Gradishar had a severely sprained ankle that had left him hobbling. Yet, Miller was hopeful. Gradishar had demonstrated that he was a quick healer. Miller felt he would be able to count on him and quarterback Craig Morton, who was still bothered with the hip injury that had forced him out of the Dallas game the week before.

December 24th dawned with excitement, but not the type normally reserved for that day. But then again, Denver was not a very normal place that year. The Broncos were in the playoffs, and that had to be a reason the sun was shining brightly. It was a perfect day for football. The sky was bright and sunny, and the temperature was a comfortable 43 degrees.

Many of those who weren't in Mile High

Randy Gradishar stops Steeler's Rocky Bleir from going anywhere.

150

Stadium that afternoon felt that the Steelers had the momentum and therefore the edge. Since their loss to Denver, the Steelers had won five of their final six games to finish with a 9-5 record. Yet, they needed help to make it to the playoffs. In the final game of the season, the Houston Oilers knocked the front running Cincinnati Bengals out of the playoff picture with a 21-16 triumph. In so doing, they earned the plaudits of the Steeler players. Their great running back, Franco Harris, expressed the sentiments of his teammates:

"What Houston did for us is greatly appreciated. I hope it is not in vain. Make no mistake about it; we've been struggling this year. But the playoffs are a whole new season, and we've been a pretty strong playoff team in the last few years."

Harris was right. The Steelers were a playoff-hardened group. Teams like the Broncos, who were getting their first exposure to such pressurized action, are never supposed to get by the initial game. But nobody ever expected Denver to reach the playoffs in the first place. And the Bronco players, or their rabid followers for that matter, never concerned themselves about that logic as Jim Turner began the game by kicking off to the veteran Steelers.

Denver's kickoff coverage was tight. The Steelers were contained on their 13-yard line. Immediately, quarterback Terry Bradshaw challenged the Bronco defense with the run. He attacked with his best runner, Franco Harris, perhaps the best in the league. The first time Harris carried the ball, he failed to gain anything as Bob Swenson stopped him. The second time he tried the left side, and Gradishar dragged him down after a 3-yard advance. An illegal procedure penalty set the Steelers back to the 11-yard line. Despite the dangerous field position, Bradshaw wasn't afraid to pass. He was successful, too. Anticipating a Denver rush, Bradshaw dropped a short screen pass to Harris, who rambled for 12 yards and a first down on the 23. At that point, the Bronco defense stiffened. After gaining only two yards on three plays, the Steelers punted.

Denver didn't have any success moving the ball either. Morton tried to open up the game quickly by throwing on first down to Haven Moses from his own 38-yard line, but the pass was incomplete. After Lytle gained three yards, Morton tried to pass once again but was unsuccessful. When Bucky Dilts's punt pinned the Steelers on the 18-yard line, the Bronco defense returned to the field.

Harris broke loose for eight yards to give Pittsburgh a little more room. Then he rushed straight up the middle for three yards and a first down on the 29. Bradshaw tried to go deep to wide receiver Lynn Swann but overthrew him. On second down, Harris tried the middle again and got another three yards. Bradshaw tried to get a first down by hitting his other wide receiver John Stallworth, but the pass was off its mark.

The Steelers' new punter, Rick Engles, dropped back to punt for the second time. The Broncos alertly noticed that Pittsburgh was more concerned with kick coverage upfield and were vulnerable to a rush. They decided to go for the ball in an attempt to block the punt. As the ball was snapped, they rushed the kicker. Reserve wide receiver John Schultz got through and blocked Engles's kick and quickly recovered the ball on the Steelers' 17-yard line. 75,011 Bronco fans roared their delight. The Broncos had forced a turnover and had an excellent chance to score.

On first down, Lytle ran over the right side and got down to the 14-yard line. Lytle carried again, this time around left end, and gained four more yards. Morton decided to keep the ball on the ground. He gave the ball to Lytle once again, and the valuable rookie slashed his way over the right side for the three yards he needed for a first down. The Broncos were getting close. Morton asked the crowd for quiet as he approached his center. He handled the snap cleanly and handed the ball to Lytle for the fourth straight time. Lytle found a hole over the left side, burst through, and went into the end zone for a touchdown. Jim Turner calmly kicked the extra point; and with 6:13 remaining in the opening quarter, the Broncos were on top, 7-0.

Pittsburgh tried to get moving after getting the ball for the third time. Harris ran for six yards from his 22-yard line. Then Rocky Bleier got a couple of yards before Harris got the two yards needed for a first down on the 32-yard line. After Harris got two more yards,

Bradshaw tried another screen pass to his big running back. But linebacker Joe Rizzo diagnosed the play correctly, came up fast, and stopped Harris after a two-yard gain. Facing a third down, Bradshaw had to pass. The Broncos knew that he would. They rushed and succeeded in trapping Bradshaw for an apparent loss. However, the gutsy quarterback broke loose and ran for 11 yards before Gradishar upended him on the 47-yard line. Bradshaw had turned a broken play into a first down.

Harris could only get two yards to the 49. Although he had been unsuccessful, Bradshaw decided to return to his passing game. His second-down pass to Stallworth was broken up by cornerback Bernard Jackson. On third down he tried a third time to go deep to Swann but missed. Of the seven passes Bradshaw attempted, he only completed two screens for 14 total yards. And for the third time in the quarter, the Steelers had to punt the ball away.

There were only 44 seconds left in the quarter when Denver put the ball in play on its own 23-yard line. Keyworth lunged ahead for six yards, but Lytle was stopped for no gain on the 29-yard line as the first period action ended. Amazingly, although the Broncos managed only one first down and had the ball for only 3:50, they were in front, 7-0, a fact that made the holiday crowd very happy.

When the second period began, Lytle was given the ball on third down; he came up empty. After Dilts's punt, the Steelers lined up on their 44-yard line, which was their best field position of the game thus far. Bradshaw looked for Swann on first down and missed connections again. After Harris could only manage a yard on a trap play, Bradshaw surveyed a third down and 9 play. This time he looked off his wide receivers and threw a 19-yard pass to his tight end, Bennie Cunningham. The Steelers had a first down on the Bronco 36 and were in Denver territory for the first time.

Now Bradshaw reverted to the ground game. That meant Harris. On first down he gained five yards and then four. On third down, Harris was handed the ball again. He needed only a yard to make a first down, but Barney Chavous was waiting for him on the right side. He stopped Harris for no gain. The

152

A happy Rob Lytle is about to slam the ball to the ground after scoring a touchdown against the Steelers.

crowd loved it. Bradshaw now looked at fourth down from the 27-yard line. The word from the bench was to go for it. Undaunted, Bradshaw inserted the ball into Harris' hands for the fourth consecutive time. The big running back responded. He shook loose around left end for 14 yards before safety Bill Thompson could stop him.

The Steelers were on the 13-yard line and posing a real threat for the first time. On first down, Bradshaw switched and gave the ball to Bleier, who moved for five yards to the 8. Setting up fast, Bradshaw then hit Swann with a quick six-yard pass. Pittsburgh had another first down on the two-yard line. They were positioned to get the tying touchdown. Bleier tried the middle and got only a yard as Gradishar tackled him. Then Harris tried; and Gradishar again made the play, stopping him short of the goal line. The fans were screaming, urging the Broncos to hold the Steeler advance. On third down Bradshaw took the snap. Only this time he kept the ball himself and leaped across the goal line for the tying touchdown. They had moved 56 yards on eleven plays.

On the kickoff, a holding penalty put the Broncos on the spot. Instead of having the ball on the 21, they had to begin from the 11. Jensen got five yards and Otis Armstrong one before Morton hit Odoms with a quickie over the middle for four yards and a first down on the 21-yard line. Throwing on first down, Morton's pass was knocked down by linebacker Jack Ham. On the next play, Pittsburgh was offside, and the ball was advanced to the 26. From there, Morton found Odoms again for seven yards this time and a first down on the 33. For the first time, the Broncos had put together two first downs in a single series.

Just as it appeared that they were beginning to move, the Broncos bogged down. Armstrong could gain only a yard. Morton's screen pass to Odoms lost four yards as Ham decked the big tight end on the 30-yard line. On third down Morton tried to go to Moses, but his pass fell incomplete. It meant that Dilts had to punt again.

When Pittsburgh set up their offense on its 34-yard line, there was only 5:58 remaining to play in the first half. Staying on the ground, Bleier made five yards, Bradshaw four, and

Harris two for a first down on the 45. Then Bradshaw reverted to the air. He tried Cunningham, who juggled the ball, then dropped it. Then he looked for Swann and threw incomplete. On third down, he decided to offset Denver's pass rush by giving the ball to Harris. Trying to find room over his left side, Harris was hit hard by Alzado, so hard that he fumbled the ball. As the ball bounced freely on the ground, Gradishar tried to pick it up. He bobbled the ball, and it fell out of his hands. However, an alert Tom Jackson pursued the loose ball and scooped it up, controlled it, and raced to the Steelers' 10-yard line before he was dragged down from behind. The defense had come up with another big turnover.

It didn't take the Bronco offensive long to capitalize on the situation. In fact, it took just one play. Armstrong found some running room around the right side and raced in for the touchdown. Turner's conversion was good; and the Broncos went back in front, 14-7.

There was 4:04 left in the half when Pittsburgh went to work on its 35-yard line. There was plenty of time for them to score, and Bradshaw went right to work. First he hit Stallworth with a 7-yard pass. Harris got a yard and then broke loose for six more for a first down on the Steelers' 49. After an incomplete pass to Bleier coming out of the backfield, Bradshaw connected with Stallworth again, this time for 21 yards. The Steelers had a first down on the Denver 30 and were threatening. Just before the two-minute warning, Bradshaw threw an 8-yard pass to Harris as the Steelers reached the 22.

Bradshaw talked over strategy with Pittsburgh coach Chuck Noll. It was decided to send Harris around right end, but the Broncos were waiting for him. However, Harris reversed his direction, ran left, found a wide open area, and bolted to the 2-yard line before he was dragged down from behind by Tom Jackson. The Steelers were two yards away from tying the game. Harris tried the left side but was halted on the 1-yard line. Then he ran over the right side and scored. The Steelers had negotiated 65 yards in just nine plays to tie the game at 14-14.

Following the kickoff, the Broncos began

play on their 24-yard line. They had a difficult time getting anywhere. Morton tried to shake Armstrong loose. But on first down the little speedster lost five yards. Then he lost two more. A delay of game penalty cost the Broncos five more yards. They now had a third down back on the 12-yard line. Armstrong tried again to no avail, but the Steelers were penalized five yards for being offside. At the same time, just about everyone, including the millions who were viewing the game on television, saw Mean Joe Greene deliver a punch to guard Paul Howard's ribs. Everyone, that is except for the officials. It incensed the fans enough for them to yell, "Get Joe Greene," as Howard was being helped off the field.

On the next play, Armstrong could only gain a yard. But, Greene found himself in the center of another altercation. This time Greene punched Montler. The Bronco center swung back but missed. This time the officials threw their penalty flag and administered a 15-yard unsportsman-like penalty against Greene. They also had to cool flaring tempers which by now were festering on both sides.

When the play was finally resumed on the Denver 33-yard line, Keyworth fumbled. The ball was recovered by, of all people, Greene on the 42-yard line. There were only 26 seconds left, and Bradshaw tried to score a quick touchdown. He wanted to collaborate with Stallworth, but Bernard Jackson intercepted on the 16-yard line to stop the threat as the gun sounded.

It was by no means a dull halftime for Bronco fans. As the two teams were trotting off the field, Miller ran after the officials and began vigorously protesting about the unnecessary style of play demonstrated by Greene. Miller was hot. Underneath the South Stands he vehemently protested to Chuck Noll. At that point, Pittsburgh's line coach, George Perles, stepped into the middle and told Miller to go back into the locker room. Understandably, Miller exploded. He challenged Perles to a fight before cooler heads prevailed and separated the two.

It was somewhat surprising that the game was also a standstill, at least when examining the statistics. Pittsburgh had controlled the ball for 20:46, while Denver only had it for 9:14. The Steelers had twelve first downs,

while the Broncos managed only six. Even more alarming was the fact that Pittsburgh ran 47 plays to Denver's 25 and gained 183 yards to just 44 by the Broncos. The difference was Denver's Orange Crush defense that had made things happen by setting up both Bronco touchdowns.

It appeared that the second half would be a wild, swinging, brawling affair; but the halftime respite had soothed tempers on both sides. Although the Broncos' fans were looking for a fight, the players were resolved to play football. There was too much involved not to. They couldn't lose sight of the fact that the game was the first step to the AFC championship and a shot at reaching the Super Bowl. That's what it was all about; and of all miracles the Broncos wanted to make happen, it was a visit to Super Bowl XII in January.

On first down from his own 27-yard line, Morton tried to change the tempo of the game. He attempted a pass to Dolbin that went incomplete. Then Armstrong brought the crowd to its feet. He scooted around the left side and almost got away before he was tackled by linebacker Jack Ham on the Pittsburgh 44-yard line. Armstrong had run for 29 yards, the biggest play of the game. Perhaps it was the spark that the offense needed. But when Lytle got only two yards and Keyworth three, Morton called time out. He went over to the sidelines and discussed a third and 5 play with Miller. They agreed on a pass to Moses. It failed, and the Broncos had to punt.

Dilts's kick pinned the Steelers on their 5-yard line. If Denver could hold at that end of the field, they would certainly have an opportunity to gain good field position once they got the ball back. But Harris broke through for six yards, Bleier for three, and then Harris got two more for a first down on the 16. Denver's defense fought back. Alzado dropped Harris for a yard loss. Bradshaw's pass to Stallworth on the next play only got four yards. On third down, the Broncos rushed Bradshaw. He tried to dump the ball to his tight end, Randy Grossman; but the ball fell short. Pittsburgh had to yield the ball.

The punt did provide the Broncos with choice field position. Morton began to operate from his own 47-yard line. He decided to strike quickly with a pass, but instead he was

The Broncos' mission on defense was to stop the Steelers' star running back Franco Harris.

sacked for a 9-yard loss. Still Morton again called pass. This time he had the time; and he was successful, too, connecting with Moses on the Steeler 35. A run by Keyworth got four more yards. Then on second down from the 31 yard line, Morton dropped back to pass. Reserve running back Jim Jensen moved out of the backfield, got free in the middle, and took Morton's pass all the way down to the 2-yard line.

Armstrong tried to take it in but was stopped on the 1-yard line. On second down, Morton's quick pass was knocked down by middle linebacker Jack Lambert. Then Lytle tried to punch the ball over. It was a crash of bodies at the goal line, and Lytle came up about three inches short. Do the Broncos go for it on fourth down or kick a tie-breaking field goal from short range? Miller decided to go for the touchdown, and the crowd roared

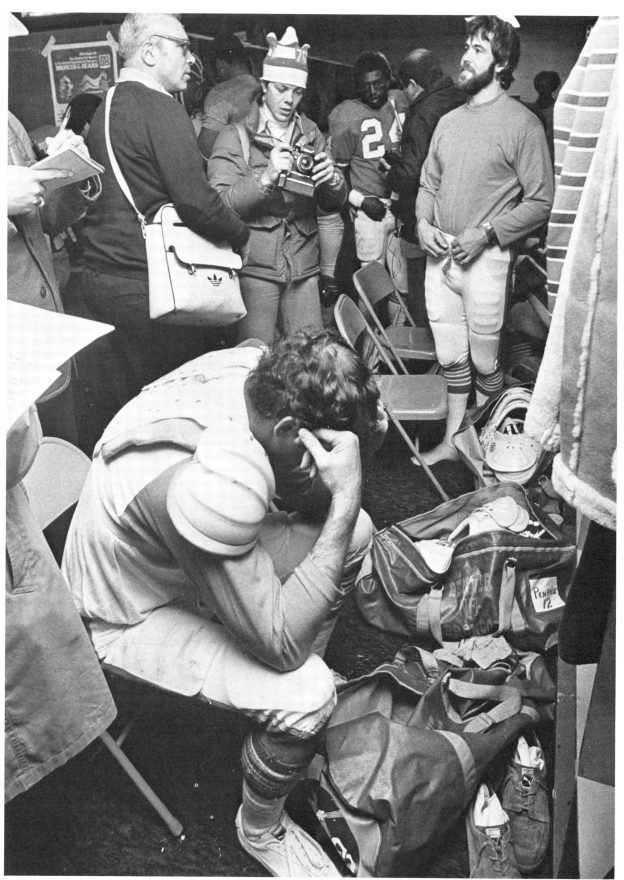

Craig Morton prays in locker room. After 1st round playoff win over the Steelers, media people converge on the Bronco players, but Morton with head bowed in prayer is unaware of the chaos behind him.

its approval. Jensen was given the opportunity to put the Broncos ahead. He drove forward but was stopped short of the goal line. The Steelers had held. In four downs, the Broncos had gained barely more than a yard.

It was now up to the Denver defense to hold the Steelers again; and they did, too. Bleier couldn't gain anything. Even after Harris gained four yards and Bradshaw five, Pittsburgh was still short of a first down by a yard. Once more the Broncos would have a chance to gain good field position.

They almost lost it. With Upchurch sidelined by a pulled muscle, Billy Thompson fumbled Dilts's punt on the Denver 48. However, Steve Foley recovered the ball on the Steeler 41. The Broncos did indeed get excellent field position for the second straight series. Morton went to work. He shot a quick, 4-yard pass to Odoms, who stepped out of bounds on the 37. Then Jensen got five yards. On third and 1, Morton kept the ball himself and picked up two yards and a first down. Denver was now on the Pittsburgh 30. In the huddle, Morton looked at Odoms. He was going to send him deep. Denver's offensive line gave Morton good protection. He looked for Odoms, saw him free on the 6-yard line, and fired. Odoms went over for a touchdown. It took Morton just four plays to drive 41 yards as Turner's conversion sent the Broncos in front, 21-14, with less than two minutes left in the third period.

When the fourth quarter action began, the Broncos were in possession on their 21-yard line. They had to play control football and avoid making mistakes. The fourth quarter was the one that Miller always exhorted his team throughout the season as the one that belonged to Denver. Keyworth gained two yards and Armstrong five. On third down, Morton found Odoms for six yards and a first down on the 34. After Armstrong got three more, Morton missed on two passes to Jensen. Dilts was sent in to punt, and Pittsburgh began its offensive series from its own 39-yard line.

Bleier ran straight ahead for a yard, and Bradshaw decided to attack the Broncos with the pass. He threw to Cunningham for 11 yards and a first down on the Denver 49. As Bradshaw faded back to pass again, his eyes opened wide. A mix-up in the Denver pass coverage enabled Stallworth to be left open on the 26-yard line. Bradshaw delivered him the ball, and the big wide receiver raced to the 1-yard line before Thompson caught him. Just like that the Steelers were looking at a game-tying touchdown—and just like that they got it. Bradshaw fooled everyone by tossing a 1-yard pass to Larry Brown on a tackle eligible, and the game was now deadlocked at 21-21. In just four plays Bradshaw had led the Steelers 61 yards, 60 of them the result of his accurate passing.

When Morton came back on the field after the kickoff, there was 10:46 left in the game. He started on the Denver 34-yard line. After Jensen ran for three yards, Morton went to the air. He hit Armstrong over the middle for nine yards and a first down on the 46. Then he sailed one to Moses for 18 yards and another first down on the Steelers' 36-yard line. The Broncos were bouncing right back. Lytle drove for three yards. Then Morton, on a bootleg, ran around right end for six yards. Denver was one yard short of a first down on Pittsburgh's 27-yard line. Morton tried to pass for it, but his ball was tipped by Ham.

On fourth down Turner made his appearance on the field. He was going to attempt a 44-yard field goal. Norris Weese, who had hurt his leg earlier and was visibly limping, knelt to place the ball for Turner. Weese handled the snap cleanly, positioned it faultlessly; and Turner stepped forward and kicked it accurately. The Broncos went back into the lead, 24-21, with only 7:17 left to play. Now it was up to the defense to make it stick.

Pittsburgh came up with good field position on the kickoff. Bradshaw moved out on the 40-yard line. He decided to stay with his passing game. On first down his pass to Swann was too low. Now the Broncos were looking for the pass. Bradshaw looked to his left and threw. Tom Jackson moved over, jumped, hit the ball with his left hand, caught it in his right hand, and took off toward the Steeler goal line behind three blockers. He made it all the way to the 9-yard line before center Mike Webster chased him down. The crowd stood and roared. The Broncos were now in control. A touchdown now would just about clinch the victory.

Lytle tried the left end and got a couple of

Linebacker Tom Jackson starts upfield after intercepting Terry Bradshaw's pass in the opening game of the AFC playoffs.

yards. Then Armstrong tried the right side and found nothing. On third down, Morton dropped back to pass. He was looking for Dolbin; but he was covered. Nearby he saw an open Moses and he threw. Dolbin leaped, but the pass landed in Moses's waiting arms. However, as the Bronco faithful were cheering at the apparent touchdown, an official ruled that it wasn't good. He claimed that Dolbin had touched the ball, which was a rules infraction in that no two receivers can touch the ball on a forward pass.

As the crowd booed and the Broncos protested in vain, Turner quietly returned to the scene. This time he was staring straight ahead at a 25-yard field goal, and he made it to give the Broncos a 27-21 edge. But the game wasn't over yet. There was still time. A Pittsburgh touchdown would be disastrous; and the Broncos realized it, too. But the Denver diehards had faith in the defense.

Pittsburgh took charge on their 20-yard line as Turner's kick soared into the end zone. There was no doubt that Bradshaw would put the ball in the air. His first pass to Harris lost two yards. Then he threw incomplete to Cunningham. Anticipating a rush on third down, Bradshaw tossed a screen pass to Cunningham who made the 12 yards necessary for the first down. After Harris lost a yard, Bradshaw returned to the pass. He hit Alvin Maxson for 10 yards which left him a yard short on the 39-yard line. An illegal motion penalty on the next play set the Steelers back to the 24, but Bradshaw got the first down with a 7-yard swing pass to Bleier on the 41. Bradshaw had the Steelers moving. He dropped to pass on first down. For the second straight time Jackson was his nemesis. The quick linebacker intercepted Bradshaw's pass at midfield and ran to the 33-yard line before he was stopped. The defense had come up with another big play.

The big clock showed only 1:57 when Morton took over. Lytle lost a yard as Pittsburgh called time out. Morton talked with Miller in front of the Denver bench. They reasoned that a deep pass to Doblin would work. So, Doblin streaked down the sideline and got behind cornerback Jim Allen. He looked up, and Morton's pass came right to his hands as he pulled it down in the end zone. It was a game clinching touchdown, and the shouts of those

seized by Broncomania reverberated throughout Mile High Stadium. It mattered little that Turner added the 34th point. The miracle was still happening. The Broncos had defeated the Steelers, 34-21, and had advanced to the AFC championship game.

"After today, nobody should doubt us," said Miller in the Bronco dressing room as he clutched the game ball given to him by his players. "Our team is earning the respect of the entire league, which is just what we wanted to do. We showed we can hang in there with anybody."

What Miller also showed the rest of the league was how much of a fighter he was. Of course his players already knew it.

"To tell you the truth, I'd have been surprised if Red *hadn't* gone after somebody," exclaimed Turner. "He's a tiger. You mess with one of his boys, and you're messing with his family. That's what he preached all season. Today he practiced it."

"Greene thought I was holding him on that play," Howard explained. "I said, 'Joe, I don't play that way.' But that didn't change Joe's mind. He hit me in the stomach and knocked the wind out of me. I told him his actions were bull. An All-Pro player shouldn't play that way."

Haven Moses

160

"I told the players at halftime that they were becoming too excited," Miller said. "I told them to calm down and play football."

"It was the right move," agreed Tom Jackson. "I think the altercations were designed to get us into a different kind of contest. We probably couldn't win a fist fight against the Steelers. We're a little smaller than they are."

That may be, but the bottom line is toughness. That's Miller's way. It was his team's way, too. It got them into the AFC championship game the following week against the Oakland Raiders, and it was a Christmas unlike any other in Denver.

PITTSBURGH	0	14	0	7	21
DENVER	7	7	7	13	34

SCORING

Denver: 6:13 First Period—Lytle 7 yard run (Turner kick).

Pittsburgh: 9:01 Second Period—Bradshaw 1 yard run (Gerela kick).

Denver: 4:15 Second Period—Armstrong 10 yard run (Turner kick).

Pittsburgh: 1:41 Second Period—Harris 1 yard run (Gerela kick).

Denver: 1:24 Third Period—Odoms 30 yard pass from Morton (Turner kick).

Pittsburgh: 10:55 Fourth Period—Brown 1 yard pass from Bradshaw (Gerela kick).

Denver: 7:17 Fourth Period—Turner 44 yard field goal.

Denver: 5:10 Fourth Period—Turner 25 yard field goal.

Denver: 1:44 Fourth Period—Dolbin 34 yard pass from Morton (Turner kick).

10
THE AFC CHAMPIONSHIP

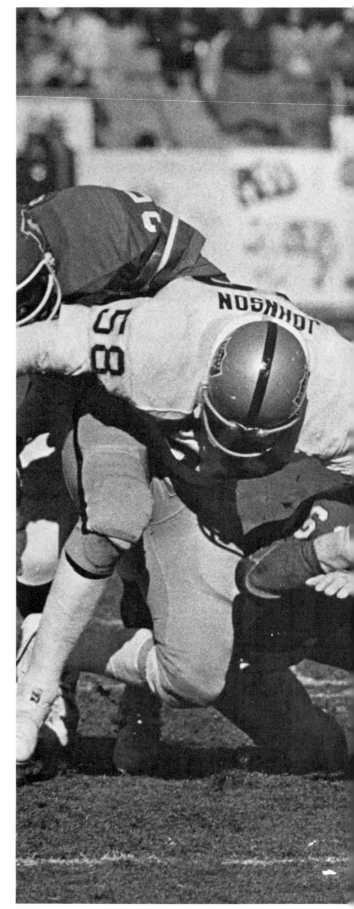

When Craig Morton awoke on Christmas morning he could hardly move. It pained him when he tried to stand up; and when he did, he found that he could hardly walk.

On Monday he called the trainer who advised him to come in for treatment, heat first and then perhaps a whirlpool. Morton slowly got into his car and drove to the Broncos' training compound. Allen Hurst, who has been the team's trainer for fifteen years, immediately gave his full attention to Morton. When he took his first good look at the quarterback, he shook his head in disbelief. Morton looked as if he had been hit by a car. The site of his injury was a massive area of discoloration the spread far beyond the injury itself. Hurst hadn't seen anything like it in all his years as a trainer.

Hurst prescribed heat treatment. All he and Morton could do was to wait, hoping the injury would respond to some extent. A short time later Hurst checked with Morton. The treatment hadn't helped. Miller was advised. All three discussed the situation. They all agreed that the best thing to do was to put Morton in a hospital. He would be completely

Otis Armstrong moves for some tough yards against the Raiders.

162

off his feet and would receive special medical care. With any luck Morton would be ready to face the Oakland Raiders in the AFC championship game on Sunday.

The Broncos were hoping for two things. One was that Morton's injury would respond to hospital attention. The other was that Morton would have the benefit of an extra day's rest. The first round playoff game against Pittsburgh was played on Saturday. The AFC championship game was scheduled for Sunday, which was a break. That extra day just might be enough. Otherwise, the Broncos would have had to play the biggest game in their history without their starting quarterback.

So, while Morton rested in a hospital, Denver began preparing for the Raiders. The week went by, and on Friday Morton was released from the hospital and reported to the training base. His hip was still tender, and he didn't participate in any of the workouts. Even the next day, Saturday, Morton didn't practice. With the exception of his teammates, nobody knew how badly hurt Morton was. That is one encouragement you don't offer a physical team like the Raiders.

There is no love lost between the two teams. For the past several years, the Raiders had prevented the Broncos from claiming any part of the Western Division title. Being members of the same division affords them the opportunity to play each other twice during the regular season. In their first meeting in Oakland, the Broncos shocked the entire professional football world by manhandling the Raiders, 30-7. It snapped the Raiders 17-game winning streak. Two weeks later in Denver, Oakland jumped into a 24-0 lead and ultimately prevailed, 24-14. The Raiders have never lost in Denver since 1963.

"I hate the Raiders," admitted Denver linebacker Tommy Jackson.

"After we beat the Broncos," countered Oakland linebacker Floyd Rice, "I'm going to get a can of orange pop, open it, and turn it upside down . . . slowly!"

While the players were heated, the coaches remained cool. They were merely concerned with the game itself and left personal innuendos to the players themselves.

"It is neither an advantage nor a disadvantage that we've already played twice," analyzed Miller. "The fact that we know each other so well and have such a mountain of information on each other really doesn't change anything. It all comes back to execution and how you carry out what you try to do.

"In the first game, we shut off their running game and forced them out of their game plan. They like to come at you and wear you down. But when we got ahead of them at the half, they had to throw more than they wanted to. The second time, they made us do what they wanted. They did gain on the ground. Their punter, Ray Guy, got us bottled up; and they got ahead of us.

"So we know what we're going to try to do, and we know what they expect us to try to do. We want to contain their running and put pressure on Ken Stabler. He's one of the premier, perhaps the premier quarterback, in the game. But he's human, and he can be rushed. The only way to play Stabler is to pressure him."

Oakland coach John Madden concurred with Miller's assessment. He knew how important the third confrontation with the Broncos was. Simply said, the winner would be in the Super Bowl. Madden had been there last year as his Raiders played practically a perfect game in easily disposing of the Minnesota Vikings, 32-14.

"It's not the theory, it's the carrying it out," Madden explained. "It doesn't matter to us where we play, or who we play, or what happened last time, or history, or records, or anything like that. We just have to do what we're supposed to do that day.

"In a way, but only in a way, this game has more tension than the Super Bowl itself. Everyone's goal is to get to the Super Bowl. When the season starts, you don't hear people say, 'We want to win the Super Bowl'; they say, 'We want to go to the Super Bowl.' It may just be semantics, but I think it reveals something about how people really feel.

"In the playoffs or the championship game, when you lose, you're out of it. There's no chance to bounce back as in the regular season. In the Super Bowl, the season is going to be over, win or lose. That doesn't mean there's any less desire to win or any less disappointment about losing. But there is no looking ahead. It's the completion of things."

Looking at it one way, Denver's season came down to a single game. The fact that they had split with the Raiders during the regular season meant nothing. Football analysts depicted the struggle as Oakland's potent offense against Denver's powerful defense. The oddsmakers established the Raiders as a 3½-4 point favorite. Bud Goode, a noted Los Angeles sports analyst, resorted to his Univac computer to get an even clearer picture of the game.

He noted that the Raiders ranked number one in the NFL in points scored (388), the average number of rushing plays per game which is a good indication of ball control (48.6), and led in first downs by rushing (156).

Defensively, the Broncos ranked number one in the following categories: opponent yards per rush (3.3), first downs allowed by rushing (77), and touchdowns allowed by rushing (five).

Goode felt that the key to Denver's success would be the commitment to their modest offense, no matter what the score. His figures showed that the Raiders' defense could be pierced by the run. Oakland was 24th out of 28 teams in opponent yards gained per play, 4.9, and 25th in opponent rushing yards per play, 4.3. He pointed out that Oakland scores so quickly and easily that its opponents often give up their game plan and play catch-up football by passing a great deal. Goode felt that the Broncos could stay close and run on Oakland which would be a good way to keep Stabler on the sidelines.

Still, all the statistics and all the theories would be worthless if Morton wasn't able to play. No one outside the Bronco organization was aware of the situation. It was a closely guarded secret. After all, there was no cause for creating panic.

On Sunday morning, several hours before the kickoff, Miller met with Morton.

"How do you feel, Craig?" asked Miller.

"Not so good, coach," replied Morton.

"Do you think you can go?" wondered Miller.

"Let's give it a whirl and see what happens," Morton said.

"Great," smiled Miller. "But if you don't feel right out there, just give me the word."

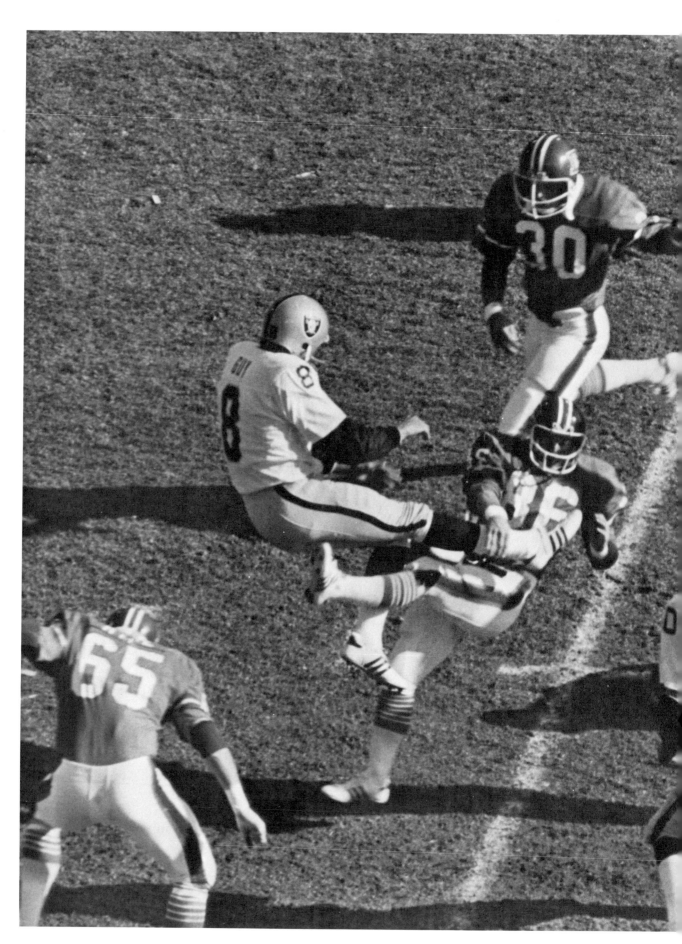

There was no way anyone could know what Morton's capabilities were. Morton himself didn't know if he could play the entire game or last for just a few plays as he had against the Dallas Cowboys in the final game of the season two weeks before. He would just have to wait and see. Even when he loosened up prior to the kickoff, he still had doubts about his physical condition. All he wanted to do was give it a shot. This was too big a game not to.

Morton wouldn't have to wait long to find out. The Broncos called the coin toss correctly and decided to receive the opening kickoff. Although it was only 18 degrees, the skies were mostly sunny; and a soft three-mile-an-hour wind was not a factor. Rick Upchurch gathered in Ray Guy's kickoff on the 14 and returned it to the 29. Slowly, Morton went out to lead the Broncos. The idea was to run. Jon Keyworth made two yards, and then Rob Lytle broke through for five. Both plays attacked Oakland's left side. On third down, Morton attempted to pass from the 36-yard line; but the ball was deflected by cornerback Lester Hayes, who covered Haven Moses on the play. Sent in to punt, Bucky Dilts didn't help Denver's cause. He got off a poor 21-yard kick that was downed on Oakland's 43-yard line. The Raiders would begin their first offensive series in excellent field position.

Immediately, Oakland tried to establish the run, which is their style. But the Broncos were ready. On Oakland's first play of the game, linebacker Randy Gradishar dropped Clarence Davis for a 4-yard loss. Then Davis tried the left side but was stopped at the line of scrimmage by linebacker Bob Swenson. On third and 14 from the 39, the Broncos played pass. Stabler tried to hit his tight end, Dave Casper; but his pass was deflected by a hard rush from defensive end Barney Chavous. The Raiders had lost four yards in three plays and were forced to punt.

But the Raiders got a break. As Guy got his kick off, he was run into by John Schultz. The mistake resulted in a 5-yard penalty, but more importantly, an automatic first down. Oakland was back in control. On first down, van Eeghen gained three yards. Then he took

Oakland punter Ray Guy is hit by John Schultz who was called for roughing the kicker.

Haven Moses dances into the end zone after taking a pass from Morton to score Denver's first touchdown.

a short pass from Stabler for three more. On third down, Stabler found wide receiver Fred Biletnikoff for nine yards and a first down on Denver's 41.

Stabler went back to the run on the left side behind tackle Art Shell and guard Gene Upshaw. Van Eeghen got three and Davis six. Then Pete Banaszak went the same way for two more. However, an offside penalty against Denver advanced the ball to the 27. The Broncos' famed Orange Crush was being tested early.

On first down Banaszak went over the left side again, this time for nine yards. Banaszak was given the ball again, and he got a first down on the 17. Then the veteran thirty-three-year-old tried the right side and gained four yards. Stabler called Banaszak's number for the fourth straight time, and this time he picked up three more yards. On third down and three, Davis followed Banaszak around the left side; but Lyle Alzado stopped him a half-yard short of a first down on the Broncos' 8-yard line. Would the Raiders go for it or kick an apparent field goal?

It was the first big decision of the game although it was only the first quarter. Stabler looked across the field to Madden. He motioned for his quarterback to go for it. The noisy crowd of 74,982 yelled for the Broncos' defense to repel the Raiders. Stabler gave the ball to Banaszak once again, and the sure-footed runner squirmed up the middle for two yards and a first down on 6. Oakland had an excellent opportunity to score a touchdown. On first down Banaszak drove over the left side for three yards. He tried it again on second down, but Bernard Jackson quickly moved in from his safety position to stop him for no gain on the 3-yard line. It was the tenth consecutive running play that Stabler had called, and Banaszak was involved in seven of them. Stabler had to throw now. He set up but couldn't find any of his receivers open and threw the ball out of the end zone. Denver's defense prevented the touchdown and yielded only a 20-yard field goal by Erroll Mann. Considering that Oakland controlled the ball for 18 plays and over eight minutes, it was a small price to pay.

On the ensuing kickoff, Denver put the ball in play on its 31-yard line. On first down they drew a 5-yard penalty for illegal procedure. Looking to pass from his 26, Morton's aerial was knocked down by safety Jack Tatum who stepped in front of Moses. Undaunted, Morton went back to Moses on second down. Getting good protection, he found Moses open on the Oakland 39 and delivered the ball into his hands. Moses side-stepped Skip Thomas and ran straight down the sidelines. There was no one in front of him. Out of nowhere, Morton and Moses had combined for a 74-yard bomb that gave the Broncos a 7-3 lead. It shocked the Raiders and delighted everyone else in Mile High Stadium.

Still, when the Raiders took the kickoff, they began controlling the ball again. When the first quarter ended, they had a first down on the Broncos' 26-yard line. They were threatening and appeared ready to score again. In the first period alone, they held the ball for 12:43, while Denver had it for only 2:17. They also had eight first downs, while the Broncos managed only one on Morton's touchdown pass. But that one pass gave Denver the edge.

When the second quarter opened, van Eeghen carried the ball three straight times and got the Raiders a first down on the 15. Tommy Jackson came up with a big play and dumped Davis for a 3-yard loss. It forced Stabler to throw. On second down he missed on a pass to Biletnikoff. He tried Biletnikoff again and hit him with a 6-yard strike on the 12-yard line. The Raiders were still seven yards short of a first down, and Mann entered the game to attempt a 19-yard field goal. He got the kick up in the air, but the ball hit the right upright and ricocheted back. The Broncos still maintained a 7-3 lead.

Then the game seemed to settle down. On Denver's next possession, they made one first down and were forced to punt. Oakland got the ball; and after three plays they, too, employed a punt. When the Broncos got the ball back, they produced a modest drive. They began in extraordinary field position, driving from the Oakland 41 to the 23 before they were stopped when Jim Turner missed on a 40-yard field goal try. So, when the first half action subsided, the Broncos still held the upper hand, 7-3, and appeared to have stopped Oakland's running game despite the fact that the Raiders had the ball forty-one times while the Broncos only had it nineteen.

But emotion can go a long way, and that's one thing the Broncos did have. Miller makes certain that his team plays with it. During the precious halftime break, he wrote on a large board, "Thirty Minutes To The Super Bowl." He knew the players would get the message. They had all season long. Now they were thirty minutes away. An entire season rested on that final half hour, and it almost came apart in the opening minute of the second half.

Carl Garrett took the kickoff on his 5-yard line and began weaving his way through the Denver pursuers. It appeared that he would run all the way for six points. Only a touchdown-saving tackle by Lonnie Perrin, who as the kicker was the last man down the field, prevented it. Perrin caught Garrett on the Broncos 33-yard line.

Still, the Raiders were in striking distance. Stabler quickly went to the air but missed on a pass to Cliff Branch. Then van Eeghen slipped and failed to gain a yard. Again Stabler went overhead, but his pass was short after throwing through the force of a Denver

rush. In just three plays, the Raiders were forced to punt.

Taking over on their 20, Morton moved the Broncos quickly. After Keyworth failed to gain even a yard, Miller reversed strategy and went to the pass. The book on the Broncos is that they never put the ball up in minus field position. So, Miller observed that the Raiders were playing the run and sent in two pass plays. On the first one he completed one for 16 yards to Perrin. On the second one, he hit Moses with a 41-yarder that brought the Broncos all the way down to the Raiders' 23-yard line. Staying on the ground three straight running plays advanced the ball nine yards to Oakland's 14-yard line. A field goal at this juncture would give the Broncos a touchdown lead. However, the usually reliable Turner missed from the 21-yard line as his kick went wide to the right.

But Denver got the ball right back again. On first down from the 20-yard line, Davis tried to move for yardage over his left side. He was hit hard, and the ball was jarred loose. Brison Manor, a rookie defensive end, pounced on it on the 17. The Broncos' opportunistic defense had created a turnover.

Joe Rizzo (59) and Lyle Alzado (rear) sack Oakland quarterback Ken Stabler.

On first down Keyworth moved for two yards to the 15. Then Morton brought the crowd to its feet when he limped back to the lineup and hit his tight end Riley Odoms with a 13-yard pass on the Raiders' 2-yard line. The Broncos were kicking open the corral door. A touchdown now would put Oakland in a dangerous catch-up situation, one which the Broncos wanted.

Morton asked the crowd for quiet as he brought his team out of the huddle. The crowd was anticipating a touchdown. Morton took the snap and quickly handed the ball to Lytle. The rookie running back hurtled through the air and was belted for no gain by Tatum, who met him head on. The ball popped from Lytle's arm and fell to the ground. The Raiders' big defensive tackle, Mike McCoy, who is employed in short yardage situations, recovered the ball; and while the Bronco players began walking slowly toward their bench, the Raiders were clapping with joy.

However, head linesman Ed Marion had ruled there was no fumble because he had blown his whistle to stop the action. The Raiders protested vehemently, so much that they were assessed a penalty of half the distance to the goal. After several minutes of quieting down the Oakland players, referee Chuck Heverling placed the ball on the 1-yard line. Again the crowd raised its voices, and once again Morton signaled for quiet. Then he took the snap, ran to his right on a gimpy leg, and tossed a pitchout to Keyworth who scored standing up. Denver had stretched its margin to 14-3. Mile High Stadium was rocking.

Oakland couldn't move after the kickoff and punted after three downs. Denver, too, couldn't produce a first down; and they also punted. However, Garrett fumbled the ball, and Larry Evans quickly fell on it on Oakland's 27-yard line. Denver had an opportunity for another score.

Morton tried to make it happen quickly. He attempted three passes, but all three fell harmlessly to the ground. Now it was Turner's turn to try another field goal, this time from the 34. Uncharacteristically, Turner missed for the third time.

Despite a lunging effort by Raiders' John Matuszak, Morton still manages to get off pass.

sacked for a 9-yard loss. Still Morton again called pass. This time he had the time; and he was successful, too, connecting with Moses on the Steeler 35. A run by Keyworth got four more yards. Then on second down from the 31 yard line, Morton dropped back to pass. Reserve running back Jim Jensen moved out of the backfield, got free in the middle, and took Morton's pass all the way down to the 2-yard line.

Armstrong tried to take it in but was stopped on the 1-yard line. On second down, Morton's quick pass was knocked down by middle linebacker Jack Lambert. Then Lytle tried to punch the ball over. It was a crash of bodies at the goal line, and Lytle came up about three inches short. Do the Broncos go for it on fourth down or kick a tie-breaking field goal from short range? Miller decided to go for the touchdown, and the crowd roared

The most disputed play in the game occurred in the third period. Officials ruled that Denver running back Rob Lytle (41) was stopped by Oakland's Jack Tatum near the Raider goal line. However, view from opposite side of the play shows the ball (arrow) pop loose from Lytle's hand. Oakland's recovery was not allowed and Denver scored its second touchdown on the next play.

172

Near the end of the quarter, Stabler had the Raiders rolling. From the Denver 48, van Eeghen ran for his biggest gain of the game. Moving over his left side, van Eeghen bolted for 13 yards before Bernard Jackson brought him down on the 35. After Stabler missed with a pass, he dropped back on second down and rifled one to Casper on the 9-yard line. Just as the third period was coming to an end, he tossed a short, 3-yard pass to Casper on the 3-yard line. The Broncos were now only fifteen minutes away from the Super Bowl.

The Raiders had to score quickly in the final quarter to get back into the game. Van Eeghen tried the left side and lost a yard. Then Stabler didn't waste any more time. He drilled a seven-yard touchdown pass to Casper that brought the Raiders to within four points of the Broncos, 14-10, with more than fourteen minutes left to play. Miller and the Broncos knew very well how Oakland comes back with a rush in the fourth quarter.

Denver wasn't about to sit on a four-point lead. They needed some more points, hopefully another touchdown; but even a field goal would help. Morton tried. In the longest drive of the game, he took the Broncos from their 25 to the Oakland 20 before they were stopped. On first down from there, Moses was smeared for a 10-yard loss on an end around play that was alertly recognized by linebacker Floyd Rice. When Morton attempted to pass on second down, Rice haunted him again. He stayed with Odoms on a pass pattern and intercepted Morton's pass on the 11-yard line and brought it back to the 22. Denver's drive was abruptly halted.

Van Eeghen picked up three yards on first down. Stabler then called a pass to the right side. Barney Chavous put on a rush and partially obstructed Stabler's view which enabled Bob Swenson to intercept the ball on Oakland's 31. Swenson rambled 14 yards to the 17 before he was tackled. The Broncos had another scoring opportunity.

Perrin gained four yards on first down. Then Otis Armstrong picked up another yard. The Broncos were now faced with a key third

Oakland's Dave Casper makes an acrobatic catch for final touchdown in front of Tommy Jackson (57).

175

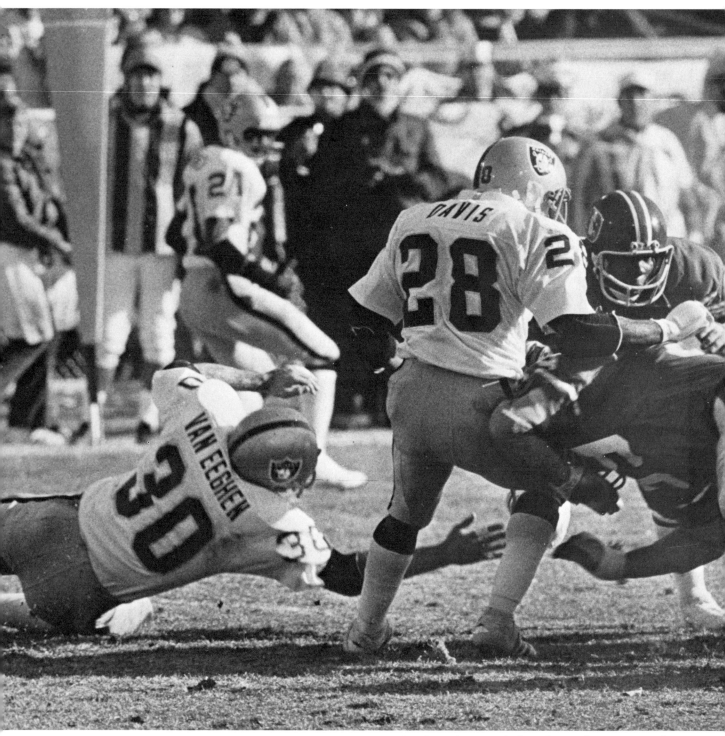

down and 5 call on the Raiders' 12-yard line. Morton called for a time out. He headed for the sidelines to discuss the strategy with Miller. Both agreed that a pass could work. They figured that Odoms would be the best shot in close. Miller told Morton to make sure, not to force the ball and create an interception.

Morton went over the play in the huddle. He wanted to be certain that everyone in-volved understood the play. The Bronco fans were cheering them on, anxiously hoping for a touchdown. There were only about eight minutes remaining, and a touchdown now would make the Raiders' mission very difficult. Morton took the snap and looked over the field as he dropped back to pass. He looked for Odoms, but he drew double coverage. He looked again, getting great protection. Finally, he saw Moses break across the middle

Rookie defensive end Brison Manor eagerly waits to grab Oakland's Clarence Davis' fumble.

of the end zone, coming over from the outside. Morton threw. The crowd leaped to its feet. Moses leaped through the air and landed on the cherished turf of the end zone with the ball cradled in his arms. Touchdown! The crowd was ecstatic. So were the Bronco players. They knew just how much that touchdown meant. Only a misplay on the extra point attempt kept the score at 20-10.

There were only 7:33 remaining on the clock when the Raiders put the ball in play on the 26-yard line. They had to score and score quickly. A touchdown would put them only a field goal away from Denver, but they couldn't afford any mistakes. Nobody counted the Raiders out just yet. If any one can get them points in a hurry, it was Stabler. He is recognized as perhaps the best quarterback in the NFL simply because he gets the job done.

Stabler went to work. On his first three

plays, he gave the ball to van Eeghen. The AFC's number one ground gainer made good yards, gaining five, six, and then five more yards. But it was not enough. Stabler knew he had to pass. On second down and 5 from the Oakland 42-yard line, Stabler connected with wide receiver Mike Siani for 12 yards and a first down on Denver's 46-yard line. He threw a short pass to Banaszak that picked up two yards. It still wasn't enough.

Then Stabler went deep. He hit wide receiver Morris Bradshaw, who had replaced the injured Fred Biletnikoff, with a 25-yard pass that gave the Raiders a first down on Denver's 19-yard line. The Raiders were moving in. Stabler handed the ball to van Eeghen, who could gain only two yards. Then Stabler called pass. He dropped back, got good protection, and zipped a 17-yard aerial to Casper in the end zone for a touchdown. Stabler had moved the Raiders 74 yards in just eight plays. Oakland had fought back to within a field goal of Denver, 20-17. The final outcome of the game was still in doubt.

Instead of gambling with an onside kick. Oakland decided to kick deep. Guy boomed the kickoff to the Denver 3-yard line where Lytle found enough room to bring it back to the 17-yard line. There was still 3:08 left to play, and the Raiders were hoping to create a turnover and move in for the kill. Time and again they have managed to pull out a victory in the closing minutes of a game as the Broncos were well aware.

Morton, tired and hurting, bent over in the huddle. He had received his instructions from Miller, to play it tight and not make mistakes. Morton looked around at his teammates.

"Just two first downs, and we win it," he stressed. "We have to run. Let's do it."

On first down Perrin ran for five yards. Then Perrin carried again and churned his way over Oakland's left side for six yards and a first down. Denver had one of the two first downs it needed. Perrin went up the middle for five more yards as the clock was automatically stopped at the two-minute mark. Morton went over to the Denver bench. He conferred with Miller just to make sure that they both were thinking the same way. The Broncos' faithful were anticipating a victory as Morton went back on the field.

Haven Moses scores Broncos' second touchdown with nobody near him.

Oakland quarterback Ken Stabler is on the way to being sacked by the Denver defense.

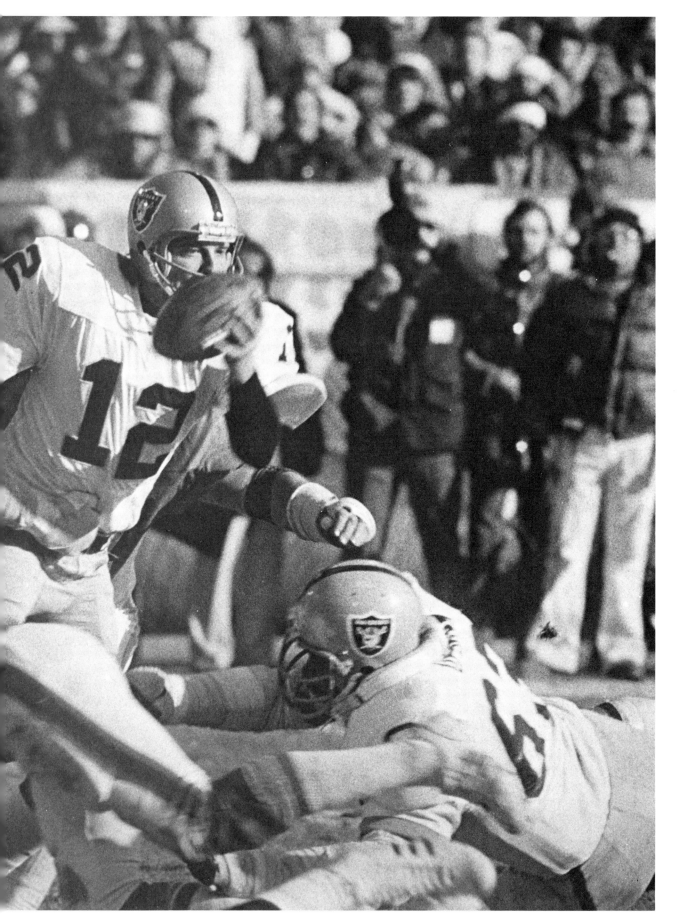

Veteran quarterback Craig Morton provided the experience and leadership needed to get the Broncos into the Super Bowl.

Perrin tried the middle on second down and fought his way for two yards. It was his fourth straight carry. Now the Broncos were faced with a third and three as Oakland called a time out with 1:48 left to play. It was perhaps the biggest play of the game. If the Raiders could stop the Broncos, they would force the Broncos into a punting situation. Then anything could happen, a blocked punt, a weak kick, or a big run back. The pressure would most definitely be on the Broncos.

Again Morton talked strategy with Miller. This one play could seal the victory. Morton returned to the huddle and called Armstrong's number. The crowd was yelling "go" as the Broncos broke from their huddle. Morton handed the ball to Armstrong; and the little running back picked his way over the right side, two, three, four yards before he finally was stopped. Armstrong had given the first down the Broncos needed, and the crowd knew its importance.

In fact, it was all but over. The look was there on the Oakland faces. After one more running play, Morton fell on the ball as the final seconds of the game flashed on the scoreboard clock. Then it was official; the game was over. The Denver fans refused to leave the stadium. They wanted to stay and savor the victory. For the first time ever in Denver's history, the Broncos were the champions of the AFC. Broncomania reigned supreme.

Morton almost collapsed as he entered the jubilant Bronco dressing room. He was spent, not only from the pain of his hip but from the emotion. Tears welled in his eyes. He spoke softly.

"This is probably the greatest thing that ever happened to me," he said. "I just want to praise the Lord. He brought us together as a team. I have to thank Him."

Alzado felt that the turning point of the game was right at the beginning when the Raiders had possession for the first time, drove all the way down to Denver's 3-yard line, and had to settle for a field goal.

"It was the moment for both sides," Alzado observed. "This was strength against strength. Guys were screaming at each other. Even the guys who normally never speak during a game were screaming."

The Denver dressing room occupants were still screaming. They chanted, "Moses, Moses, Moses." The lithe receiver had caught five of the ten passes Morton completed for 168 yards and two touchdowns. It was his biggest day of the season. He was awarded the game ball by his teammates in recognition of his contribution to the team's victory.

"I'm going to keep this in a vault," beamed Moses. "After ten years, I was wondering if I was ever going to get a chance to go to the Super Bowl."

So were the Bronco fans, and they had been waiting for seventeen years.

OAKLAND	3	0	0	14	17
DENVER	7	0	7	6	20

SCORING

Oakland: 4:26 First Period—Mann 20 yard field goal.

Denver: 3:59 First Period—Moses 74 yard pass from Morton (Turner kick).

Denver: 8:37 Third Period—Keyworth 1 yard run (Turner kick).

Oakland: 14:21 Fourth Period—Casper 7 yard pass from Stabler (Mann kick).

Denver: 7:43 Fourth Period—Moses 12 yard pass from Morton (Kick failed).

Oakland: 3:16 Fourth Period—Casper 17 yard pass from Stabler (Mann kick).

11
SUPER BOWL XII

The distractions were there. Despite all precautions to maintain a normal routine, it wasn't possible. The Super Bowl hype is a definite deterrent to a team's concentration. For the Denver Broncos, it was a new experience in a strange town. It was living in a hotel for a week, makeshift meeting rooms, unfamiliar practice fields, and the incessant daily pressure of the news media. No single American sporting event rivals it in total intensity. The fusilade of publicity that accompanies the game is staggering. So much so that for Super Bowl XII, a commercial minute on television reached a record $325,000.

Super Bowl XII had a circus atmosphere because, for one thing, New Orleans is an all-night town. It's a beautiful city with a historic French Quarter and excellent restaurants. On a normal weekend it can be most enjoyable, but Super Bowl weekend is something else. Over 60,000 people crowd into the grand old city, making hotel rooms and restaurant reservations impossible.

Dallas quarterback Roger Staubach prepares to call the first play of Super Bowl XII.

185

In the confinement of the French Quarter, one could feel the excitement of the game. As at every other bar in town, the talk at the Absynthe House, an all-night drinking spa, was about the game. While everybody expected the Dallas Cowboys to be in the Super Bowl, almost everyone else was surprised that the Broncos made it. Tickets were the scarcest of any previous eleven Super Bowls. Ticket gougers were asking and getting as much as $200 for a ducat. Some 50-yard line seats were attracting $250. The presence of the Broncos had a great bearing on the inflated ticket prices. As the sharpies admitted, the Broncs "made" the ticket. The appearance of the Cowboys was half the ticket. Anytime the Cowboys are involved in a big game, ticket scalpers have a shot at a big pay day because Texas money is big and loose. The wave of Denver sentiment guaranteed the scalpers a bonanza.

"I need all the tickets I can get," exhorted restaurateur Jimmy Moran. "I have a lot of friends I have to cover."

"The tickets are going for $150 and up," offered a listener.

"No way," insisted Moran. "I won't pay more than what's printed on the ticket, and that's only $30."

"It's gonna be tough," shot back the other.

"Well, I'll see what happens by the end of the week," Moran said confidently. "I have a lot of friends among the owners and players, and I've never come up short yet."

By week's end, Moran had miraculously covered his ticket commitments. Others weren't so fortunate. A Denver travel agency had difficulty filling its ticket allotment. So did another from California. They were willing to pay whatever the rate was to reach their quota. One Philadelphia agency never did supply its group with the precious game tickets. That's how bullish the Broncos were on the ticket market.

The analysts, who dictate betting prices established the Cowboys as favorites. The point spread opened at Dallas -5 and went as high as six in some bet parlors. The underdog roles assigned to Denver appealed to Danny Sheridan, a football analyst for ABC television's *Good Morning America* program. In his own way, Sheridan is unique. He had correctly picked 10 straight Super Bowl games with the points. For a bettor, that's big dollars. The big money was on Dallas. On paper, they graded out with far too many plusses than Denver. But Sheridan liked the Broncos with the points.

"But," cautioned Sheridan, "it is imperative that the Broncos not only force mistakes but to score first as they are not capable of playing catch-up football against Dallas. Denver also has to force four turnovers by the Cowboy running backs. It is very important for the Broncos to achieve this. I can't see them covering the points if they don't accomplish this. They will quickly fall behind, and the game could turn into a rout."

There were others who offered respected opinions. Allie Sherman for one. The former coach of the New York Giants was considered a brilliant offensive innovator. He strongly felt that the Broncos had to pass to win.

"Denver has to come out throwing," observed Sherman just three days before the extravaganza. "They have to throw on first down, use a lot of play action passes to slow down the rush and freeze the linebackers. There is no way they can run successfully against Dallas's flex defense."

It was the same view shared by Len Dawson, an analyst for NBC television. A former premier quarterback with the Kansas City Chiefs until he retired three years ago, Dawson played against the Broncos frequently and was quite familiar with the Denver personnel.

"I'd come out throwing early," Dawson told an interviewer; "not the bomb but short, working on their linebackers.

"I'd use my tight end a lot; and in Riley Odoms, the Broncos have an outstanding one. And I'd throw to my backs quite a bit, screens and outlet passes to pick up five or six yards; and I wouldn't hesitate to do it on first down. In fact, I'd prefer throwing on first down to pick up four, five, six yards at a clip. If I'm successful this way, then the Cowboys will have to play defense; and they'll be the ones doing the guessing.

"Denver has good receivers with good speed in Haven Moses, Rick Upchurch, and Jack Dolbin. Moses, especially, is a good pattern runner. I'd throw to him deep early because the Dallas secondary will be looking for him to

Before the game, Red Miller shakes hands with Dallas coach Tom Landry.

run intermediate patterns. By sending him deep early, it'll keep their secondary honest.

"In throwing deep, I'd do so to the outside. This will prevent their safeties from getting involved in the play. In Charlie Waters and Cliff Harris, Dallas has a pair of great safeties; and it's not smart to challenge them too much.

"On defense the Cowboys do blitz occasionally. They don't have to blitz much because they get a great deal of penetration from their front four. They have great size up front, Too Tall Jones (6'9"), Jethro Pugh (6'6"), Harvey Martin (6'5"), and Randy White (6'4"). They are really big and quick, and they come at you with their hands up which makes it difficult to throw over them. If you're in a third and long situation and they play pass, they come at you all out; and it's murder. It places the quarterback in jeopardy of getting sacked or having to throw the ball before he's ready, which increases the percentage of interceptions.

"The flex is tough to run on. On the ground, I would attack them more straight ahead than sideways. Sweeps don't work against them because they are so big, so quick, and so well disciplined. There is no question

that the Denver offensive line is going to have their hands full controlling the Dallas front four and linebackers.

"Denver's strength has been that they don't turn the ball over on offense. That's been demonstrated all season long. It is a big reason why they are in the Super Bowl. The other team has to earn what it gets against the Broncos' defense, and that hasn't been much. But the main thing is that Morton has to avoid turning over the football to the Cowboys. That would be a primary objective. You just can't give the Cowboys too many chances with the football. They have a lot of offense and can put points on the board in a hurry. And if Denver falls behind early, it could be a long night."

Even before the game itself, Miller had to guard against distractions. This was the one element that was new to him although long before he arrived in New Orleans with his squad he was aware of it. He spoke at great length over the telephone with Al Locasale, the assistant general manager of the Oakland Raiders. In the previous year's Super Bowl, the Raiders had glorified themselves with an

Rick Upchurch almost gets away down the sidelines.

easy 32-14 triumph over the Minnesota Vikings. Miller sought Locasale's advice on how to cope with all the pre-game pressure. It's hard to merely dismiss it.

Only four Broncos had been exposed to the pressure of a Super Bowl. Kicker Jim Turner had experienced it when he was a member of the New York Jets in Super Bowl III. Morton experienced it twice during his career with the Cowboys in Super Bowl V and VI. Offensive tackle Andy Maurer and defensive back Randy Poltl both played with the Vikings in Super Bowl IX. However, it's only been in the last five years or so that the Super Bowl has reached such a crescendo of pre-game puff.

It all begins when each competing team, on league orders, arrives on the same day, Monday preceding the game itself. League thinking is to keep things uniform for both clubs so that one won't gain an advantage over the other. Such might have been the case when the 1969 Jets, flew to Florida ten days before the game. To avoid the freezing cold of New York and insure decent practice sessions, the Jets toiled in the Florida sun three days ahead of the Colts, who didn't arrive until Sunday night.

"I didn't impose any immediate curfew on the players," disclosed Ewbank. "I wanted them to have some fun. They deserved it. I didn't want to regiment them right away; but on Tuesday, we began to clamp down."

Miami coach Don Shula, who coached the Colts in the 1969 Super Bowl, has appeared in four world championship games. Yet, the first one always holds a special memory.

"You have to learn to live with Super Bowl week," disclosed Shula. "It's never easy, especially the first time."

Former Washington Redskins' coach George Allen, who lost to Shula, 14-7, in the 1973 Super Bowl, still has bitter memories.

"It's hard for the players to concentrate on what they're there for," frowned Allen. "There are so many distractions. If you're not careful, you don't realize what's taking place."

This was what Miller had to contend with. It was new to him. He really didn't have the control he had throughout the season. Unlike other games, where he could regiment his own schedule the previous week, the Super Bowl schedule was dictated by the league. Even though the game was being played in an NFC city, the Broncos were nevertheless designated as the home team. All that merely did was to allow them to wear orange jerseys, which pleased the Orange Crush people to no end. Although the soft drink popularized by the Broncos was not sold in New Orleans, the beverage company propitiously flew in 400 cases of the stuff.

Yet, despite the fact that the Broncos were labeled as the home team, they were not allowed to use the training facilities of the home-standing New Orleans Saints in nearby Meterie. That fine facility was awarded to the Cowboys simply because, like the Saints, they were an NFC team. So, the Broncos were assigned to practice in antiquated Tulane Stadium, a venerable structure that was made famous by the Sugar Bowl in years past but now faces demolition.

Every morning for three days beginning on Tuesday, Miller had to breakfast with the large press corps in a banquet room of the Sheraton Hotel where the league quartered them. The session would last from 8:30 A.M. until about 9:45. After breakfast, Miller would stand behind the podium and patiently answer question after question from inquisitive writers. After the first day, the questions really never changed, only the way they were presented.

Following the question and answer period, the press were allowed 45 minutes to interview the players. The setting, resembling a carnival show, was in an adjacent room. Each player sat behind a small table. On top of the table was a long pole. Attached to the pole was a sign identifying the player's number. The only thing missing was a program, identifying the numbers. The more popular numbers like Lyle Alzado, Randy Gradishar, Tom Jackson, Haven Moses, and Otis Armstrong drew the biggest crowds. The lesser known reserves usually didn't attract anyone. They sadly had to sit and endure the attention their more popular teammates were getting.

Quite naturally, the quarterback draws the biggest crowd. It is the glamour position on any football team, and Morton was given star treatment. In the vacated breakfast room, he faced a bevy of reporters on a platform behind the same microphone that Miller had used earlier. This is how it went, morning after morning, for three consecutive days.

By Friday morning, Miller had grown weary; but this day was different for him. Instead of the regular morning breakfast sessions with the writers, he was scheduled to appear at 9 A.M. for a press conference downtown in the Hyatt Regency. Following that press conference, Miller was scheduled for a television interview. His only day when he could be Red Miller, coach, would be on Saturday. Then, and only then, could he get totally involved with his players and coaches and concentrate on the game itself.

It was almost too easy to get immersed in the distractions that he faced all week. One unexpected event occurred on Wednesday when running back Jon Keyworth received a threatening phone call. Denver club officials reacted quickly. They placed extra security around him, and Keyworth was instructed not to attend Thursday morning's regular player interviews with the press. However, by Friday the seriousness of the threat was diminished when Denver police discovered it had been made after a lover's spat. However until it was resolved, Keyworth admittedly was a bit edgy. During those two days, his concentration for Sunday's game had been seriously interrupted.

It also presented Miller with a worry he didn't need. During the drive downtown to his Friday conference, Miller's voice appeared weary. He sat in the back seat of the car, his legs crossed, and appeared at ease. An emotional individual, Miller was now speaking calmly.

"From the very beginning of camp I knew

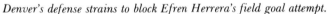
Denver's defense strains to block Efren Herrera's field goal attempt.

we had the makings of a good team. How good remained to be seen. Then it all began to happen. Pretty soon we were nine and one, then ten and one, then eleven and one, and twelve and one. Then we knew we'd be in the playoffs for the first time.

"But you know something odd? Nobody ever gave us any credit. After each victory, none of the rival coaches would compliment us. They'd come up after a game and say, 'Boy, we played a bad game today,' or 'Wow, we sure got a lot of work ahead of us.' It's funny in a way. All along you're doing the job, winning games week after week—and nobody seems to recognize it."

All week long the weather was cold and damp. The winds that buffeted the French Quarter made it feel even colder. But Super Sunday dawned sunny and warm. Not that it

mattered as far as the game was concerned. The indoor facility of the Superdome offered comfort from both cold and wind.

Spectators began arriving early for the contest. They were in a mood to frolic, or perhaps they were just continuing where they left off from the night before. One thing was certain. They definitely had more time to recover from a long night of partying. For the first time ever in Super Bowl history, the game was being played in the early evening hours. The kickoff was scheduled for 5 P.M. New Orleans time which is in the Central Time Zone.

Right up until game time, fans were looking for tickets. If they weren't asking out loud, they held up small cardboard signs indicating the number needed to buy. As with any great sporting event, ticket transactions took place and large bills were exchanged, despite the fact that the game was being shown on television in New Orleans. Although the police tried to prevent the scalping of the coveted tickets, there was no way they could stop it completely. There was just too much of it going on, and the price of the ticket hadn't dropped even as kickoff time approached.

Inside the Dome, the anticipation of the game itself created an electric current. Anything that caught the crowd's fancy drew a cheer. Every visible seat was filled. There was such a large list of writers than an auxiliary press box was situated on the third level of the end zone. One special observer, Joe Namath, attended the spectacle with an entourage that included two beautiful women. Nattily dressed and deeply tanned, the handsome Namath was underneath the large stadium waiting for an elevator to take him and his party to a private box.

"This Denver team is something like the Jets in Super Bowl III," a friend began.

"Only we were a bigger underdog," answered Namath.

"That's true. Besides that, they don't have somebody like you at quarterback."

"You're very kind," smiled Namath. "Who do you like in the game?"

"On paper it's all Dallas, but . . ."

"Forget on paper," interrupted Namath. "I'm talking about on the field. No way form won't hold up. They have too much going."

While Namath obviously favored Dallas, the

big crowd seemed to be with Denver. Along with the Jets in 1969 and the Kansas City Chiefs in 1970, they were perhaps the best loved underdogs in the history of the post-season extravaganza.

Besides being noticeably vocal, the Denver diehards were extremely visible. It looked as if one section of the huge Superdome had been painted orange. Bright orange shirts, sweaters, and hats were much in evidence in the sections behind the Denver bench.

The Cowboys were introduced first. One by one the Dallas offensive team trotted on to the field. Extremely disciplined, the Cowboys ran to a spot on the field marked by the television crew, paused for a moment, and then continued toward the Dallas bench. The biggest cheers were for Roger Staubach and Tony Dorsett.

Next came the Broncos, and their introduction was something else. A deafening din greeted each player, a din that seemed to reverberate off the massive dome almost as a second roar. Nothing in professional sports was ever like it. The well of sound and emotion was almost too much to be contained under one roof. Broncomania had reached its highest decibel in New Orleans.

As expected, the Denver defensive unit was introduced. One by one they ran out to the appointed spot. However, instead of running off the field, each player that was introduced stepped to one side, waiting to glad-hand the next teammate coming out of the tunnel. By the time the defensive backfield was introduced to the noisy crowd, the backs were leaping into the arms of the linemen. The current of emotion was exhausting. Two weeks after their dramatic victory over Oakland in the AFC championship game, the Broncos were still on a Rocky Mountain high. Miller had his team up!

After the noise finally quieted down the officials signalled for the ritualistic toss of the coin at midfield. The Denver players made the call but guessed wrong. Dallas elected to receive. It didn't matter in the least to the Bronco backers. After all, the pride of the team all year long was the defense.

Deep down, perhaps the Denver coaches wanted it that way. Not that the offense was anything to be ashamed of, but the strength of the Broncos was their defense. The offense was at best opportunistic. So maybe, just maybe, in the early minutes of the biggest game in Denver's history, the defense could create a turnover and position the ball for the offense.

Turner's opening-game kickoff did not carry very far. Butch Johnson caught it on the 15 and returned it to the Dallas 29. On the very first play from scrimmage, Dallas coach Tom Landry felt he would open up the game right from the start with a double reverse. It almost cost him. Johnson, from his flanker position, swept wide into his backfield on the end of a double reverse. He fumbled the ball. However, he managed to recover the fumble as Tom Jackson dropped him for a 9-yard loss. The crowd roared its delight.

When Dorsett failed to gain a yard on the next play, the crowd cheered again. The Denver defense looked as awesome as ever. Even the fact that Preston Pearson gained eight yards on a screen pass from Staubach meant nothing. Dallas was forced to punt.

Danny White's punt carried only 40 yards. Denver's deluxe kick returner, Rick Upchurch, set to catch the ball on his own 40-yard line. However, he was interfered from making a clean catch of the ball by Dallas linebacker Tom Henderson. The penalty advanced the ball to the Bronco's 47-yard line. Denver had excellent field position.

On first down, Morton tested Dallas's right side. He handed the ball to Keyworth, who was stopped for a 5-yard loss by Henderson. On second down, Morton again gave the ball to Keyworth. The big running back gained three yards before he once again was tackled by Henderson. Morton was now faced with third and long. He looked over the Dallas defense. He looked down into the huddle and called for a pass. He knew the Cowboys would be coming in an obvious passing situation. Yet, he wanted Moses to start ouside and cut in the middle. The play worked. Morton took the snap and fired quickly into the pass route. Moses caught the ball on the Dallas 34 and was immediately hit by cornerback Benny Barnes.

Cowboys' rookie whiz Tony Dorsett scores game's first touchdown.

Randy Hughes (42) intercepts Craig Morton's pass in first period.

The 21-yard pass brought the crowd to its feet. Suddenly, after three minutes had gone by, the Broncos were in striking distance. If Morton could get Denver on the board, then the Cowboys would have to challenge the Denver defense. It was just what the Broncos wanted, and the crowd was expecting as much.

However, the Dallas defense stiffened. Otis Armstrong tried the left side and got only a yard. On second down, Morton tried to pass. He was rushed, and his pass was deflected by Jones. He attempted to pass once again on third down, but the Dallas rush was again too much. Morton didn't even get the chance to set up as he was sacked for an 11-yard loss by White.

Bucky Dilts booted a high punt that Tony Hill circled under on the 1-yard line. Instead of letting the ball bounce into the end zone for an apparent touchback, Hill tried to catch the ball and run with it. He fumbled the ball as the crowd rose to its feet and roared once again. For a split second, a Denver player covered the loose ball. Somehow Hill reached under the pileup and recovered the ball on the 1-yard line. For the second straight time, the ball didn't bounce right for the Broncos. Was Dame Fortune, who had been with Denver all season long, about to jilt them?

The Cowboys were in serious trouble. Yet, Staubach remained cool. On first down he didn't hesitate to pass. He flipped a short 2-yard pass to Dorsett on the three, and the swift rookie reached the 16-yard line before he was brought down by Jackson. That daring play got Dallas out of the hole. On the next play, Dorsett ran inside for three yards to the 19 before Alzado grabbed him. For the third play in a row, Staubach called Dorsett's number. This time he sent him up the middle. After reaching the 22-yard line, the ball popped loose. Quickly, center John Fitzgerald recovered the ball. Three times Dallas had misplayed the ball, and all three times they retained possession.

Denver fans got their hopes up again on the next play when Rubin Carter sacked Staubach for a 6-yard loss on the 16. For the second time in two series, White was sent in to punt. So far, Denver held the Cowboys in check, even though they didn't benefit from any of Dallas's three mistakes. White's punt didn't

196

carry very far, only to the Broncos' 47. Up-church could only bring it back to the Dallas 46 before he was tackled. However, Denver was penalized 15 yards on the return when Randy Poltl was detected for holding.

Morton wanted to get on the scoreboard fast. On first down from his own 39, he sent Moses deep down the left side. Releasing the ball under a strong rush, Morton overthrew him. Morton called for another pass. This time he sent Upchurch on a quick turn in up the middle. Once more the Dallas front four, led by Harvey Martin, applied pressure; and once again Morton overthrew his receiver.

Determinedly, Morton challenged Dallas' rush a third time. It was no easy task. This

He knew they would be coming. How fast he never realized. As soon as he took the snap and dropped back to pass, he was pressured. Instead of taking the loss, Morton let the pass go. It softly left his hand as he was going down and landed into the waiting arms of Dallas defensive back Randy Hughes who caught it at his shoe tops on the Denver 25.

The Cowboys moved quickly to capitalize on the mistake. On first down, Staubach looked to his left and then threw a bullet to tight end Billy Joe DuPree on the right side. The big tight end ran 13 yards to the Broncos' 12 before he was finally halted. Staubach then handed the ball to Robert Newhouse, who moved the ball to the 10. Dorsett came right back over the right side and picked up six yards before he was downed on the 4-yard line. For the third straight time, Staubach called for a run over the right side. This time Dorsett got only a yard before he was buried by Randy Gradishar and Joe Rizzo.

Now came the first big decision of the scoreless game. The Cowboys were confronted with a fourth and 1 on the Denver 3-yard line. Should they go for an almost sure field goal or try for a first down? Staubach looked over at Dallas coach Tom Landry. He waved for Staubach to stay on the field and sent in a play. Landry was going all the way.

The Cowboys broke the huddle. The crowd was imploring the famed Denver defense to stop the Dallas threat. Staubach took the snap, turned, and handed the ball to Dorsett. This time he broke over the left side and went in for a touchdown. Dallas jumped into a 7-0 lead after Efren Herrera's conversion. It was a big advantage for the Cowboys, both psychologically and tactically.

On the ensuing kickoff, John Schultz provided the Broncos with good field position when he ran the ball back 37 yards to the Denver 40. After a run by Rob Lytle gained only two yards, Morton dropped back to pass on second down. Pressured again under a fierce rush, Morton threw up the middle. The pass was deflected by Dallas's middle linebacker Bob Breunig and picked off by cornerback

time he was attempting to penetrate Dallas's 4-1-6 defense. It is the defense they employ on certain passing downs, taking out two linebackers and inserting two extra backs. Nobody but Dallas executes it so well. The key is a big rush from the front four.

Leaning over his center, Mike Montler, Morton looked over the Cowboys' alignment.

With his right foot barely on the field, Staubach prepares to throw second quarter pass that was intercepted by Billy Thompson in the end zone. However, referee ruled that Staubach was out of bounds and on next play Herrera kicked a field goal.

Aaron Kyle at the Dallas 46. Kyle shook loose for 19 yards before he was tackled on the Denver 35.

Suddenly the Cowboys were threatening again, less than two minutes after scoring their first touchdown. Newhouse tried the right side and busted through for nine yards to the Denver 26. With the Broncos' defense bunched in tight, Dorsett made a move inside and then cut to the outside for 18 yards before Louis Wright caught him from behind on the 8-yard line.

Denver was in trouble. But the doughty Bronco defense dug in. On first down they stopped Dorsett for no gain. Staubach tried to hit DuPree with a pass in the end zone but missed as DuPree fell down. In an obvious passing situation, the Bronco defense called for a blitz. Linebacker Joe Rizzo stormed in from the left side. Staubach turned to his right and was sacked by Lyle Alzado on the 18-yard line. Dallas now had to settle for a 35-yard field goal by Herrera which pushed their advantage to 10-0.

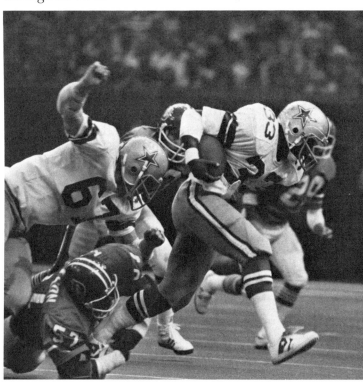

Dorsett slips through the grip of Bob Swenson for a short gain.

On their first series of downs after the kick-off, the Broncos couldn't do anything. They were forced to give up the ball again. Dilts's punt wasn't good. It only went 32 yards where it was downed on the Cowboys' 43-yard line. The Cowboys had good field position once more. Mixing his plays, Staubach produced two first downs and reached the Broncos' 19-yard line. Facing a third and six, Staubach scrambled to his right before throwing a pass in the Denver end zone that was intercepted by Bill Thompson.

However, the interception was nullified. The referee ruled that Staubach had stepped out of bounds on the 25-yard line and ruled the play a 6-yard loss. More importantly, Dallas retained possession. Miller ran up the sidelines chiding the official for blowing the call. Photographs showed later that Staubach did not step out. By keeping possession, Herrera was able to boot a 43-yard field goal that sent Dallas into a 13-0 lead.

Things certainly didn't look good for Denver. Especially when Morton was intercepted for the third time on the second play after the kickoff. Then everything began to go wrong for the Broncos. First, Schultz fumbled a punt on the Dallas 40-yard line. Later, Morton completed a 15-yard pass to Jack Dolbin, who fumbled the ball on the Denver 42. Still later, tight end Riley Odoms caught a 10-yard pass from Morton, only to fumble it on the Denver 28. Finally, as the half was near completion, Morton yielded his fourth interception. Only the fact that Herrera missed three field goals prevented the score from being more than 13-0 as the first half ended. It left the Denver fans shaking their heads in disbelief.

Morton did not look like the same quarterback that had led the Broncos to fourteen victories during the 1977 season. Something was wrong. He didn't appear to have command. He kept glancing over at Harvey Martin as if wondering what the big Dallas defensive end would do next. His interception total of four was astronomical. Throughout the entire campaign of sixteen games, he had surrendered only eight passes, or an average of only one every two games. Yet, against Dallas, before millions of people watching over television, he had been intercepted four times in only half a game.

Denver could not generate any offense at all, and it wasn't that Morton was hampered by a painful hip pointer as he had been in the championship game two weeks earlier. Dallas's defensive strategy was obvious. They decided to put pressure on Morton on every play, and they were succeeding. The Denver offensive line was getting beaten in the pits.

The Broncos' halftime stats were woeful. They had only produced three first downs. Their total yardage was 72 yards, 44 rushing and only 28 passing. Virtually a mistake-free team all season, the Broncos committed a total of seven turnovers. Besides Morton's four interceptions, the Broncos lost the ball three times on fumbles. It was miraculous that in allowing a team like Dallas seven turnovers they weren't further behind than 13-0.

That was the only consolation that Miller had in the locker room. That, along with the fact that his defense had played well. He kept reminding his squad that despite the seven turnovers they were still in the game. He stressed that the second half was a new game, to keep hitting out there, to stay close on the scoreboard, that the breaks would finally come their way.

Then he did something else. After his talk, he called Morton off to one side. It was a private conversation between a coach and his quarterback. He placed his arm on Morton's shoulder and whispered.

"Craig," began Miller, "I'm going to let you start the second half. However, if we can't get something started quickly, I'm going to see what Weese can do. You understand?"

Morton nodded his head. For a moment he was alone with his thoughts. He was thinking that the Broncos would get the second half kickoff and that he had to get them on the board. He tried to forget about the nightmarish first half. The second half was the half that counted, the one in which most games are won.

Everybody was wondering if they were going to see a different Bronco team in the second half when Morton trotted onto the field. Schultz's kickoff return had given the Broncos fair field position on the 35-yard line.

Quarterback Craig Morton spent a most frustrating afternoon against the Dallas Cowboys. He was intercepted four times during the game.

202

Morton and the offense had room to operate. The veteran quarterback realized all too well the significance of the first series of plays. He had to get the Broncos moving toward the goal line.

On the first play, Keyworth was denied even a yard. However, on second down, Armstrong broke loose around right end and ran for 18 yards before Cliff Harris knocked him over. The Broncos had a first down on the Cowboys' 48-yard line. Morton decided to go to the air. He tried to hit Dolbin with a pass in the middle but failed. Then on a keeper play, Morton moved to his right and pitched out to Keyworth for a 6-yard gain. Denver was faced with a third and 4 on the Dallas 41-yard line. Morton called a screen right. Martin applied pressure from the left side, and Morton's pass to Armstrong fell harmlessly to the ground. Morton started to walk off the field, turning his head behind him for a brief second.

It appeared as if the Broncos would have to give up the ball. Dilts was sent in to punt, but the Cowboys were suspicious. Miller has been known to call a trick play at an opportune time, and Dallas was looking for something. Dilts handled the long snap cleanly, faked a punt, brought his arm back to pass, and couldn't find anyone open. The Dallas defenders had the Denver receivers covered. Dilts did the only thing left. He tucked the ball under his arm and began to run, but he didn't get very far. Kyle swarmed all over him on the 41-yard line for a 4-yard loss.

Nothing seemed to be going right for the Broncos. But then an official's flag fell commandingly to the ground, and Denver finally got their break. The Cowboys were cited for an illegal formation. They were assessed a 5-yard penalty, which gave the Broncos a first down on the Cowboys' 36-yard line. They had new life.

Morton returned to the lineup. He quickly went to work. On first down he tried to connect with Moses down the left side but threw the ball short. Anticipating a Dallas rush on the next play, Morton called a draw; and Keyworth advanced the ball five yards. Once again Morton was confronted with a key third-down play. Instead of a pass, however, he dispatched Armstrong around the right

end. He figured Dallas would be playing pass, but the Cowboys were braced for a run and stopped Armstrong after a 1-yard gain.

With a fourth down and needing four yards for a first, there was nothing left for the Broncos to do but attempt a field goal. They desperately had to get some points on the board to get back into the game. A field goal at this point would leave the Broncos only 10 points behind with plenty of time left. Besides, psychologically, the Broncos needed something. A field goal would do just nicely.

The reliable veteran Jim Turner was asked to give the Broncos that needed lift. During the season, Turner had been successful on 13 of 19 field goal attempts. His longest one was 48 yards. Now, under pressure, he was attempting a kick from 47 yards away. The placement was perfect; and Turner booted it accurately, and the ball split the crossbar. The Broncos now trailed 13-3, and their hopes began to rise. After all, they scored the first time they got their hands on the ball in the second half; and time was still on their side.

They almost received another break on the kickoff. Johnson fumbled the ball on the six-yard line, but he recovered in time to run to the 21 before he was swarmed on. Excitement began to envelop the crowd. They felt that perhaps the momentum was about to swing in Denver's favor. Their boisterous cheers implored the Bronco defense to contain the Cowboys. Even the Denver bench was up and yelling for the defensive brigade.

Playing aggressively, the Denver defense stymied the Cowboys. The Superdome fans were on their feet. On the field below, the momentum of the game was changing. Dallas was in an awkward position. They were looking at a fourth and 11 situation on their own 20-yard line. There was nothing left for them to do but punt the ball out of danger.

With pressure resting on his talented right foot, Danny White, the Cowboys' reserve quarterback, came through admiringly. He boomed a 53-yard punt. It not only had distance but was high enough to allow his teammates proper coverage. It resulted in limiting the dangerous Upchurch to only an 8-yard advance to the Denver 35.

Still, Morton had good field position from which to maneuver his team. In fact, it was the same spot he opened the second half. He knew if he could take his team down field again and this time score a touchdown, then the momentum most decidedly would be with the Broncos. Everybody realized it. And now it was the Denver defense on the sidelines that was cheering the offense on. Morton didn't waste any time. On first down he tried to deliver a pass to his favorite receiver, Haven Moses, but failed. Then he reverted to a run on the right side, but Dallas linebacker Bob Breunig came up quickly and smothered Lytle on the line of scrimmage. Now Morton had to pass. Dallas knew it. They came hard and fast on Morton. The irrepressible Martin led the way and sacked Morton for a 9-yard loss. The Broncos were stopped unceremoniously and were forced to surrender the ball. Their brief courtship with momentum was broken.

Dilts's weak punt didn't help the situation. It only traveled 32 yards where Tony Hill signaled for a fair catch on the Dallas 42-yard line. As Staubach returned on the field, he realized that he must seize the momentum back. The most propitious way to do it would be to score a touchdown or a field goal. He kept the ball himself on first down and ran for five yards. After an illegal motion penalty set the Cowboys back to the original line of scrimmage, Staubach fired a 13-yard pass to Drew Pearson for a first down on Denver's 45-yard line.

Dorsett failed to gain a yard as linebacker Joe Rizzo read the play and popped him on the line of scrimmage. On second down, Staubach wanted to go all the way for a touchdown. He dropped back and heaved a long pass to Golden Richards that went over the fleet receiver's head in the end zone. It looked as if the Denver defense was about to reject the Cowboys' thrust.

On third down and 10, Staubach was thinking "pass." So were the Broncos. But instead of calling for a medium-range pass, Staubach was determined to go all the way. Butch Johnson replaced Richards in the lineup, and Staubach called his pattern. Johnson ran straight down the left sideline and then cut toward the center of the end zone after he crossed the goal line. Staubach's long pass came flying toward him. Johnson had crossed the goal line. Intuitively, Johnson leaped towards the ball. While soaring through the air laterally with the ground, Johnson stretched out and clutched the pigskin in his hands. As soon as he made contact with the ground, the ball popped loose from Johnson's grasp. It was a legal catch since he had possession when he crossed the goal line. The official threw his hands high into the air to indicate a touchdown. Suddenly, Dallas went ahead 19-3. The play was a shocker.

In the first place, nobody expected Staubach to try for a touchdown on third down from 45 yards out. Not with his team 10 points in front. Then, before Herrera's conversion pushed Dallas's margin to 20-3, many had wondered if Johnson's catch should have been ruled a touchdown. The official's call was totally accurate. Once an offensive player breaks the imaginary plane on the goal line, he doesn't have to maintain possession of the ball once he crosses it; and that's exactly what Johnson did.

The touchdown shook the Denver bench. Their task now became exceedingly difficult. They were 17 points behind, and playing catch-up football was not their style. Their game was to jump out in front and then force their opponents to make mistakes. That was not the case now. Certainly they couldn't expect Dallas to make that many mistakes now, but they had to hope. Besides, they have never been accused of quitting. The Broncos had too much character for that.

Upchurch demonstrated the battling spirit that epitomized the Broncos throughout the 1977 season. He brought the crowd to its feet in unison when he ran back the kickoff 67 yards to the Dallas 26. It was the longest kickoff return in Super Bowl history. More important, it provided the Broncos with a tremendous lift. They had to strike back swiftly, and Morton didn't hesitate. He wanted to score quickly while the adrenalin was flowing. That meant a pass. On first down he looked for Lytle. However, the rookie running back was nowhere near the ball; but Ed "Too Tall" Jones was. Shocked momentarily at seeing the ball delivered right into his hands, the big defensive end dropped it. It very nearly was Morton's fifth interception. The large crowd looked on disbelievingly at what had almost happened and then began to buzz as

Running back Rob Lytle breaks loose for a sizeable game against the Cowboys, but it was not enough.

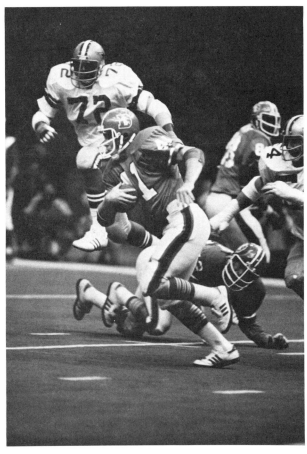

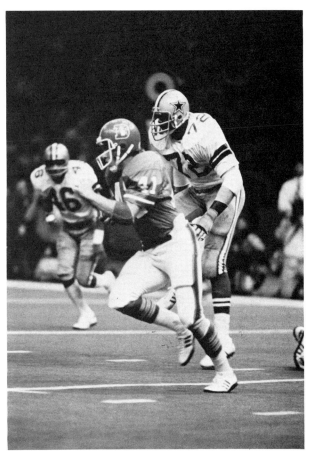

Dallas wide receiver Butch Johnson lands in end zone with dramatic 45-yard touchdown catch in third quarter.

Staubach raises his arms for joy after Johnson's catch.

Morton walked toward the sideline. Reserve quarterback Norris Weese was trotting on the field. It was bold move by Red Miller. Weese was listed not as the second string but the third reserve on the Denver depth chart. But Miller had to do something. He had to try and change the tempo of the game and get his team moving.

Morton stood alongside Miller as Weese took control. It was a tough assignment, coming in cold in a game as big as the Super Bowl. The first call was a handoff to Lytle, who advanced the ball four yards to the Dallas 22. Now Weese had first taste of action, one designed to relieve him of any nervousness. He didn't wait long to pass. On third down, he tossed a little pass to his running back Jim Jensen that gained five yards. The Broncos were just one yard short of a first down. Weese was experiencing his first clutch play of the game.

210

The second-year youngster exhorted his teammates in the middle. He took the fourth down snap and kept the ball. He moved to his right laterally along the line of scrimmage. Then he made a quick pitch to Jensen, who found running room on the outside. Jensen accelerated and almost made it to the end zone before he was pulled down on the one-yard line. On the very next play, Lytle went in from one yard out.

The Broncos finally scored a touchdown. Remarkably, Weese got them in on only four plays; but time was now becoming a factor. There was only a little more than five minutes left in the third quarter after Turner's conversion made the score 20-10. It was almost imperative that the Broncos would have to hold Dallas and come back with another score.

As the third quarter ended, the Cowboys were mounting a drive. They began on their

Ed "Too Tall" Jones of Cowboys calmly walks away after sacking Morton.

Quarterback Norris Weese feels the pressure of the Cowboys' famed "Doomsday Defense" as Harvey Martin grabs him.

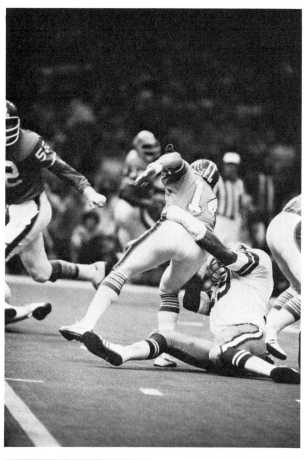

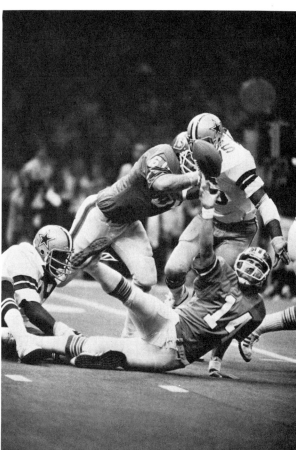

own 14-yard line and had moved to the Denver 36. Dropping back to pass on third and nine, Tom Jackson blitzed and sacked Staubach for a 9-yard loss. He hit the veteran quarterback so hard that he jarred the ball loose. As it dropped out of Staubach's hands, Rubin Carter pounced on the ball at the Denver 45. The Denver partisans loved it.

Weese assumed control in good field position. If he could put some points on the board, any amount, then anything could happen the rest of the way. Certainly Dallas would be under pressure. With 14 minutes left to play, a 20-10 lead wasn't impossible to overcome, not with the fight the Broncos had in them and the Bronco backers cheering them on.

Lytle had lost eight yards on first down, but a face mask infraction on Charlie Waters gave the Broncos a first down on their 42. Weese then went overhead and hit Upchurch with a 9-yard pass on the Dallas 49. He gave the ball to Armstrong, who moved forward for three yards and a first down on the Cowboys' 46. Just as it appeared that the Broncos were putting it together, they stalled. It was the result of three consecutive pass plays that failed to reach fruition.

On all three occasions, Weese challenged cornerback Mark Washington on the right side of the Dallas secondary. The first time, he tried to hit Dolbin but threw out of bounds. The second pass was intended for Upchurch in the end zone but missed. The third occasion he went back to Dolbin, this time up the middle, but failed. On three incompleted pass plays Denver's attack was abruptly halted. No one seemed to care that Dilts's punt carried into the Dallas end zone.

When the Cowboys put the ball in play on the 20-yard line, Staubach was not among them. On the play in which Jackson sacked him, Staubach had injured the index finger of his right hand. So, White was dispatched to play quarterback; and Bronco fans were just hoping that perhaps he would fall victim to a turnover. Denver needed something to get the ball back in good attack position.

Undaunted, White threw a pass on his very first play that gained five yards. After a running play gained two yards, White had to execute a third and three play. He did so brazenly. On a quarterback draw, he darted up the middle for 13 yards. However, on a third down and nine situation, he was replaced by Staubach, who had had his finger treated with a pain killer. Staubach failed to complete a pass from the Cowboy 41-yard line, and Dallas had to yield the ball.

One play later, White returned to punt. He kicked a high punt that Upchurch gathered on the Denver 17, Dallas's punt coverage was good and contained Upchurch on the 24. The Broncos had a long way to go with only 8:50 left on the clock.

Denver sought to move through the air on first down. Odoms was tackled after a reception that lost one yard. Weese was pressured on the play and did well to avoid being sacked for still a bigger loss. Then, on a keeper play, Weese maneuvered his way for seven yards before meeting the ground on the 30-yard line. On third down, Denver shifted into the shotgun formation that Dallas made famous. Apparently, the Cowboys know its weaknesses as well as its strengths. The untiring Martin tore after Weese, sacked him, and caused him to fumble. Kyle covered the loose ball on the 29, and Denver was in trouble again.

The Cowboys didn't waste any time in going for the kill, and they achieved it in an unusual way. On what began as a sweep to the left, Newhouse stopped and fired a 29-yard touchdown pass to Richards who beat Foley in the end zone. Richards had made a remarkable over-the-shoulder catch, and the touchdown broke the game wide open as Herrera's conversion sent Dallas into an unsurmountable 27-10 advantage.

Still, the Broncos didn't quit. With less than seven minutes remaining before the game was over, Weese gave the Bronco fans a bit more excitement. In the Broncos' final offensive effort, he got his team as far as the Dallas 24-yard line. He just missed securing another touchdown when his fourth-down pass went in and out of Upchurch's hands on the 5-yard line.

All that was left was for Dallas to run out the clock. With just 3:14 left on the big electric clocks on both ends of the Superdome, they succeeded without incident.

Even in defeat, the Broncos were beautiful.

Dallas linebacker Mike Hegman signals his team's victory.

They were beautiful in the sense that they showed their emotions. Although most look at professional athletes as cold and synthetic, the Broncos project a rare quality of humaness. As they came off the field in a strange town, in an indoor stadium for a football field, they held their heads high. But as they were walking into their dressing room, their faces told the story. They bit their lips and held back the tears that welled in their eyes. Some appeared glassy-eyed, staring into space as if not actually knowing where they really were. Despite its sadness, it was all that much more beautiful, only because the Broncos portrayed the human side of professional football.

Inside the dressing room, Red Miller himself was suppressing the tears. He stood on a platform in the middle of the subdued room, waiting to be interviewed on television. CBS sportscaster Paul Hornung told him that they would be on the air in three minutes. Miller excused himself and said that he would be back in time.

It was a tough moment for him. It was the first time the Broncos had lost a big game all year. They had finally made believers out of a lot of people by winning the Western Division of the AFC and then by beating Pittsburgh and then Oakland in the playoffs.

Although the atmosphere changed, the man didn't. At that very moment, while waiting to be interviewed on television, all Miller could think about was his players. That's when he decided to leave the makeshift platform and be with them.

"Coach, where are you going? You have to be on television," shouted an aide.

"I know that," he replied, "but I have three minutes, and I want to make use of them."

And so while the television crew wondered where Miller had gone, he quietly did what he wanted to do. He walked over to each of his players and offered some words of encouragement. He was proud of the fact that they had won fourteen games and had made it to the Super Bowl.

"I just wish that things would have turned out differently today," Miller said. "We lost to a fine football team, and I am proud of our players. Despite the setbacks, they never quit.

Miller congratulates Landry on Cowboys' 27-10 victory.

217

"We just couldn't get started. Our players weren't at all tight. I felt that we were plenty loose when the game began, but it was a great defense that did us in. It is the best defense in football. Nobody plays the 4-1-6 better than Dallas. It was a clean, hard game. Broncomania carried us all the way down here, and I felt we were ready to play. But we couldn't overcome all those fumbles and interceptions in the first half. You can't do that to a team like Dallas. But this team is a great bunch. I'm real proud of them. We have nothing to be ashamed of, and we don't have to apologize to anybody."

Indeed he doesn't. The Broncos were something else. Nobody believed they would ever reach the Super Bowl. Week after week they kept surprising their severest critics. They did it by being resourceful. They would force their opponents into mistakes and quickly capitalize on them. That was their style. Broncomania swept across the country. Everybody knew about the Orange Crush. By the season's end, every little guy in America was pulling for the Denver Broncos. It was almost un-American not to.

Emotion had a great deal to do with the Broncos' success. In professional sports, that's such a refreshing ingredient. Unfortunately, in a very big game like the Super Bowl, emotion is not quite enough. It can carry talent just so far. The bottom line is quality players, and offensively, the Broncos didn't have that many.

But they'll be back. Any Bronco fan in America will bet their last can of Orange Crush on that.

DALLAS	10	3	7	7	27
DENVER	0	0	10	0	10

SCORING

Dallas: 4:29 First Period—Dorsett 3 yard run (Herrera kick).

Dallas: 1:31 First Period—Herrera 35 yard field goal.

Dallas: 11:16 Second Period—Herrera 43 yard field goal.

Denver: 12:32 Third Period—Turner 47 yard field goal.

Dallas: 6:59 Third Period—Johnson 45 yard pass from Staubach (Herrera kick).

Denver: 5:39 Third Period—Lytle 1 yard run (Turner kick).

Dallas: 7:04 Fourth Period—Richards 29 yard pass from Newhouse (Herrera kick).

Bronco defensive end Barney Chavous shows the pain of defeat.

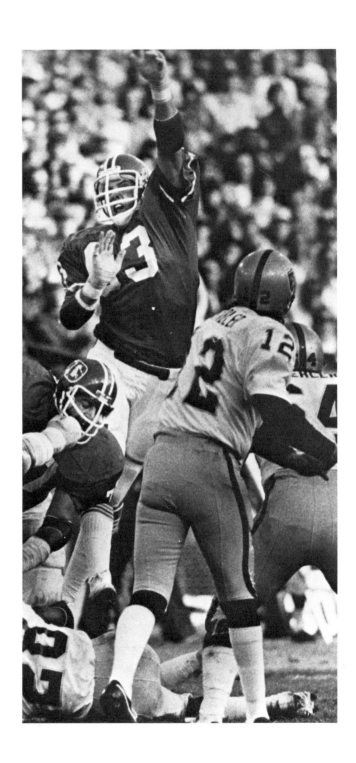

APPENDIX

RESULTS AND ATTENDANCE

at Denver 7, St. Louis 0	75,002
at Denver 26, Buffalo 6	74,897
Denver 24, at Seattle 13	53,108
at Denver 23, Kansas City 7	74,878
Denver 30, at Oakland 7	53,616
Denver 24, at Cincinnati 13	54,305
Oakland 24, at Denver 14	75,007
at Denver 21, Pittsburgh 7	74,967
Denver 17, at San Diego 14	45,211
Denver 14, at Kansas City 7	54,050
Denver 27, at Baltimore 13	74,939
Denver 24, at Houston 14	46,875
Denver 17, San Diego 9	74,905
at Dallas 14, Denver 6	63,752

Team Statistics

	Broncos	Opponent
TOTAL FIRST DOWNS	223	217
Rushing	101	77
Passing	107	123
Penalty	15	17
Third Down Made/Att.	72/210	71/221
Third Down Efficiency	34%	32%
TOTAL NET YARDS	3906	3774
Avg. Per Game	279.0	269.6
Total Plays	887	941
Avg. Per Play	4.4	4.0
NET YARDS RUSHING	2043	1530
Avg. Per Game	145.9	109.3
Total Rushes	523	470
Avg. Per Rush	3.9	3.3
NET YARDS PASSING	1863	2244
Avg. Per Game	133.1	160.3
Tackled/Yards Lost	50/402	35/312
Gross Yards	2265	2556
Attempts/Completions	314/163	426/235
Pct. of Completions	.519	.552
Had Intercepted	12	25
PUNTS/AVERAGE	91/39.2	95/40.7
NET PUNTING AVERAGE	33.7	31.3
PUNT RETURNS/AVERAGE	58/12.3	54/7.4
KICKOFF RETURNS/AVERAGE	34/21.5	50/21.7
INTERCEPTIONS/AVG. RETURN	25/19.6	12/14.3
PENALTIES/YARDS	91/883	97/718
FUMBLES/LOST BALL	28/15	27/14
TOUCHDOWNS	34	18
Rushing	16	5
Passing	15	11
Returns	3	2
EXTRA POINTS/ATTEMPTS	31/34	16/18
FIELD GOALS/ATTEMPTS	13/19	8/22
TOTAL POINTS	274	148

Score by Periods

	1	2	3	4	OT	Total
Broncos	68	72	60	74	0	274
Opponents	45	46	40	17	0	148

Rushing

	No.	Yds.	Avg.	LG	TD
Armstrong	130	489	3.8	35	4
Perrin	110	456	4.1	62	3
Lytle	104	408	3.9	21	1
Keyworth	83	311	3.7	16	1
Jensen	40	143	3.6	12	1
Morton	31	125	4.0	15	4
Weese	11	56	5.1	21	1
Penrose	4	24	6.0	17	0
Upchurch	1	19	19.0	19T	1
Dolbin	2	12	6.0	14	0
Kiick	1	1	1.0	1	0
Dilts	1	0	0.0	0	0
Moses	5	-1	-0.2	8	0
Broncos Total	523	2043	3.9	62	16
Opponents Total	470	1530	3.3	65	5

Passing

	Att.	Comp.	Yards	Pct.	Avg./Att.	TD
Morton	254	131	1929	.516	7.59	14
Penrose	40	21	217	.525	5.43	0
Weese	20	11	119	.550	5.95	1
Broncos Total	314	163	2265	.519	7.21	15
Opponents Total	426	235	2556	.552	6.00	11

	Pct. TD	Int.	Pct. Int.	LG	Lost/Att.	Rating
Morton	.055	8	.031	81T	43/338	82.1
Penrose	.000	4	.100	35	5/49	28.9
Weese	.050	0	.000	31	2/15	89.4
Broncos Total	.048	12	.038	81T	50/402	75.6
Opponents Total	.026	25	.059	51	35/312	57.2

Receiving

	No.	Yds.	Avg.	LG	TD
Odoms	37	429	11.6	33	3
Moses	27	539	20.0	35	4
Dolbin	26	443	17.0	81T	3
Armstrong	18	128	7.1	20	0
Lytle	17	198	11.6	47T	1
Upchurch	12	245	20.4	45	2
Keyworth	11	48	4.4	14	0
Perrin	6	106	17.8	41T	1
Jensen	4	63	15.8	34	0
Egloff	2	27	13.5	20	0
Kiick	2	14	7.0	11	0
Turner	1	25	25.0	25T	1
Broncos Total	163	2265	13.9	81T	15
Opponents Total	235	2556	10.9	51	9

Interceptions

	No.	Yds.	Avg.	LG	TD
Thompson	5	122	24.4	38	0
T. Jackson	4	95	23.8	73T	1
Wright	3	128	42.7	59	1
Gradishar	3	56	18.7	28	0
Rizzo	3	49	16.3	38	0
Foley	3	22	7.3	11	0
B. Jackson	1	13	13.0	13	0
Smith	1	6	6.0	6	0
Evans	1	0	0.0	0	0
Swenson	1	0	0.0	0	0
Broncos Total	25	491	19.6	73T	2
Opponents Total	12	172	14.3	29	0

Punting

	No.	Yds.	Avg.	TB	In 20	LG
Dilts	90	3525	39.2	5	20	63
Weese	1	38	38.0	0	0	38
Broncos Total	91	3563	39.2	5	20	63
Opponents Total	95	3868	40.7	9	13	74

Scoring

	TDR	TDP	TDRt	PAT	FG	TP
Turner		1		31/34	13/19	76
Armstrong	4					24
Moses		4				24
Morton	4					24
Perrin	3	1				24
Upchurch	1	2	1			24
Dolbin		3				18
Odoms		3				18
Lytle	1	1				12
Wright			1			6
Keyworth	1					6
Jensen	1					6
Weese	1					6
Jackson			1			6
Broncos Total	16	15	3	31/34	13/19	274
Opponents Total	5	11	2	16/18	8/22	148

Punt Returns

	No.	FC	Yds.	Avg.	LG	TD
Upchurch	51	6	653	12.8	87T	1
Schultz	1	0	11	11.0	11	0
Pane	6	2	48	8.0	14	0
Broncos Total	58	8	712	12.3	87T	1
Opponents Total	54	8	397	7.4	29	0

Kickoff Returns

	No.	Yds.	Avg.	LG	TD
Perrin	3	72	24.0	32	0
Upchurch	20	456	22.8	32	0
Schultz	6	135	22.5	33	0
Pane	1	16	16.0	16	0
Keyworth	1	15	15.0	15	0
Hyde	1	15	15.0	15	0
Grant	1	8	8.0	8	0
Nairne	1	1	1.0	1	0
Dolbin	0	14	—	—	—
Broncos Total	34	732	21.5	33	0
Opponents Total	50	1084	21.7	41	0

Field Goals

	1-19	20-29	30-39	40-49	50+	Total
Turner	0-0	3-4	7-10	3-5	0-0	13-19
Opponents Total	1-1	2-3	1-5	4-9	0-4	8-22

GAMES PLAYED (REGULAR SEASON)

Allison 3, Alzado 14, Armstrong 10, Baska 4, Bryan 1, Carter 14, Chavous 13, Dilts 14, Dolbin 14, Egloff 13, Evans 14, Foley 13, Glassic 14, Gradishar 14, Grant 14, Howard 14, Hyde 14, B. Jackson 14, T. Jackson 13, Jensen 11, Keyworth 11, Kiick 3, Lytle 14, Manor 13, Maples 14, Maurer 13, Minor 14, Montler 14, Morton 14, Moses 14, Nairne 13, Odoms 14, Pane 11, Penrose 8, Perrin 14, Poltl 14, Riley 5, Rizzo 13, Schindler 14, Schultz 14, Smith 12, Swenson 14, Thompson 14, Turk 13, Turner 14, Upchurch 14, Weese 14, Wright 14.

PLAYOFF STATISTICS

RESULTS AND ATTENDANCE

at Denver 34, Pittsburgh 21	75,011
at Denver 20, Oakland 7	74,982
Super Bowl at New Orleans, Jan. 15, 1978	
Dallas 27, Denver 10	76,400

Team Statistics

	Broncos	Opponent
TOTAL FIRST DOWNS	42	55
Rushing	19	24
Passing	18	27
Penalty	5	4
Third Down: Made/Att.	12/40	24/55
Third Down Efficiency	30%	44%
TOTAL NET YARDS	722	927
Avg. Per Game	240.7	309.0
Total Plays	177	219
Avg. Per Play	4.1	4.2
NET YARDS RUSHING	315	364
Avg. Per Game	105.0	121.3
Total Rushes	103	113
Avg. Per Rush	3.1	3.2
NET YARDS PASSING	407	563
Avg. Per Game	135.7	187.7
Tackled/Yards Lost	6/42	6/46
Gross Yards	449	609
Attempts/Completions	68/29	100/55
Pct. of Completions	.426	.550
Had Intercepted	5	4
PUNTS/AVERAGE	13/38.8	15/39.5
NET PUNTING AVERAGE	34.5	33.7
PUNT RETURNS/AVERAGE	10/4.6	7/5.1
KICKOFF RETURNS/AVERAGE	14/23.2	12/24.3
INTERCEPTIONS/AVG. RETURN	4/19.5	5/11.4
PENALTIES/YARDS	19/126	24/167
FUMBLES/BALL LOST	7/5	10/5
TOUCHDOWNS	8	8
Rushing	4	3
Passing	4	5
Returns	0	0
EXTRA POINTS/ATTEMPTS	7/8	8/8
FIELD GOALS/ATTEMPTS	3/6	3/7
TOTAL POINTS	64	65

Score by Periods

	1	2	3	4	OT	Total
Broncos	14	7	24	19	—	64
Opponents	13	17	7	28	—	65

Scoring

	TDR	TDP	TDRt	PAT	FG	TP
Turner				7/7	3/6	16
Moses		2				12
Lytle	2					12
Armstrong	1					6
Odoms		1				6
Dolbin		1				6
Keyworth	1					6
Team				0-1		
Broncos Total	4	4	0	7/8	3/6	64
Opponents Total	3	5	0	8/8	3/7	65

Rushing

	No.	Yds.	Avg.	LG	TD
Armstrong	25	87	3.5	29	1
Lytle	29	87	3.0	16	2
Perrin	14	50	3.6	10	0
Keyworth	18	48	2.7	7	1
Jensen	6	31	5.2	16	0
Weese	3	26	8.7	10	0
Morton	7	-4	-0.6	6	0
Moses	1	-10	-10.0	-10	0
Broncos Total	103	315	3.1	29	4
Opponents Total	113	364	3.2	20	3

Receiving

	No.	Yds.	Avg.	LG	TD
Moses	8	234	29.3	74T	2
Odoms	8	65	8.1	30T	1
Jensen	4	58	14.5	29	0
Dolbin	3	58	19.3	34T	1
Perrin	3	13	4.3	9	0
Armstrong	1	9	9.0	9	0
Upchurch	1	9	9.0	9	0
Keyworth	1	3	3.0	3	0
Broncos Total	29	449	15.5	74T	4
Opponents Total	55	609	11.1	45T	5

Interceptions

	No.	Yds.	Avg.	LG	TD
T. Jackson	2	49	24.5	32	0
B. Jackson	1	15	15.0	15	0
Swenson	1	14	14.0	14	0
Broncos Total	4	78	19.5	32	0
Opponents Total	5	57	11.4	27	0

Punting

	No.	Yds.	Avg.	TB	In 20	LG
Dilts	13	504	38.8	1	3	55
Broncos Total	13	504	38.8	1	3	55
Opponents Total	15	592	39.5	2	0	55

Punt Returns

	No.	FC	Yds.	Avg.	LG	TD
Upchurch	6	1	37	6.2	9	0
Thompson	2	0	5	2.5	3	0
Schultz	2	0	4	2.0	4	0
Broncos Total	10	1	46	4.6	9	0
Opponents Total	7	2	36	5.1	17	0

Kickoff Returns

	No.	Yds.	Avg.	LG	TD
Schultz	4	109	27.3	37	0
Upchurch	8	185	23.3	67	0
Jensen	1	17	17.0	17	0
Lytle	1	14	14.0	14	0
Broncos Total	14	325	23.2	69	0
Opponents Total	12	291	24.3	62	0

Field Goals

	1-19	20-29	30-39	40-49	50+	Total
Turner	0-0	1-1	0-1	2-4	0-0	3-6
Opponents Total	0-1	1-1	1-2	1-3	0-0	3-7

Turner: (44, 25) (40-WL, 31-WL, 44-WL) (47)

Passing

	Att.	Comp.	Yards	Pct.	Avg./Att.	TD
Morton	58	25	427	.431	7.36	4
Weese	10	4	22	.400	2.20	0
Broncos Total	68	29	449	.426	6.60	4
Opponents Total	100	55	609	.550	6.09	5

	Pct. TD	Int.	Pct. Int.	LG	Lost/Att.	Rating
Morton	6.9	5	8.6	74T	4/36	—
Weese	0.0	0	0.0	9	2/6	—
Broncos Total	5.9	5	7.4	74T	6/42	—
Opponents Total	5.0	4	4.0	48	6/46	—

TOP PERFORMANCES OF 1977

Individual

RUSHING—Otis Armstrong, 21-120, at Kansas City (11/20). **PASSING**—Craig Morton, 19-32-1, 242 yards, 1 TD, vs. Oakland (10/30). **RECEIVING**—Catches: Riley Odoms, 6 for 86 yards, at Houston (12/4), and 6 for 69 yards, vs. San Diego (12/11). Yards: Haven Moses, 5 for 92 yards, at Seattle (10/2). **INTERCEPTIONS**—Joe Rizzo, 3, at Oakland (10/16). **KICKOFF RETURNS**—John Schultz, 3 for 71, vs. Baltimore (11/27). Rick Upchurch, 3 for 71, vs. San Diego (12/11). **PUNT RETURNS**—Rick Upchurch, 5 for 167, vs. Pittsburgh (11/6). **SCORING**—Jim Turner, 12, at Oakland (10/16). Haven Moses, 12, at San Diego (11/13).

Team

TOTAL OFFENSE—376 (249 rush, 127 pass) at Kansas City (11/20). **RUSHING**—249 at Kansas City (11/20). **PASSING**—180 vs. Oakland (10/30). **SCORING**—30 at Oakland (10/16). **TOTAL DEFENSE**—129, Buffalo (9/25). **RUSHING DEFENSE**—64, San Diego (12/11). **PASSING DEFENSE**—63, Buffalo (9/25). **SCORING DEFENSE**—0, St. Louis (9/18).

Longest Plays

RUN FROM SCRIMMAGE—Lonnie Perrin, 62 yards, vs. Baltimore (11/27). **PASS PLAY**—Craig Morton to Jack Dolbin, 81 yards (touchdown), at Cincinnati (10/23). **KICKOFF RETURN**—John Schultz, 33 yards, at Cincinnati (10/23). **PUNT RETURN**—Rick Upchurch, 87 yards (touchdown), vs. Pittsburgh (11/6). **INTERCEPTION RETURN**—Tom Jackson, 73 yards (touchdown), vs. Baltimore (11/27). **PUNT**—Bucky Dilts, 63 yards, vs. Pittsburgh (11/6). **FIELD GOAL**—Jim Turner, 48 yards, vs. Buffalo (9/25).

DEFENSIVE STATISTICS

FIRST HITS—Gradishar 145, Swenson 89, Alzado 80, T. Jackson 77, Rizzo 72, Carter 71, Thompson 69, Foley 58, Wright 57, Chavous 51, B. Jackson 42, Grant 39, Manor 25, Smith 19, Turk 16, Poltl 12, Evans 4, Pane 1, Nairne 1, Baska 1.

ASSISTS—Gradishar 74, Rizzo 51, Swenson 46, Carter 42, Alzado 39, T. Jackson 39, Chavous 31, B. Jackson 30, Thompson 26, Wright 20, Manor 13, Foley 13, Grant 12, Smith 7, Turk 6, Pane 4, Poltl 4, Evans 2, Nairne 1.

Broncos 1977

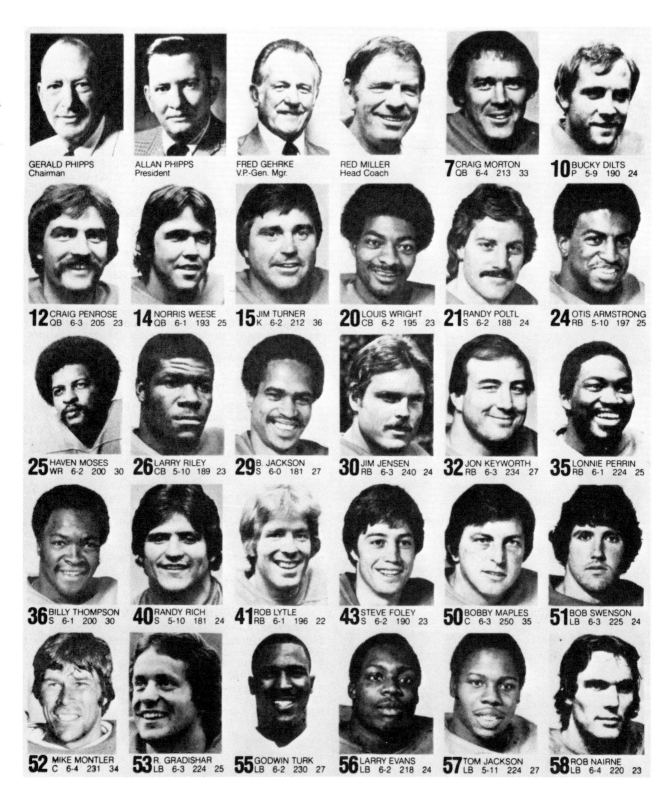

GERALD PHIPPS
Chairman

ALLAN PHIPPS
President

FRED GEHRKE
V.P.-Gen. Mgr.

RED MILLER
Head Coach

7 CRAIG MORTON
QB 6-4 213 33

10 BUCKY DILTS
P 5-9 190 24

12 CRAIG PENROSE
QB 6-3 205 23

14 NORRIS WEESE
QB 6-1 193 25

15 JIM TURNER
K 6-2 212 36

20 LOUIS WRIGHT
CB 6-2 195 23

21 RANDY POLTL
S 6-2 188 24

24 OTIS ARMSTRONG
RB 5-10 197 25

25 HAVEN MOSES
WR 6-2 200 30

26 LARRY RILEY
CB 5-10 189 23

29 B. JACKSON
S 6-0 181 27

30 JIM JENSEN
RB 6-3 240 24

32 JON KEYWORTH
RB 6-3 234 27

35 LONNIE PERRIN
RB 6-1 224 25

36 BILLY THOMPSON
S 6-1 200 30

40 RANDY RICH
S 5-10 181 24

41 ROB LYTLE
RB 6-1 196 22

43 STEVE FOLEY
S 6-2 190 23

50 BOBBY MAPLES
C 6-3 250 35

51 BOB SWENSON
LB 6-3 225 24

52 MIKE MONTLER
C 6-4 231 34

53 R. GRADISHAR
LB 6-3 224 25

55 GODWIN TURK
LB 6-2 230 27

56 LARRY EVANS
LB 6-2 218 24

57 TOM JACKSON
LB 5-11 224 27

58 ROB NAIRNE
LB 6-4 220 23

224

 **59** JOE RIZZO
LB 6-1 223 27

 **60** PAUL HOWARD
G 6-3 260 26

 **62** TOM GLASSIC
G 6-4 248 23

 **63** JOHN GRANT
DE 6-3 246 27

 **65** GLENN HYDE
OT 6-3 255 26

 **66** BRISON MANOR
DE 6-4 247 24

67 STEVE SCHINDLER
G 6-3 252 23

 **68** RUBIN CARTER
DT 6-0 254 25

 **70** PAUL SMITH
DT 6-3 250 31

 **71** CLAUDIE MINOR
OT 6-4 280 26

 **73** HENRY ALLISON
OT 6-3 263 30

 **74** ANDY MAURER
OT 6-3 265 28

 **77** LYLE ALZADO
DE 6-3 250 28

 **79** BARNEY CHAVOUS
DE 6-3 250 26

 **80** RICK UPCHURCH
WR 5-10 180 25

 **82** JACK DOLBIN
WR 5-10 183 28

 **85** RON EGLOFF
TE 6-5 227 21

 **86** JOHN SCHULTZ
WR 5-10 183 24

 **88** RILEY ODOMS
TE 6-4 232 27

 MARV BRADEN
Special Teams

 JOE COLLIER
Defensive Coordinator

 BOB GAMBOLD
Defensive Backs

 KEN GRAY
Offensive Line

STAN JONES
Defensive Line

 MYREL MOORE
Linebackers

 BABE PARILLI
Quarterbacks

 FRAN POLSFOOT
Wide Receivers

 PAUL ROACH
Offensive Backfield

 ALLEN HURST
Trainer

 LARRY ELLIOTT
Equipment Manager

BRONCOS DEPARTMENTAL LEADERS

Category	Player	AFC Rank	NFL Rank	AFC Leader	NFL Leader
Scoring	Turner—76	7th	12th	Mann, Oak—99	Mann, Oak—99
Rushing	Armstrong—489	22nd	40th	van Eeghen, Oak—1273	Payton, Chi—1852
Passing	Morton—131-254, 1929 yards, 14 TD, 8 int., 82.1 rating	2nd	4th	Griese, Mia—88.0	Griese, Mia—88.0
Receiving	Odoms—37	T-18th	T-31st	Mitchell, Bal—71	Mitchell, Bal—71
	Moses—539 yards	19th	32nd	Burrough, Hou—816	Burrough, Hou—816
Punting	Dilts—39.2 ave.	7th	15th	Guy, Oak—43.3	Guy, Oak—43.3
Interceptions	Thompson—5	T-10th	T-16th	Blackwood, Bal—10	Blackwood, Bal—10
Kickoff returns	Upchurch—22.8 ave.	T-8th	T-19th	Clayborn, NE—31.0	Clayborn, NE—31.0
Punt returns	Upchurch—12.8 ave.	5th	5th	Johnson, Hou—15.4	Johnson, Hou—15.4

HOW THE BRONCOS RANKED

OFFENSE

Category	Bronco total	AFC Rank	NFL Rank	AFC Leader	NFL Leader
Points scored	274	8th	10th	Oakland—351	Oakland—351
First downs	223	13th	T-20th	Oakland—305	Oakland—305
Total plays	887	8th	17th	Oakland—1030	Oakland—1030
Total yards	3906	12th	17th	Oakland—4736	Dallas—4812
Rushing yards	2043	7th	11th	Oakland—2627	Chicago—2811
Passing yards	2265	11th	15th	Buffalo—2803	Buffalo—2803
Penalties	91	6th	12th	Cleveland—125	Cleveland—125
Penalty yards	883	4th	5th	Cleveland—1046	Cleveland—1046
Fumbles	28	T-8th	T-14th	Pittsburgh—41	Pittsburgh—41
Fumbles lost	15	T-8th	T-14th	Pittsburgh—28	Pittsburgh—28

DEFENSE

Category	Bronco total	AFC Rank	NFL Rank	AFC Leader	NFL Leader
Points allowed	148	1st	3rd	Denver—148	Atlanta—129
Touchdowns rushing	5	1st	1st	Denver—5	Denver—5
Total first downs	217	4th	10th	Oakland—204	Atlanta—192
Rushing	77	1st	1st	Denver—77	Denver—77
Passing	123	11th	25th	Buffalo—98	Atlanta—76
Penalty	17	5th	14th	Miami—9	Detroit—10
Total yards allowed	3774	4th	9th	New England—3638	Dallas—3213
Rushing	1531	1st	1st	Denver—1531	Denver—1531
Passing	2244	12th	25th	Pittsburgh—1969	Atlanta—1384
Interceptions	25	5th	6th	Pittsburgh—31	Pittsburgh—31

NOTABLE PERFORMANCES

THE LAST TIME . . .

PUNT RETURN FOR TOUCHDOWN—

Broncos:	Rick Upchurch, 87 yards, vs. Pittsburgh, 11/6/77.
Opponent:	Mike Haynes, 62 yards, at New England, 11/28/76.

KICKOFF RETURN FOR TOUCHDOWN—

Broncos:	Randy Montgomery, 94 yards, at San Diego, 9/24/72.
Opponent:	Cullen Bryant, 84 yards, vs. Los Angeles, 9/15/74.

INTERCEPTION RETURN FOR TOUCHDOWN—

Broncos:	Tom Jackson, 73 yards, vs. Baltimore, 11/27/77.
Opponent:	Allan Ellis, 22 yards, at Chicago, 12/12/76.

FUMBLE RETURN FOR TOUCHDOWN (DEFENSE)—

Broncos:	Randy Poltl, 26 yards (lateral from Swenson) vs. Tampa Bay, 11/7/76.
Opponent:	Fred Dean, 11 yards, at San Diego, 11/13/77.

BLOCKED PUNT RETURN FOR TOUCHDOWN—

Broncos:	John Griffin, 10 yards, vs. Houston, 10/17/65.
Opponent:	Jim Stienke, 1 yard, vs. New York Giants, 11/21/76.

BLOCKED FIELD GOAL RETURN FOR TOUCHDOWN—

Broncos:	John Bramlett, 86 yards, vs. San Diego, 11/27/66.
Opponent:	Les Duncan, 72 yards, at San Diego, 11/23/67.

SAFETY—

Broncos:	Ken Criter blocked punt out of end zone, at San Diego, 12/9/73.
Opponent:	Willie Lanier tackled Otis Armstrong in end zone, vs. Kansas City, 11/18/74.

SHUTOUT—

Broncos:	Denver 7, St. Louis 0, 9/18/77.
Opponent:	Denver 0, at San Diego 17, 12/15/74.

100 YARDS RUSHING—

Broncos:	Otis Armstrong, 21-120 yards, at Kansas City, 11/20/77.
Opponent:	Clarence Davis, 20-105, vs. Oakland, 10/30/77.

300 YARDS PASSING—

Broncos:	Charley Johnson, 12-20, 329 yards, 3 TD, vs. Kansas City, 9/21/75.
Opponent:	Joe Gilliam, 31-50, 348 yards, 1 TD, vs. Pittsburgh, 9/22/74. (Overtime game; at end of regulation play, Gilliam was 29-44 for 339 yards and 1 TD.)

100 YARDS RECEIVING—

Broncos:	Haven Moses, 5-168 yards, 2 TD, vs. Oakland, 1/1/78. (Playoff game.) Rick Upchurch, 3-153 yards, 1 TD, vs. Kansas City, 9/21/75.
Opponent:	Don McCauley, 11-112 yards, 0 TD, vs. Baltimore, 11/27/77.

1,000-YARD RUSHING SEASONS

OTIS ARMSTRONG, 1974—1,407 yards and 9 TDs

		Carries	Yards	Cumulative
9/15	vs. Los Angeles	12	31	12-31
9/22	vs. Pittsburgh	19	131	31-162
9/30	at Washington	11	32	42-194
10/6	at Kansas City	14	48	56-242
10/13	vs. New Orleans	13	57	69-299
10/20	vs. San Diego	20	98	89-397
10/27	at Cleveland	17	142	106-539
11/3	vs. Oakland	20	88	126-627
11/10	at Baltimore	19	110	145-737
11/18	vs. Kansas City	16	55	161-792
11/24	at Oakland	29	146	190-938
11/28	at Detroit	24	144	214-1,082
12/8	vs. Houston	31	183	245-1,265
12/15	at San Diego	18	142	263-1,407

1,000-YARD RUSHING SEASONS (Continued)

FLOYD LITTLE, 1971 — 1,133 yards and 6 TDs

		Carries	Yards	Cumulative
9/19	vs. Miami	23	70	23-70
9/26	at Green Bay	16	53	39-123
10/3	vs. Kansas City	13	27	52-150
10/10	vs. Oakland	16	39	68-189
10/17	vs. San Diego	17	62	85-251
10/24	at Cleveland	25	113	110-364
10/31	at Philadelphia	24	123	134-487
11/7	vs. Detroit	22	91	156-578
11/14	vs. Cincinnati	22	101	178-679
11/21	at Kansas City	13	63	191-742
11/28	at Pittsburgh	22	91	213-833
12/5	vs. Chicago	29	125	242-958
12/12	at San Diego	18	96	260-1,054
12/19	at Oakland	24	79	284-1,133

OTIS ARMSTRONG, 1976 — 1,008 yards and 5 TDs

		Carries	Yards	Cumulative
9/12	at Cincinnati	24	96	24-96
9/19	vs. New York Jets	17	94	41-190
9/26	vs. Cleveland	18	23	59-213
10/3	vs. San Diego	23	91	82-304
10/10	at Houston	12	47	94-351
10/17	vs. Oakland	21	70	115-421
10/24	at Kansas City	16	101	131-522
10/31	at Oakland	14	63	145-585
11/7	vs. Tampa Bay	18	116	163-701
11/14	at San Diego	13	35	176-736
11/21	vs. New York Giants	24	97	200-833
11/28	at New England	4	14	204-847
12/5	vs. Kansas City	17	45	221-892
12/12	at Chicago	26	116	247-1,008

100-YARD RUSHING GAMES

Player	Performance	Opponent
Don Stone	17-104, 1 TD	Oct. 6, 1963 vs. San Diego
Billy Joe	20-105, 0 TD	Nov. 17, 1963 vs. New York
Billy Joe	16-108, 1 TD	Nov. 15, 1964 vs. New York
Cookie Gilchrist	32-142, 0 TD	Sept. 24, 1965 at Boston
Cookie Gilchrist	16-119, 0 TD	Nov. 14, 1965 at Houston
Floyd Little	25-126, 1 TD	Oct. 27, 1968 vs. Miami
Floyd Little	30-147, 1 TD	Nov. 3, 1968 at Boston
Floyd Little	21-105, 1 TD	Sept. 14, 1969 vs. Boston
Floyd Little	15-104, 1 TD	Sept. 21, 1969 vs. New York Jets
Floyd Little	29-166,1 TD	Oct. 19, 1969 at Cincinnati
Floyd Little	16-140, 1 TD	Oct. 25, 1970 at San Francisco
Bobby Anderson	25-106, 1 TD	Oct. 17, 1971 vs. San Diego
Floyd Little	25-113, 1 TD	Oct. 24, 1971 at Cleveland
Floyd Little	24-123, 1 TD	Oct. 31, 1971 at Philadelphia
Floyd Little	22-101, 0 TD	Nov. 14, 1971 vs. Cincinnati
Floyd Little	29-125, 0 TD	Dec. 5, 1971 vs. Chicago
Floyd Little	22-101, 0 TD	Sept. 17, 1972 vs. Houston
Floyd Little	18-100, 2 TD	Oct. 15, 1972 vs. Minnesota
Floyd Little	14-124, 1 TD	Nov. 5, 1972 at New York Giants
Joe Dawkins	30-117, 0 TD	Oct. 28, 1973 at New York Jets
Floyd Little	19-123, 1 TD	Oct. 14, 1973 at Houston
Floyd Little	22-109, 2 TD	Nov. 11, 1973 vs. San Diego
Otis Armstrong	19-131, 0 TD	Sept. 22, 1974 vs. Pittsburgh
Otis Armstrong	17-142, 1 TD	Oct. 27, 1974 at Cleveland
Otis Armstrong	19-110, 1 TD	Nov. 10, 1974 at Baltimore
Otis Armstrong	29-146, 0 TD	Nov. 24, 1974 at Oakland
Jon Keyworth	15-148, 1 TD	Nov. 24, 1974 at Oakland
Otis Armstrong	24-144, 1 TD	Nov. 28, 1974 at Detroit

100 YARD RUSHING GAMES (Continued)

Otis Armstrong	31-183, 3 TD	Dec. 8, 1974 vs. Houston
Otis Armstrong	18-142, 0 TD	Dec. 15, 1974 at San Diego
Jon Keyworth	20-132, 0 TD	Nov. 30, 1975 vs. San Diego
Otis Armstrong	16-101, 1 TD	Oct. 24, 1976 at Kansas City
Otis Armstrong	18-116, 0 TD	Nov. 7, 1976 vs. Tampa Bay
Otis Armstrong	26-116, 1 TD	Dec. 12, 1976 at Chicago
Norris Weese	12-120, 0 TD	Dec. 12, 1976 at Chicago
Otis Armstrong	21-120, 0 TD	Nov. 20, 1977 at Kansas City

TOTALS—Floyd Little 15, Otis Armstrong 11, Billy Joe 2, Cookie Gilchrist 2, Jon Keyworth 2, Donnie Stone 1, Bobby Anderson 1, Joe Dawkins 1, Norris Weese 1.

300-YARD PASSING GAMES

Player	Performance	Opponent
Frank Tripucka	30-52-2, 375 yards and 3 TD	Nov. 6, 1960 vs. Houston
Frank Tripucka	19-41-5, 328 yards and 3 TD	Nov. 27, 1960 vs. Buffalo
Frank Tripucka	28-47-2, 376 yards and 2 TD	Sept. 7, 1962 vs. San Diego
Frank Tripucka	29-56-3, 447 yards and 2 TD	Sept. 15, 1962 at Buffalo
Frank Tripucka	26-40-1, 308 yards and 1 TD	Oct. 21, 1962 vs. Houston
Jacky Lee	11-36-1, 370 yards and 1 TD	Dec. 5, 1965 at Oakland
John McCormick	13-37-3, 328 yards and 3 TD	Dec. 18, 1966 at Buffalo
Marlin Briscoe	12-29-2, 335 yards and 4 TD	Nov. 24, 1968 vs. Buffalo
Steve Tensi	19-26-1, 301 yards and 3 TD	Nov. 23, 1969 at San Diego
Charley Johnson	20-28-0, 361 yards and 3 TD	Oct. 22, 1972 at Oakland
Charley Johnson	24-39-2, 326 yards and 1 TD	Sept. 20, 1973 vs. Chicago
Charley Johnson	28-42-2, 445 yards and 2 TD	Nov. 18, 1974 vs. Kansas City
Charley Johnson	12-20-2, 329 yards and 3 TD	Sept. 21, 1975 vs. Kansas City

TOTALS—Frank Tripucka 5, Charley Johnson 4, Jacky Lee 1, John McCormick 1, Marlin Briscoe 1, Steve Tensi 1.

100-YARD RECEIVING GAMES

Player	Performance	Opponent
Al Carmichael	6-130, 1 TD	Sept. 9, 1960 at Boston
Lionel Taylor	6-125, 1 TD	Sept. 23, 1960 at New York
Lionel Taylor	7-101, 2 TD	Oct. 2, 1960 vs. Oakland
Al Carmichael	3-109, 2 TD	Oct. 23, 1960 vs. Boston
Lionel Taylor	10-106, 1 TD	Oct. 23, 1960 vs. Boston
Lionel Taylor	10-140, 1 TD	Nov. 6, 1960 vs. Houston
Al Carmichael	7-117, 2 TD	Nov. 6, 1960 vs. Houston
Lionel Taylor	10-138, 0 TD	Nov. 20, 1960 at Houston
Lionel Taylor	9-199, 3 TD	Nov. 27, 1960 vs. Buffalo
Lionel Taylor	9-171, 1 TD	Dec. 10, 1960 at Los Angeles
Lionel Taylor	7-132, 2 TD	Sept. 10, 1961 at Buffalo
Lionel Taylor	11-126, 0 TD	Sept. 24, 1961 at New York
Lionel Taylor	9-118, 0 TD	Oct. 1, 1961 at Oakland
Lionel Taylor	7-120, 1 TD	Oct. 8, 1961 vs. Dallas
Al Frazier	7-166, 1 TD	Oct. 15, 1961 vs. Oakland
Al Frazier	6-126, 1 TD	Oct. 22, 1961 vs. New York
Al Frazier	5-125, 1 TD	Nov. 12, 1961 vs. San Diego
Lionel Taylor	10-119, 0 TD	Nov. 12, 1961 vs. San Diego
Donnie Stone	9-137, 1 TD	Dec. 3, 1961 vs. Boston
Lionel Taylor	9-133, 0 TD	Sept. 15, 1962 at Buffalo
Al Frazier	4-125, 1 TD	Sept. 15, 1962 at Buffalo
Lionel Taylor	12-119, 0 TD	Sept. 21, 1962 at Boston
Jerry Tarr	4-152, 2 TD	Sept. 21, 1962 at Boston
Lionel Taylor	7-110, 0 TD	Dec. 9, 1962 at Dallas
Lionel Taylor	7-169, 1 TD	Sept. 29, 1963 vs. Boston
Lionel Taylor	7-142, 2 TD	Oct. 6, 1963 vs. San Diego
Bob Scarpitto	4-134, 2 TD	Oct. 13, 1963 vs. Houston
Lionel Taylor	10-116, 1 TD	Dec. 15, 1963 at Oakland
Gene Prebola	4-106, 1 TD	Dec. 15, 1963 at Oakland
Lionel Taylor	8-149, 1 TD	Sept. 27, 1964 vs. Houston
Hewritt Dixon	4-109, 0 TD	Oct. 25, 1964 at Oakland
Hewritt Dixon	5-121, 1 TD	Nov. 1, 1964 at Kansas City

228

100-YARD RECEIVING GAMES (Continued)

Al Denson	3-113, 1 TD	Nov. 1, 1964 at Kansas City
Lionel Taylor	13-112, 0 TD	Nov. 29, 1964 vs. Oakland
Bob Scarpitto	11-111, 1 TD	Dec. 20, 1964 at Houston
Bob Scarpitto	5-108, 2 TD	Sept. 11, 1965 at San Diego
Lionel Taylor	9-172, 1 TD	Sept. 19, 1965 vs. Buffalo
Lionel Taylor	7-114, 0 TD	Nov. 7, 1965 vs. San Diego
Lionel Taylor	11-141, 2 TD	Nov. 21, 1965 vs. Oakland
Lionel Taylor	8-164, 0 TD	Dec. 5, 1965 at Oakland
Wendell Hayes	5-126, 1 TD	Dec. 5, 1965 at Oakland
Al Denson	5-158, 1 TD	Oct. 2, 1966 vs. Houston
Charlie Mitchell	4-126, 1 TD	Dec. 4, 1966 vs. Miami
Bob Scarpitto	5-123, 3 TD	Dec. 18, 1966 at Buffalo
Al Denson	4-131, 2 TD	Sept. 3, 1967 vs. Boston
Al Denson	7-134, 1 TD	Sept. 24, 1967 vs. New York Jets
Eric Crabtree	6-123, 1 TD	Oct. 22, 1967 vs. San Diego
Al Denson	4-107, 1 TD	Oct. 29, 1967 at Kansas City
Al Denson	7-102, 2 TD	Nov. 19, 1967 at Buffalo
Eric Crabtree	8-107, 1 TD	Nov. 23, 1967 at San Diego
Eric Crabtree	6-129, 1 TD	Dec. 17, 1967 vs. Kansas City
Al Denson	8-115, 0 TD	Sept. 15, 1968 at Cincinnati
Eric Crabtree	7-113, 0 TD	Sept. 22, 1968 at Kansas City
Eric Crabtree	5-148, 1 TD	Oct. 13, 1968 at New York Jets
Jimmy Jones	8-128, 2 TD	Oct. 20, 1968 at San Diego
Floyd Little	4-165, 1 TD	Nov. 24, 1968 vs. Buffalo
Al Denson	31, 2 TD	Dec. 8, 1968 at Oakland
Mike Haffner	4-122, 0 TD	Dec. 14, 1968 vs. Kansas City
Al Denson	6-138, 1 TD	Sept. 28, 1969 at Buffalo
Mike Haffner	6-102, 1 TD	Oct. 26, 1969 at Houston
Al Denson	6-140, 2 TD	Nov. 23, 1969 at San Diego
John Embree	9-122, 1 TD	Nov. 23, 1969 at San Diego
Jerry Simmons	6-153, 0 TD	Nov. 21, 1971 at Kansas City
Rod Sherman	4-110, 0 TD	Sept. 17, 1972 vs. Houston
Jerry Simmons	6-118, 1 TD	Oct. 22, 1972 at Oakland
Bobby Anderson	13-143, 0 TD	Sept. 10, 1973 vs. Chicago
Riley Odoms	5-114, 1 TD	Nov. 4, 1973 at St. Louis
Haven Moses	5-108, 2 TD	Nov. 25, 1973 vs. Kansas City
Haven Moses	5-132, 0 TD	Oct. 13, 1974 vs. New Orleans
Floyd Little	7-127, 0 TD	Oct. 20, 1974 vs. San Diego
Riley Odoms	7-125, 0 TD	Nov. 18, 1974 vs. Kansas City
Rick Upchurch	3-153, 1 TD	Sept. 21, 1975 vs. Kansas City
*Haven Moses	5-168, 2 TD	Jan. 1, 1978 vs. Oakland

TOTALS—Lionel Taylor 24, Al Denson 10, Eric Crabtree 5, Al Frazier 4, Bob Scarpitto 4, Al Carmichael 3, Haven Moses 3 (includes one playoff game), Hewritt Dixon 2, Mike Haffner 2, Floyd Little 2, Jerry Simmons 2, Riley Odoms 2, Jimmy Jones 1, Gene Prebola 1, Jerry Tarr 1, Donnie Stone 1, Wendell Hayes 1, Charlie Mitchell 1, John Embree 1, Rod Sherman 1, Bobby Anderson 1, Rick Upchurch 1.

ALL-TIME SCORES

REGULAR SEASON RESULTS

1960
Coach: Frank Filchock 4-9-1

			Attend.
13	At Boston	10	21,597
27	At Buffalo	21	15,229
24	At New York	28	20,462
31	Oakland	14	18,372
19	Los Angeles	23	19,141
31	Boston	24	12,683
14	Dallas	17	13,002
25	Houston	45	14,489
7	At Dallas	34	21,000
10	At Houston	20	20,778
38	Buffalo	38	7,785
27	New York	30	5,861
33	At Los Angeles	41	9,928
10	At Oakland	48	7,000

1961
Coach: Frank Filchock 3-11-0

			Attend.
22	At Buffalo	10	16,636
17	At Boston	45	14,479
28	At New York	35	14,381
19	At Oakland	33	8,361
12	Dallas	19	14,500
27	Oakland	24	11,129
27	New York	10	12,508
0	At San Diego	37	32,584
14	Houston	55	11,564
16	San Diego	19	7,859
10	Buffalo	23	7,645
14	At Houston	45	27,874
24	Boston	28	9,303
21	At Dallas	49	8,000

1962
Coach: Jack Faulkner 7-7-0

			Attend.
30	San Diego	21	28,000
23	At Buffalo	20	30,577
16	At Boston	41	21,038
32	At New York	10	17,213
44	Oakland	7	22,452
23	At Oakland	6	7,000
20	Houston	10	34,496
38	Buffalo	45	26,051
23	At San Diego	20	20,827
29	Boston	33	28,187
3	Dallas	24	23,523
45	New York	45	15,776
17	At Houston	34	30,650
10	At Dallas	17	19,137

1963
Coach: Jack Faulkner 2-11-1

			Attend.
7	Kansas City	59	21,115
14	At Houston	20	23,047
14	Boston	10	18,636
50	San Diego	34	19,137
24	Houston	33	24,896
21	At Boston	40	25,418
35	At New York	35	22,553
28	Buffalo	30	19,424
17	At Buffalo	27	30,989
9	New York	14	14,247
10	Oakland	26	14,763
21	At Kansas City	52	17,433
31	At Oakland	35	15,223
20	At San Diego	58	31,312

1964
Coach: Jack Faulkner (4 games) and Mac Speedie (10 games)
2-11-1

			Attend.
6	At New York	30	45,665
13	At Buffalo	30	25,141
17	Houston	38	22,155
10	Boston	39	17,851
33	Kansas City	27	16,885
14	At San Diego	42	23,242
7	At Oakland	40	16,825
39	Kansas City	49	15,053
20	San Diego	31	19,670
20	New York	16	11,309
7	At Boston	12	24,979
20	Oakland	20	15,958
19	Buffalo	30	14,431
15	At Houston	34	15,839

1965
Coach: Mac Speedie 4-10-0

			Attend.
31	At San Diego	34	27,022
15	Buffalo	30	30,656
27	At Boston	10	26,782
16	New York	13	34,988
23	Kansas City	31	31,001
28	Houston	17	32,492
13	At Buffalo	31	45,046
10	At New York	45	55,572
21	San Diego	35	33,073
31	At Houston	21	28,126
20	Oakland	28	30,369
13	At Oakland	24	19,023
20	Boston	28	27,207
35	At Kansas City	45	14,421

1966
Coach: Mac Speedie (2 games) and Ray Malavasi (12 games)
4-10-0

			Attend.
7	At Houston	45	30,156
10	Boston	24	25,160
7	New York	16	28,770
40	Houston	38	27,203
10	At Kansas City	37	33,929
7	At Miami	24	23,393
10	Kansas City	56	26,196
17	At San Diego	24	25,819
17	At Boston	10	18,154
3	Oakland	17	26,703
20	San Diego	17	24,860
17	Miami	7	33,306
10	At Oakland	28	31,765
21	At buffalo	38	40,583

1967
Coach: Lou Saban 3-11-0

			Attend.
26	Boston	21	35,488
0	At Oakland	51	25,423
21	At Miami	35	29,381
24	New York	38	35,565
6	At Houston	10	21,798
16	Buffalo	17	35,188
21	San Diego	33	34,465
9	At Kansas City	52	44,002
17	Oakland	21	29,043
18	Houston	20	30,392
21	At Buffalo	20	30,891
20	At San Diego	24	34,586
33	At New York	24	61,615
24	Kansas City	38	31,660

REGULAR SEASON RESULTS

<table>
<tr><th colspan="4">1968</th><th colspan="4">1969</th></tr>
<tr><td colspan="4">Coach: Lou Saban   5-9-0   Attend.</td><td colspan="4">Coach: Lou Saban   5-8-1   Attend.</td></tr>
</table>

1968 Coach: Lou Saban	5-9-0	Attend.	1969 Coach: Lou Saban	5-8-1	Attend.
10 At Cincinnati	24	25,049	26 Boston	21	35,488
2 At Kansas City	34	45,821	21 New York	19	50,583
17 Boston	20	37,024	28 At Buffalo	41	40,302
10 Cincinnati	7	41,257	13 Kansas City	26	50,564
21 At New York	13	62,052	14 Oakland	24	49,511
24 At San Diego	55	42,953	30 At Cincinnati	23	27,920
21 Miami	14	44,115	21 At Houston	24	45,348
35 At Boston	14	18,304	13 San Diego	0	45,511
7 Oakland	43	50,002	10 At Oakland	41	54,416
17 At Houston	38	36,075	20 Houston	20	45,002
34 Buffalo	32	35,201	24 At San Diego	45	34,664
23 San Diego	47	35,312	17 At Kansas City	31	48,773
27 At Oakland	33	47,754	24 At Miami	27	25,332
7 Kansas City	30	38,463	27 Cincinnati	16	42,196

1970 Coach: Lou Saban	5-8-1	Attend.	1971 Coach: Lou Saban (9 games) and Jerry Smith (5 games)	4-9-1	Attend.
25 At Buffalo	10	34,882	10 Miami	10	51,200
16 Pittsburgh	13	50,705	13 At G. Bay (Milw.)	34	47,957
26 Kansas City	13	50,705	3 Kansas City	16	51,200
23 At Oakland	35	54,436	16 Oakland	27	51,200
24 Atlanta	10	50,705	20 San Diego	16	51,200
14 At San Francisco	19	39,515	27 At Cleveland	0	75,674
3 Washington	19	50,705	16 At Philadelphia	17	65,358
21 At San Diego	24	48,327	20 Detroit	24	51,200
19 Oakland	24	50,959	10 Cincinnati	24	51,200
31 At New Orleans	6	66,837	10 At Kansas City	28	49,945
21 At Houston	31	35,733	22 At Pittsburgh	10	39,710
0 At Kansas City	16	50,454	6 Chicago	3	51,200
17 San Diego	17	50,959	17 At San Diego	45	44,347
13 Cleveland	27	51,001	13 At Oakland	21	54,651

1972 Coach: John Ralston	5-9-0	Attend.	1973 Coach: John Ralston	7-5-2	Attend.
30 Houston	17	51,656	28 Cincinnati	10	49,059
14 At San Diego	37	49,048	34 San Francisco	36	50,966
24 Kansas City	45	51,656	14 Chicago	33	51,159
10 At Cincinnati	21	55,812	14 At Kansas City	16	71,414
20 Minnesota	23	51,656	48 At Houston	20	32,801
30 At Oakland	23	53,551	23 Oakland	23	51,270
20 Cleveland	27	51,656	40 at N.Y. Jets	28	55,108
17 At N.Y. Giants	29	62,689	17 At St. Louis	17	46,567
16 At Los Angeles	10	65,398	30 San Diego	19	51,034
20 Oakland	37	51,656	23 At Pittsburgh	13	48,580
20 At Atlanta	23	58,850	14 Kansas City	10	51,331
21 At Kansas City	24	66,725	10 Dallas	22	51,508
38 San Diego	13	51,473	42 At San Diego	28	44,954
45 New England	21	51,656	17 At Oakland	21	51,910

1974 Coach: John Ralston	7-6-1	Attend.	1975 Coach: John Ralston	6-8-0	Attend.
10 Los Angeles	17	51,121	37 Kansas City	33	51,858
35 Pittsburgh	35	51,068	23 Green Bay	13	51,621
3 At Washington	30	54,395	14 At Buffalo	38	79,864
17 At Kansas City	14	67,298	9 At Pittsburgh	20	49,164
33 New Orleans	17	50,881	16 Cleveland	15	52,590
27 San Diego	7	50,928	13 At Kansas City	26	70,043
21 At Cleveland	23	60,478	17 Oakland	42	5,505
17 At Baltimore	6	33,244	16 Cincinnati	17	49,919
34 Kansas City	42	50,236	27 At San Diego	17	26,048
20 At Oakland	17	51,224	21 At Atlanta	35	28,686
31 At Detroit	27	51,157	13 San Diego (OT)	10	46,802
37 Houston	14	47,142	10 At Oakland	17	51,075
0 At San Diego	17	36,571	25 Philadelphia	10	37,080
			13 At Miami	14	43,064

REGULAR SEASON RESULTS

1976 Coach: John Ralston	9-5-0	Attend.	1977 Coach: Red Miller	12-2-0	Attend.
7 At Cincinnati	17	53,464	7 St. Louis	0	75,002
46 New York Jets	3	62,669	26 Buffalo	6	74,897
44 Cleveland	13	62,975	24 At Seattle	13	53,108
26 San Diego	0	63,369	23 Kansas City	7	74,878
7 At Houston	17	47,928	30 At Oakland	7	53,616
10 Oakland	17	63,431	24 At Cincinnati	13	54,305
35 At Kansas City	26	57,961	14 Oakland	24	75,007
6 At Oakland	19	52,169	21 Pittsburgh	7	74,967
48 Tampa Bay	13	62,703	17 At San Diego	14	45,211
17 At San Diego	0	32,017	14 At Kansas City	7	54,050
14 New England	13	63,151	27 Baltimore	13	74,939
14 At New England	38	61,128	24 At Houston	14	46,875
17 Kansas City	16	58,170	17 San Diego	9	74,905
28 At Chicago	14	44,459	6 At Dallas	14	63,752
			Playoffs		
			34 Pittsburgh	21	75,011
			20 Oakland	17	74,982
			Super Bowl		
			10 Dallas	27	76,400

ALL-TIME PRE-SEASON RESULTS

1960 (0-5)
6 Boston 43 (Providence, R.I.)
14 Buffalo 31 (Rochester)
3 At Houston 42
0 Dallas 48 (Little Rock)
30 At Los Angeles 36

1961 (1-4)
13 At Dallas 31 (Midland, Tex.)
48 Oakland 21 (Spokane)
27 At Dallas 29 (Ft. Worth)
10 Houston 42 (Mobile)
12 At Oakland 49

1962 (2-2)
17 Houston 33 (Atlanta)
24 At San Diego 31
27 At Dallas 24
41 At Oakland 12 (Stockton, Calif.)

1963 (2-3)
27 Houston 10
10 At Oakland 35
31 San Diego 25
16 At Kansas City 30
14 Buffalo 21 (Winston-Salem)

1964 (2-3)
20 At San Diego 34
7 Oakland 20
32 At Houston 20
10 Kansas City 14 (Ft. Worth)
28 Boston 17

1965 (1-4)
24 Kansas City 30
27 Oakland 17 (Salt Lake City)
6 San Diego 21
3 Houston 25 (San Antonio)
20 Oakland 30 (Saramento)

1966 (1-3)
30 Kansas City 32
3 At Buffalo 25
28 Miami 16 (Memphis)
21 Oakland 52

1967 (3-1)
2 Miami 19 (Akron)
13 Detroit 7
14 Minnesota 9
21 Oakland 17 (N. Platte, Neb.)

1968 (2-3)
15 Cincinnati 13
16 Minnesota 39
6 San Francisco 22
6 San Diego 3 (San Antonio)
7 Oakland 23 (Portland)

1969 (1-4)
6 At Minnesota 26
22 New Orleans 28
19 San Francisco 15
10 Boston 26 (Jacksonville)
11 At Cincinnati 13

1970 (3-2)
26 St. Louis 16
7 Baltimore 24
7 S. Francisco 23 (Eugene, Ore.)
30 Chicago 17
16 Boston 14 (Salt Lake City)

1971 (1-4)
13 Washington 17
10 Atlanta 27 (Memphis)
17 San Francisco 33 (Spokane)
14 Minnesota 7
17 At Chicago 33

1972 (2-3)
0 At Washington 41
13 At St. Louis 17
27 At San Francisco 24
49 New England 24
13 Baltimore 20

1973 (2-3)
10 At Washington 14
38 St. Louis 17
7 At San Francisco 43
16 Buffalo 14
10 Baltimore 17

ALL-TIME PRE-SEASON RESULTS (Continued)

1974 (4-2)
19	New York Jets 41
27	Minnesota 21
10	At San Francisco 3
31	At Green Bay 21
27	New England 21 (At Spokane)
14	Atlanta 20

1975 (3-3)
20	Baltimore 23
21	At New Orleans 24
27	Houston 21
13	At Chicago 0
10	At San Francisco 44
21	St. Louis 17

1976 (5-2)
10	Detroit 7 (Hall of Fame Game at Canton, Ohio)
14	Chicago 15
7	At San Francisco 17
13	At Dallas 9
52	Seattle 7
21	At St. Louis 17
30	Minnesota 17

1977 (5-1)
14	Baltimore 8
15	St. Louis 7
10	At Atlanta 2
24	At Philadelphia 28
27	At Seattle 10
20	At San Francisco 0

REGULAR SEASON SERIES RECORDS

ATLANTA FALCONS
1970—At Den 24, Atl 10
1972—At Atl 23, Den 20
1975—At Atl 35, Den 21
(Broncos 1, Falcons 2)

BALTIMORE COLTS
1974—Den 17, At Bal 6
1977—At Den 27, Bal 13
(Broncos 2, Colts 0)

BUFFALO BILLS
1960—Den 27, At Buf 21
1960—At Den 38, Buf 38 (tie)
1961—Den 22 At Buf 10
1961—Buf 23, At Den 10
1962—Den 23, At Buf 20
1962—Buf 45, At Den 38
1963—Buf 30, At Den 28
1963—At Buf 27, Den 17
1964—At Buf 30, Den 13
1964—Buf 30, At Den 19
1965—Buf 30, At Den 15
1965—At Buf 31, Den 13
1966—At Buf 38, Den 21
1967—Buf 17, At Den 16
1967—Den 21, At Buf 20
1968—At Den 34, Buf 32
1969—At Buf 41, Den 28
1970—Den 25, At Buf 10
1975—At Buf 38, Den 14
1977—At Den 26, Buf 6
(Broncos 7, Bills 12, 1 tie)

CHICAGO BEARS
1971—At Den 6, Chi 3
1973—Chi 33, At Den 14
1976—Den 28, At Chi 14
(Broncos 2, Bears 1)

CINCINNATI BENGALS
1968—At Cin 24, Den 10
1968—At Den 10, Cin 7
1969—Den 30, At Cin 23
1969—At Den 27, Cin 16
1971—Cin 24, At Den 10
1972—At Cin 21, Den 10
1973—At Den 28, Cin 10
1975—Cin 17, At Den 16
1976—At Cin 17, Den 7
1977—Den 24, At Cin 13
(Broncos 5 Bengals 5)

CLEVELAND BROWNS
1970—Cle 27, At Den 13
1971—Den 27, At Cle 0
1972—Cle 27, At Den 20
1974—At Cle 23, Den 21
1975—At Den 16, Cle 15
1976—At Den 44, Cle 13
(Broncos 3, Browns 3)

DALLAS COWBOYS
1973—Dal 22, At Den 10
1977—At Dal 14, Den 6
(Broncos 0, Cowboys 2)

DETROIT LIONS
1971—Det 24, At Den 20
1974—Den 31, At Det 27
(Broncos 1, Lions 1)

GREEN BAY PACKERS
1971—At GB 34, Den 13
1975—At Den 23, GB 13
(Broncos 1, Packers 1)

HOUSTON OILERS
1960—Hou 45, At Den 25
1960—At Hou 20, Den 10
1961—Hou 55, At Den 14
1961—At Hou 45, Den 14
1962—At Den 20, Hou 10
1962—At Hou 34, Den 17
1963—At Hou 20, Den 14
1963—Hou 33, At Den 24
1964—Hou 38, At Den 17
1964—At Hou 34, Den 15
1965—At Den 28, Hou 17
1965—Den 31, At Hou 21
1966—At Hou 45, Den 7
1966—At Den 40, Hou 38
1967—At Hou 10, Den 6
1967—Hou 20, At Den 18
1968—At Hou 38, Den 17
1969—At Hou 24, Den 21
1969—At Den 20, Hou 20
1970—At Hou 31, Den 21
1972—At Hou 30, Den 17
1973—Den 48, At Hou 20
1974—At Den 37, Hou 14
1976—At Hou 17, Den 3
1977—Den 24, At Hou 14
(Broncos 8, Oilers 16, 1 tie)

SERIES RECORDS (CONTINUED)

KANSAS CITY CHIEFS
(Dallas Texans 1960-62)
1960—Dal 17, At Den 14
1960—At Dal 34, Den 7
1961—Dal 19, At Den 12
1961—At Dal 49, Den 21
1962—Dal 24, At Den 3
1962—At Dal 17, Den 10
1963—KC 59, At Den 7
1963—At KC 52, Den 21
1964—At Den 33, KC 27
1964—At KC 49, Den 39
1965—KC 31, At Den 23
1965—At KC 45, Den 35
1966—At KC 37, Den 10
1966—KC 56, At Den 10
1967—At KC 52, Den 9
1967—KC 38, At Den 24
1968—At KC 34, Den 2
1968—KC 30, At Den 7
1969—KC 26, At Den 13
1969—At KC 31, Den 17
1970—At Den 26, KC 13
1970—At KC 16, Den 0
1971—KC 16, At Den 3
1971—At KC 28, Den 10
1972—KC 45, At Den 24
1972—At KC 24, Den 21
1973—At KC 16, Den 14
1973—At Den 14, KC 10
1974—Den 17, At KC 14
1974—KC 42, At Den 34
1975—At Den 37, KC 33
1975—At KC 26, Den 13
1976—At KC 35, Den 26
1976—At Den 17, KC 16
1977—At Den 23, KC 7
1977—Den 14, At KC 7
(Broncos 9, Chiefs 27)

LOS ANGELES RAMS
1972—Den 16, At LA 10
1974—LA 17, Den 10
(Broncos 1, Rams 1)

MIAMI DOLPHINS
1966—At Mia 24, Den 7
1966—At Den 17, Mia 7
1967—At Mia 35, Den 21
1968—At Den 21, Mia 14
1969—At Mia 27, Den 24
1971—At Den 10, Mia 10
1975—At Mia 14, Den 13
(Broncos 2, Dolphins 4, 1 tie)

MINNESOTA VIKINGS
1972—Min 23, At Den 20
(Broncos 0, Vikings 1)

NEW ENGLAND PATRIOTS
(Boston Patriots 1960-70)
1960—Den 13, At Bos 10
1960—At Den 31, Bos 24
1961—At Bos 45, Den 17
1961—Bos 28, At Den 24
1962—At Bos 41, Den 16
1962—Bos 33, At Den 29
1963—At Den 14, Bos 10
1963—At Bos 40, Den 21
1964—Bos 39, At Den 10
1964—At Bos 12, Den 7
1965—Den 27, At Bos 10
1965—Bos 28, At Den 20
1966—Bos 24, At Den 10
1966—Den 17, At Bos 10
1967—At Den 26, Bos 21
1968—Bos 20, At Den 17
1968—Den 35, At Bos 14
1969—At Den 35, Bos 7
1972—At Den 45, NE 21
1976—At NE 38, Den 14
(Broncos 9, Patriots 11)

NEW ORLEANS SAINTS
1970—Den 31, At NO 6
1974—At Den 33, NO 17
(Broncos 2, Saints 0)

NEW YORK GIANTS
1972—At NY 29, Den 17
1976—At Den 14, NY 13
(Broncos 1, Giants 1)

NEW YORK JETS
(New York Titans 1960-62)
1960 At NY 28, Den 24
1960—NY 30, At Den 27
1961—At NY 35, Den 28
1961—At Den 27, NY 10
1962—Den 32, At NY 10
1962—NY 46, At Den 45
1963—Den 35, NY 35
1963—NY 14, At Den 9
1964—At NY 30, Den 6
1964—At Den 20, NY 16
1965—At Den 16, NY 13
1965—At NY 45, Den 10
1966—NY 16, At Den 7
1967—NY 38, At Den 24
1967—Den 33, At NY 24
1968—Den 21, At NY 13
1969—At Den 21, NY 19
1973—Den 40, At NY 28
1976—At Den 46, NY 3
(Broncos 9, Jets 9, 1 tie)

SERIES RECORD (CONTINUED)

OAKLAND RAIDERS
1960—At Den 31, Oak 14
1960—At Oak 48, Den 10
1961—At Oak 33, Den 19
1961—At Den 27, Oak 24
1962—At Den 44, Oak 7
1962—Den 23, At Oak 6
1963—Oak 26, At Den 10
1963—At Oak 35, Den 31
1964—At Oak 40, Den 7
1964—At Den 20, Oak 20
1965—Oak 28, At Den 20
1965—At Oak 24, Den 13
1966—Oak 17, At Den 3
1966—At Oak 28, Den 10
1967—At Oak 51, Den 0
1967—Oak 21, At Den 17
1968—Oak 43, At Den 7
1968—At Oak 33, Den 27
1969—Oak 24, At Den 14
1969—At Oak 41, Den 10
1970—At Oak 35, Den 23
1970—Oak 24, At Den 19
1971—Oak 27, At Den 16
1971—At Oak 21, Den 13
1972—Den 30, At Oak 23
1972—Oak 37, At Den 20
1973—At Den 23, Oak 23
1973—At Oak 21, Den 17
1974—Oak 28, At Den 17
1974—Den 20, At Oak 17
1975—Oak 42, At Den 17
1975—At Oak 17, Den 10
1976—Oak 17, At Den 10
1976—At Oak 19, Den 3
1977—Den 30, At Oak 7
1977—Oak 24, At Den 14
    (Broncos 7, Raiders 27, 2 ties)

SAN DIEGO CHARGERS
(Los Angeles Chargers 1960)
1960—LA 23, At Den 19
1960— At LA 41, Den 33
1961—At SD 37, Den 0
1961—SD 19, At Den 16
1962—At Den 30, SD 21
1962—Den 23, At SD 20
1963—At Den 50, SD 34
1963—At SD 58, Den 20
1964—At SD 42, Den 14
1964—SD 31, At Den 20
1965—At SD 34, Den 31
1965—SD 35, At Den 21
1966—At SD 24, Den 17
1966—At Den 20, SD 17
1967—SD 38, At Den 21
1967—At SD 24, Den 20
1968—At SD 55 Den 24
1968—SD 47, At Den 23
1969—At Den 13, SD 0
1969—At SD 45, Den 24
1970—At SD 24, Den 21
1970—At Den 17, SD 17
1971—At Den 20, SD 16
1971—At SD 45, Den 17
1972—At SD 37, Den 14
1972—At Den 38, SD 13
1973—At Den 30, SD 19
1973—Den 42, At SD 28
1974—At Den 27, SD 7
1974—At SD 17, Den 0
1975—Den 27, At SD 17
1975—At Den 13, SD 10 (OT)
1976—At Den 26, SD 0
1976—Den 17, At SD 0
1977—Den 14, At SD 10
1977—At Den 17, SD 9
    (Broncos 16, Chargers 19, 1 tie)

PHILADELPHIA EAGLES
1971—At Phi 17, Den 16
1975—At Den 25, Phi 10
    (Broncos 1, Eagles 1)

SAN FRANCISCO 49ERS
1970—At SF 19, Den 14
1973—SF 36, At Den 34
    (Broncos 0, 49ers 2)

PITTSBURGH STEELERS
1970—At Den 16, Pit 13
1971—Den 22, At Pit 10
1973—Den 23, At Pit 13
1974—At Den 35, Pit 35 (OT)
1975—At Pit 20, Den 9
1977—At Den 21, Pit 7
    (Broncos 4, Steelers 1, 1 tie)

SEATTLE SEAHAWKS
1977—Den 24, At Sea 13
    (Broncos 1, Seahawks 0)

TAMPA BAY BUCCANEERS
1976—At Den 48, TB 13
    (Broncos 1, Buccaneers 0)

ST. LOUIS CARDINALS
1973—Den 17, at SL 17 (tie)
1977—At Den 7, SL 0
    (Broncos 1, Cardinals 0, 1 tie)

WASHINGTON REDSKINS
1970—Was 19, At Den 3
1974—At Was 30, Den 3
    (Broncos 0, Redskins 2)

BRONCOS COACHING HISTORY

BRONCO COACHING RECORDS

Season	Coach	Record	
1960	Frank Filchock	4-9-1	
1961	Frank Filchock	3-11-0	
	Filchock's totals	**7-20-1**	.268
1962	Jack Faulkner	7-7-0	
1963	Jack Faulkner	2-11-1	
1964	Jack Faulkner	0-4-0	
	Faulkner's totals	**9-22-1**	.297
1964	Mac Speedie	2-7-1	
1965	Mac Speedie	4-10-0	
1966	Mac Speedie	0-2-0	
	Speedie's totals	**6-19-1**	.250
1966	Ray Malavasi	4-8-0	
	Malavasi's totals	**4-8-0**	.333
1967	Lou Saban	3-11-0	
1968	Lou Saban	5-9-0	
1969	Lou Saban	5-8-1	
1970	Lou Saban	5-8-1	
1971	Lou Saban	2-6-1	
	Saban's totals	**20-42-3**	.331
1971	Jerry Smith	2-3-0	
	Smith's totals	**2-3-0**	.400
1972	John Ralston	5-9-0	
1973	John Ralston	7-5-2	
1974	John Ralston	7-6-1	
1975	John Ralston	6-8-0	
1976	John Ralston	9-5-0	
	Ralston's totals	**34-33-3**	.507
1977	Red Miller	12-2-0	
	Playoffs	2-1-0	
	Miller's totals	**12-2-0**	.857
		14-3-0	.824

ASSISTANT COACH ROSTER

Ken Carpenter 1961; Jim Cason 1960; Max Coley 1972-1976; Joe Collier 1969-1977; Dick Coury 1972-1973; Kay Dalton 1974-1976; George Dickson 1964-1965; Dale Dodrill 1960-1963, 1966; Whitey Dovell 1967-1971; Hunter Enis 1967-1971; Jerry Frei 1972-1975; Bob Gambold 1972-1977; Mike Giddings 1976; Gary Glick 1962; Ken Gray 1977; Ed Hughes 1963; Charley Johnson 1976; Stan Jones 1967-1971, 1976-1977; Dick MacPherson 1967-1970; Ray Malavasi 1964-1966; Jim Martin 1962; Marv Matuszak 1966; Bus Mertes 1965-1966; Bob Miller 1963-1965; Myrel Moore 1972-1977; Babe Parilli 1977; Fran Polsfoot 1977; Paul Roach 1977; Sam Rutigliano 1967-1970; Jerry Smith 1971; Mac Speedie 1962-1964; Doc Urich 1972-1976.

ATTENDANCE MARKS

BRONCOS LARGEST CROWDS

At Home — Mile High Stadium

75,011	vs. Pittsburgh (Playoffs)	Dec. 24, 1977
75,007	vs. Oakland	Oct. 30, 1977
75,002	vs. St. Louis	Sept. 18, 1977
74,982	vs. Oakland (Playoffs)	Jan. 1, 1978
74,967	vs. Pittsburgh	Nov. 6, 1977
74,939	vs. Baltimore	Nov. 27, 1977
74,905	vs. San Diego	Dec. 11, 1977
74,897	vs. Buffalo	Sept. 25, 1977
74,878	vs. Kansas City	Oct. 9, 1977
63,431	vs. Oakland	Oct. 17, 1976

On the Road

79,864	at Buffalo	Oct. 5, 1975
76,400	at New Orleans (Super Bowl XII)	Jan. 15, 1978
75,674	at Cleveland	Oct. 24, 1971
71,414	at Kansas City	Oct. 7, 1973
70,043	at Kansas City	Oct. 26, 1975
67,298	at Kansas City	Oct. 6, 1974
66,837	at New Orleans	Nov. 22, 1970
66,725	at Kansas City	Dec. 3, 1972
65,398	at Los Angeles	Nov. 12, 1972
65,358	at Philadelphia	Oct. 31, 1971

ATTENDANCE BY SEASON

Year	Home	Road	Total
1960	91,333	115,994	207,327
1961	74,508	122,315	196,823
1962	178,485	146,442	324,927
1963	132,218	165,995	298,213
1964	118,259	166,744	285,003
1965	219,786	215,992	435,778
1966	192,198	203,799	395,997
1967	231,801	247,696	479,497
1968	281,374	278,008	559,382
1969	326,851	276,755	603,606
1970	355,739	330,184	685,923
1971	358,400	377,642	736,042
1972	361,414	*412,073	773,487
1973	356,327	351,334	707,661
1974	347,322	354,367	701,689
1975	342,375	347,944	690,319
1976	436,468	349,126	785,594
1977	*524,595	370,917	*895,512
Totals	4,929,453	4,833,327	9,762,780

*Bronco records

SEASON TICKET SALES

1960 — 2,675	1969 — 31,936
1961 — 5,775	1970 — 43,580
1962 — 5,042	*1971 — 47,500
1963 — 7,624	*1972 — 48,000
1964 — 8,002	*1973 — 48,000
1965 — 22,905	*1974 — 49,000
1966 — 18,898	*1975 — 49,000
1967 — 24,650	*1976 — 62,215
1968 — 27,348	*1977 — 73,089
	*1978 —

*Season tickets sold out. Since and including the 1970 season, every Bronco game at Mile High Stadium has been a sellout, giving the Broncos 56 consecutive sellouts in the regular season through the final game of the 1977 season.

BRONCOS STATISTICAL HISTORY

OFFENSE YEAR-BY-YEAR

	Total Plays	First Downs	Rush Yards	Pass Yards	Total Yards	Total Points
1960	958	248	1195	3247	4442	309
1961	934	219	1091	2720	3811	251
1962	885	270	1298	3404	4702	353
1963	832	230	1508	2487	3995	301
1964	905	211	1311	2021	3332	240
1965	959	255	1829	2640	4469	303
1966	816	171	1173	1995	3168	196
1967	852	172	1265	1682	2947	256
1968	897	217	1614	2357	3971	255
1969	841	243	1637	2524	4161	297
1970	883	217	1802	2025	3827	253
1971	891	217	2093	2065	4158	203
1972	831	237	1838	2634	4472	325
1973	893	253	1954	2519	4473	354
1974	861	258	2157	2328	4485	302
1975	964	268	1993	2541	4534	254
1976	901	239	1932	2204	4136	315
1977	887	223	2043	1863	3906	274

DEFENSE YEAR-BY-YEAR

	Total Plays	First Downs	Rush Yards	Pass Yards	Total Yards	Total Points
1960	927	254	2145	2987	5132	393
1961	899	233	1633	2785	4418	432
1962	862	234	1868	2670	4538	332
1963	828	254	1687	3394	5081	473
1964	902	270	2064	2906	4970	438
1965	850	244	1337	2960	4297	392
1966	871	251	2029	2515	4544	381
1967	921	276	2076	3125	5201	409
1968	916	251	1861	3163	5024	404
1969	918	278	1709	2932	4641	344
1970	838	199	1351	2354	3705	264
1971	825	206	1834	1985	3819	275
1972	876	251	1668	2183	3851	350
1973	872	239	1795	2440	4235	296
1974	945	265	1808	2583	4391	294
1975	901	247	1974	2032	4006	307
1976	903	222	1709	2026	3735	206
1977	941	217	1530	2244	3774	148

YEARLY LEADERS

Rushing

	Yards	Attempts	Average	TDs
1960	Rolle—501	Rolle—130	Mingo—3.9	Mingo—4
1961	Stone—505	Stone—127	Stone—4.0	Bukaty—5
1962	Stone—360	Stone—94	Stone—3.8	Mingo—4
1963	Joe—649	Joe—154	Joe—4.2	Joe—4
1964	Mitchell—590	Mitchell—177	Joe—3.7	Mitchell—5
1965	Gilchrist—954	Gilchrist—252	Hayes—4.1	Gilchrist—6
1966	Hayes—411	Haynes—129	Hayes—3.9	Haynes—2
				Choboian—2
1967	Little—381	Little—130	Mitchell—3.8	Hickey—4
				Hayes—4
1968	Little—584	Little—158	Little—3.7	Lynch—4
1969	Little—729	Little—146	Little—5.0	Little—6
1970	Little—901	Little—209	Anderson—4.4	Crenshaw—5
1971	Little—1133	Little—284	Dawkins—4.4	Little—6
1972	Little—859	Little—216	Anderson—4.4	Little—9
1973	Little—979	Little—256	Dawkins—4.4	Little—12
1974	Armstrong—1407	Armstrong—263	Armstrong—5.3	Keyworth—10
1975	Keyworth—725	Keyworth—182	Keyworth—4.0	Keyworth—3
				Lynch—3
1976	Armstrong—1008	Armstrong—247	Armstrong—4.1	Armstrong—5
1977	Armstrong—489	Armstrong—130	Perrin—4.1	Armstrong—4
				Morton—4

233

Passing

	Yards	Attempts	Completions
1960	Tripucka—3038	Tripucka—478	Tripucka—248
1961	Tripucka—1690	Tripucka—344	Tripucka—167
1962	Tripucka—2917	Tripucka—440	Tripucka—240
1963	Slaughter—1689	Slaughter—223	Slaughter—112
1964	Lee—1611	Lee—265	Lee—133
1965	McCormick—1292	McCormick—253	McCormick—103
1966	Choboian—1110	McCormick—193	Choboian—82
1967	Tensi—1915	Tensi—325	Tensi—131
1968	Briscoe—1589	Briscoe—224	Briscoe—93
1969	Tensi—1990	Tensi—286	Tensi—131
1970	Liske—1340	Liske—238	Liske—112
1971	Ramsey—1120	Ramsey—178	Horn—89
1972	Johnson—1783	Johnson—238	Johnson—132
1973	Johnson—2465	Johnson—346	Johnson—184
1974	Johnson—1969	Johnson—244	Johnson—136
1975	Ramsey—1562	Ramsey—233	Ramsey—128
1976	Ramsey—1931	Ramsey—270	Ramsey—128
1977	Morton—1929	Morton—254	Morton—131

	Pct.	TD	Int.
1960	Tripucka—.519	Tripucka—24	Tripucka—34
1961	Tripucka—.486	Tripucka—10	Herring—22
1962	Tripucka—.545	Tripucka—17	Tripucka—25
1963	Slaughter—.502	Slaughter—12	Slaughter—14
1964	Slaughter—.513	Lee—11	Lee—20
1965	Slaughter—.510	McCormick—7	McCormick—14
1966	Choboian—.503	McCormick—6	McCormick—15
1967	Tensi—.403	Tensi—16	Tensi—17
1968	Briscoe—.415	Briscoe—14	Briscoe—13
1969	Tensi—.458	Tensi—14	Tensi—12
1970	Liske—.471	Liske—7	Liske—11
1971	Horn—.514	Ramsey—5	Horn—14
1972	Johnson—.555	Johnson—14	Johnson—14
1973	Johnson—.532	Johnson—20	Johnson—17
1974	Johnson—.557	Johnson—13	Johnson—9
1975	Ramsey—.549	Ramsey—9	Ramsey—14
1976	Ramsey—.474	Ramsey—11	Ramsey—13
1977	Morton—.516	Morton—14	Morton—8

Receiving

	No.	Yards	Average	TD
1960	Taylor—92	Taylor—1235	Carmichael—19.3	Taylor—12
1961	Taylor—100	Taylor—1176	Frazier—17.0	Frazier—6
1962	Taylor—77	Taylor—908	Scarpitto—19.0	Scarpitto—6
1963	Taylor—78	Taylor—1101	Groman—16.2	Taylor—10
1964	Taylor—76	Taylor—873	Dixon—15.4	Taylor—7
1965	Taylor—85	Taylor—1131	Scarpitto—18.3	Taylor—6
1966	Haynes—46	Denson—725	Denson—20.1	Scarpitto—4
1967	Denson—46 Crabtree—46	Denson—899	Denson—19.5	Denson—11
1968	Crabtree—35	Crabtree—601	Denson—17.2	Crabtree—5 Denson—5
1969	Denson—53	Denson—809	Embree—16.2	Denson—10
1970	Denson—47	Denson—646	Whalen—14.0	Whalen—3
1971	Anderson—37	Simmons—403	Simmons—16.1	Harrison—2
1972	Sherman—38	Sherman—661	Sherman—17.4	Moses—5
1973	Odoms—43	Odoms—629	Moses—18.5	Moses—8
1974	Odoms—42	Odoms—639	Moses—16.4	Odoms—6
1975	Keyworth—42	Odoms—544	Moses—17.4	Dolbin—3 Odoms—3
1976	Armstrong—39	Moses—498	Moses—19.9	Moses—7
1977	Odoms—37	Moses—539	Moses—20.0	Moses—4

Interceptions

	No.	Ret. Yards
1960	Gonsoulin—11	Gonsoulin—98
1961	Nugent—7	McNamara—85
1962	Gonsoulin—7	Zeman—133
1963	Gonsoulin—6	Gonsoulin—64

Interceptions

	No.	Yards
1964	Brown—9	Brown—140
1965	Gonsoulin—6	Wilson—118
1966	Brown—3 Sellers—3	Brown—37
1967	Sellers—7	Wilson—153
1968	Jaquess—5	Jaquess—64
1969	Thompson—3	Thompson—92
1970	Martha—6	Martha—99
1971	Thompson—5	Thompson—83
1972	Mitchell—3	Preece—30
1973	Jones—4	Thompson—96
1974	Jones—5 Thompson—5	Thompson—105
1975	Gradishar—3	Thompson—97
1976	Jackson—7	Jackson—136
1977	Thompson—5	Wright—128

Interception Returns For Touchdowns

	Date	Opponent	Yards
Jackson	11/27/77	vs. Baltimore	73
Wright	10/16/77	at Oakland	18
Jackson	11/14/76	at San Diego	46
Rowser	11/7/76	vs. Tampa Bay	32
Gradishar	11/7/76	vs. Tampa Bay	31
Rowser	9/19/76	vs. N. Y. Jets	41
Gradishar	9/29/75	vs. Green Bay	44
Thompson	10/13/74	vs. New Orleans	38
Mitchell	10/28/73	at N.Y. Jets	40
Thompson	10/14/73	at Houston	59
Forsberg	10/24/71	at Cleveland	40
Burrell	12/7/69	at Miami	38
Thompson	11/16/69	vs. Houston	57
Wilson	12/17/67	vs. Kansas City	70
Wilson	10/22/67	vs. San Diego	40
Sellers	9/3/67	vs. Boston	24
Bramlett	11/14/65	at Houston	25
Wilson	11/7/65	vs. San Diego	65
Griffin	10/17/65	vs. Houston	44
Janik	11/1/64	at Kansas City	22
Gonsoulin	10/6/63	vs. San Diego	43
McMillin	11/22/62	vs. New York	59
McGeever	10/5/62	vs. Oakland	48
Gonsoulin	10/5/62	vs. Oakland	64
Zeman	9/30/62	at New York	30
Yelverton	10/2/60	vs. Oakland	20
Pyeatt	9/18/60	at Buffalo	40

Other Defensive Returns For Touchdowns

	Date	Opponent	Yards
Poltl (fumble-lateral from Swenson)	11/7/76	vs. Tampa Bay	26
Jones (fumble)	9/23/76	vs. Cleveland	43
Smith (fumble)	11/23/75	at Atlanta	80
Thompson (fumble)	10/22/73	vs. Oakland	80
Bramlett (blocked FG)	11/27/66	vs. San Diego	86
Griffin (blocked punt)	10/17/65	vs. Houston	10
Bramlett (fumble)	9/24/65	at Boston	(recovered in end zone)
McMillin (fumble)	11/8/64	vs. San Diego	(recovered in end zone)
Cooke (fumble)	11/1/64	at Kansas City	46
McFadin (fumble)	10/13/63	vs. Houston	6
McMillin (fumble)	12/9/62	at Dallas	9
McFadin (fumble)	11/22/62	vs. New York	69
Gavin (blocked punt)	12/10/61	at Dallas	23

YEARLY LEADERS (CONTINUED)

Punt Returns

	No.	Yards	Average
1960	Carmichael—15	Carmichael—101	Carmichael—6.7
1961	Frazier—18	Frazier—231	Frazier—12.8
1962	Mingo—7	Zeman—59	Zeman—11.8
1963	Mitchell—12	Mitchell—141	Mingo—12.1
1964	Barry—16	Barry—149	Mitchell—12.0
1965	Barry—21	Barry—210	Barry—10.0
1966	Haynes—10	Haynes—119	Haynes—11.9
1967	Little—16	Little—270	Little—16.9
1968	Little—24	Little—261	Little—10.9
1969	Thompson—25	Thompson—288	Thompson—11.5
1970	Thompson—23	Thompson—233	Thompson—10.1
1971	Thompson—29	Thompson—274	Thompson—9.4
1972	Sherman—10	Sherman—89	Sherman—8.9
1973	Thompson—30	Thompson—366	Thompson—12.2
1974	Thompson—26	Thompson—350	Thompson—13.5
1975	Upchurch—27	Upchurch—312	Thompson—12.2
1976	Upchurch—39	Upchurch—536	Upchurch—13.7
1977	Upchurch—51	Upchurch—653	Upchurch—12.8

Punt Returns For Touchdowns

	Date	Opponent	Yards
Upchurch	11/6/77	vs. Pittsburgh	87
Upchurch	10/24/76	at Kansas City	55
Upchurch	10/3/76	vs. San Diego	92
Upchurch	9/26/76	vs. Cleveland	47
Upchurch	9/26/76	vs. Cleveland	73

(Upchurch's two punt returns for touchdowns in one game and four punt returns for touchdowns in one season tie NFL records.)

	Date	Opponent	Yards
Greer	12/10/72	vs. San Diego	65
Little	11/17/68	at Houston	67
Little	12/3/67	at N. Y. Jets	72
Haynes	11/14/65	at Houston	57
Griffin (blocked punt)	10/17/65	vs. Houston	10
Barry	11/15/64	vs. N. Y. Jets	52
Frazier (lateral from McNamara)	12/3/61	vs. Boston	55
Gavin (blocked punt)	12/10/61	at Dallas	23
Mingo	9/9/60	at Boston	76

Kickoff Returns

	No.	Yards	Average
1960	Carmichael—22	Carmichael—581	Carmichael—26.4
1961	Frazier—18	Frazier—504	Frazier—28.0
1962	Frazier—19	Frazier—388	Frazier—20.4
1963	Mitchell—37	Mitchell—954	Mitchell—25.7
1964	Barry—47	Barry—1245	Barry—26.5
1965	Haynes—34	Haynes—901	Haynes—26.5
1966	Sellers—19	Sellers—540	Sellers—28.4
1967	Little—35	Little—942	Little—26.9
1968	Little—26	Little—649	Little—25.0
1969	Williams—23	Williams—574	Thompson—28.5
1970	Anderson—21	Anderson—520	Anderson—24.8
1971	Anderson—8	Little—199	Little—28.3
1972	Montgomery—29	Montgomery—756	Montgomery—26.1
1973	Armstrong—20	Armstrong—472	Armstrong—23.6
1974	Armstrong—16	Armstrong—386	Armstrong—24.1
1975	Upchurch—40	Upchurch—1084	Upchurch—27.1
1976	Upchurch—22	Upchurch—514	Perrin—27.9
1977	Upchurch—20	Upchurch—456	Upchurch—22.8

Kickoff Returns For Touchdowns

	Date	Opponent	Yards
Montgomery	9/24/72	at San Diego	94
Wilson	10/8/66	at Kansas City	100
Sellers	10/2/66	vs. Houston	100
Sellers	9/3/66	at Houston	88
Mitchell	9/14/63	at Houston	90
Frazier	12/3/61	vs. Boston	90

PLAYER HISTORY

ALL-TIME DRAFT CHOICES

1960 (First selections)—Harry Ball, T, Boston College; Charley Britt, QB, Georgia; Dave Canary, E, Cincinnati; Paul Candro, HB, Boston U.; Bill Carrico, G, N. Texas St.; Larry Cundiff, C, Mich. State; Bernard Darre, T, Tulane; Roger Davis, T, Syracuse; Lonnie Dennis, G, Brig. Young; John Dingens T-G, Detroit; Maurice Doke, G, Texas; Mike Dowdle, FB, Texas; Wayne Hawkins, T, COP; Gary Huber, C, Miami (O.); Dave Hudson, E, Florida; Claude King, HB, Houston; Don Klochak, FB, N. Carolina; Roger LeClerc, C, Trinity; Dean Look, QB, Mich. State; Bill Mathis, HB, Clemson; Ken McNeece, T-G, San Jose St.; James Monroe, QB, Arkansas; Ray Norton, HB, San Jose St.; Robert Rosbaugh, HB, Miami (Fla.); Mel Semenko, E, Colorado; Lebron Shields, T, Tennessee; Jack Spikes, FB, TCU; Howard Turley, E, Louisville; Jim Walden, QB, Wyoming; Willie West, HB, Oregon; John Willener, G, Oregon; Bob Yates, T, Syracuse; Ken Young, E, Valparaiso; Bob Zimpter, T-G, Bowling Gr.

1960 (Second selections)—Mel Branch, T-G, LSU; Ronnie Cain, E, Kentucky; Jack Campbell, E, Toledo; Tom Chapman, E, Detroit; LaVelle Coleman, HB, West Mich.; Jim Colvin, T-G, Houston; Teddy Foret, T-G, Auburn; Bobby Green, HB, Florida; Jack Hanlon, HB, Penn.; G. Hershberger, T-G, Wichita; Sam Homer, HB, VMI; Bob Hudson, E, Lamar Tech.; Vic Jones, HB, Indiana; Billy Luplow, T-G, Arkansas; George Phelps, HB, Cornell C. Ia.; Tom Roberts, T-G, Georgia Tech; Sam Stenger, C, Denver; Olin Treadway, QB, Iowa; John Wilkins, T-G, So. California; Emmet Wilson, T-G, Georgia Tech.

1961—1, Bob Gaiters, HB, N. Mex. St. 2, Jerry Hill, HB, Wyoming. 3, Chas. Strange, C, LSU. 4, Roland McDale, T, Nebraska. 4a, (NY), Sonny Davis, E, Baylor. 5, Charles Cowan, E, NM H'lds. U. 6, Dale Evans, HB, Kansas State. 7, Pat Patchen, E, Florida. 9, Phil Nugent, QB, Tulane. 10, Chas. Sturgeon, HB, Kentucky. 11, John Simko, E, Augustana. 12, Jerry Miller, E, H. Payne. 13, Ron Greene, G, Wash. St. 14, Bill Cooper, FB, Muskingum. 15, Willie Crafts, G, Texas A&I. 16, Jim Larkin, T, Hillsdale. 17, Chuck Weiss, FB, Colorado. 18, Chick Graning, HB, Georgia Tech. 19, John Hobbs, G, Maryland St. 20, Buck McLeod, T, Baylor. 21, Jim Morgan, HB, Iowa St. Tech. 22, Tom Hackler, E, Tenn. Tech. 23, Tom Jewell, T, Idaho St. 24, E. A. Simms, E, N. Mex. St. 25, Pete Samms, T, Central Okla. 26, Sam Smith, HB, Florence St. 27, Donald Olson, HB, Nebraska. 28, Wayne Lee, G, Colo. St. Col. 29, Archie Cobb, T, Nebraska. 30, Dave Mills, HB, NE Mo. St. Tech.

1962—1, Merlin Olsen, T. Utah St. 2, Jerry Hillebrand, E, Colorado. 3, Charles Holmes, FB, Maryland St. 4, John Furman, QB, Texas Western. 7, John McGeever, HB, Auburn. 8, Elbert Harris, HB, S.E. Louisiana. 9, Larry Jepson, C, Furman. 10, Gale Weidner, QB, Colorado. 11, Mike Kline, G, Oregon St. 13, Bob Cegelski, C, Montana St. 14, Sonny Gibbs, QB, TCU. 15, Bill Louden, G, Benedict Coll. 16, Gary Ballman, HB, Mich. St. 17, Jerry Tarr, E, Oregon. 18, Pete Schenk, E, Washington St. 20, Mike Martin, E, Washington St. 21, Jim Perkins, T, Colorado. 22, Don Kasso, HB, Oregon St. 23, Ken Tureaud, HB, Michigan. 24, Neil Thomas, G, Hillsdale. 25, Dave Edwards, E, Auburn. 26, Jim Roberts, T. Mississippi. 27, A. Von Sonn, C, UCLA. 28, Paul Holmes, T, Georgia. 29, Lynn Hoyem, C, Long Beach St. 30, Walter Mince, HB, Arizona. 31, Bill Williamson, T, Bakersfield JC. 32, Vester Flanagan, T, Humboldt St. 33, Duane Allen, E, Mt. S.A. Coll. 34, S. Stonebraker, E, Detroit.

1963—1, K. Alexander, HB,UCLA. 2a, (NY), Ray Poage, FB, Texas. 2b, Tom Nomina, T, Miami (O.). 3, Tommy Janik, HB, Texas A&I. 4, Lou Slaby, LB, Pittsburgh. 5, Ray Mansfield, C, Washington. 6, Anton Peters, T, Florida. 7a, (San Diego), M. Slaughter, QB, Louisiana Tech. 7b, Paul Flatley, E, Northwestern. 8a, (Buf.), H. Dixon, FB, Florida A&M. 8b, John Griffin, HB, Memphis St. 9, Marv Fleming, E, Utah. 10a, Lonnie Sanders, HB, Michigan St. 10b, (Hous.), Pat Richter, E, Wisconsin. 11, Billy Joe, FB, Villanova. 12, John Gamble, E, U. of Pacific. 13, James Maples, C, Baylor. 15, W. Freeman, E, North Texas. 16, Dave Crossan, G, Maryland. 17, Bob Paremore, HB, Florida A&M. 18, Charles Mitchell, HB, Washington. 19a, Frank Baker, FB, Toledo. 19b, (Dallas), Bruce Starling, HB, Florida. 20, Dan Grimm, G, Colorado. 21, Ross Nolan, E, NE Louisiana. 22, Dave Mathiesen, QB, Washington St. 23, Billy Mooty, HB, Arkansas. 24, C. B. Simons, LB, Stanford. 25, Forest Farmer, LB, Purdue. 26, Monte Day, T, Fresno St. 27, John Sellers, T, Bakersfield JC. 28, Bill Reddell, HB, Occidental. 29, Kern Carson, HB, San Diego St.

ALL-TIME DRAFT CHOICES (CONTINUED)

1964—1, Bob Brown, T, Nebraska. 3, Marv Woodson, DB, Indiana. 3a, Matt Snorton, DE-E, Michigan St. 6, Don Shackleford, T, Pacific. 6a, Al Denson, FL, Florida A&M. 7, Ray Kubala, C-T, Texas A&M. 7a, Jerry Richardson, LB, W. Texas St. 8, W. Hilgenberg, G-LB, Iowa. 9, John Mims, T, Rice. 12, Paul Krause, DB, Iowa. 13, Charley Parker, G, So. Mississippi. 14, Bob Hayes, HB, Florida A&M. 15, Chuck Logan, E, Northwestern. 16, Bob Cherry, E, Wittenburg. 17, J. McNaughton, E, Utah St. 18, George Mira, QB, Miami. 19, Odell Barry, FL, Findlay. 21, Dick Herzing, T, Drake. 22, Gary Lewis, HB, Arizona St. 23, Ken Brusvan, T, Oregon St. 24, Mickey Bitsko, LB, Dayton. 25, Jim Jones, E, Wisconsin. 26, Bob Berry, QB, Oregon.

1965—2, Dick Butkus, LB, Illinois. 3, Glen Ressler, C, Penn St. 4, Geo. Donnelly, DB, Illinois. 5a, Bob Breitenstein, T, Tulsa. 5b, Max Leetzow, DT, Idaho. 6, Tom Wilhelm, T, Syracuse. 7, Jim Garcia, DE, Purdue. 8, John Holman, G, Wisconsin. 9, Gary Bussell, DB, Georgia Tech. 10, Gene Jeter, LB, Arkansas AM&N. 11, Tom Vaughan, HB, Iowa St. 12, Tom Myers, QB, Northwestern. 13, Mike Strofalino, LB, Villanova. 14, John Frick, G, Ohio U. 15, Jeff Jordan, DB, Tulsa. 16, Brian Schweda, T, Kansas. 18, Larry Dupree, HB, Florida. 19, R. Oelschlager, HB, Kansas. 20, Terry Metchner, G, Albion.

1966—1, Jerry Shay, T, Purdue. 2, Freeman White, E, Nebraska. 3, Bob Hadrick, E, purdue. 4, Randy Johnson, QB, Texas A&I. 5, Billy Clay, DB, Mississippi. 6, James Fulgham, T, Minnesota. 7, Jerry Jone, G, Bowling Green. 7a, (Buf.), Scotty Glacken, QB, Duke. 8, Goldie Sellers, DB, Grambling. 9, Ron Sbranti, LB, Utah St. 10, Larry Cox, T, Abilene CC. 11, James Burns, G, Northwestern. 13, Eric Crabtree, DB, Pittsburgh. 14, Fred Forsberg, DT, Washington. 15, Mike Ringer, DB, Oklahoma. 16, Frank Rogers, K, Colorado. 17, Gary Eickman, DE, Illinois. 18, Tom Talaga, T, Notre Dame. 19, Tom Coughlin, DE, Miami. 20, Cliff Hysell, T, Montana St.

1967—1, Floyd Little, HB, Syracuse. 2, Thomas Beer, TE, Houston. 3a, Mike Current, T, Ohio State. 3b, Geo. Goeddeke, C, Notre Dame. 4, C. Cunningham, DE, Houston. 5a, Fran Lynch, FB, Hofstra. 5b, John Huard, LB, Maine. 6, Neal Sweeney, E, Tulsa. 7, Frank Richter, G, Georgia. 8, Tom Cassese, E, C. W. Post. 9, James Summers, DB, Michigan St. 10, Paul Krause, QB, Dubuque. 11, Lou Andrus, DE, Brigham Young. 13, Dennis Furjanic, DE, Houston. 14, Tom Francisco, HB, Virginia Tech. 15, Donald Smith, G, Florida A&M. 16, Jack Lentz, QB, Holy Cross. 17, W. Valley, Jr., T, Oregon St.

1968—2, Curley Culp, DE, Arizona St. 3a, Garrett Ford, RB, West Virginia. 3b, (K.C.), Robert Vaughan, T, Mississippi. 4b, (Miami), Gordon Lambert, LB, Tenn. Martin. 4c, (K.C.) Drake Garrett, DB, Michigan St. 4d, (Cincy), Gus Holloman, DB, Houston. 8, Steve Holloway, DB, Weber St. 9, Paul Smith, LB, New Mexico. 10, Bob Langford, T, Middle Tenn. 12, Robert Hendrix, T, Mississippi. 13, Charles Greer, DB, Colorado. 14, Marlin Briscoe, RB, Omaha. 15, Jeff Kuhman, LB, Vermont. 16, Adin Brown, LB, William & Mary. 17, Steve Grady, RB, So. California.

1969—2, Grady Cavness, DB, Texas-El Paso. 3, Bill Thompson, DB, Maryland St. 4a, Mike Schnitker, LB, Colorado (From Boston thru K.C.). 4b, Edward Hayes, DB, Morgan St. 5, Frank Quayle, RB, Virginia. 6a, (Buf.), Wandy Williams, RB, Hofstra. 6b, Mike Coleman, RB, Tampa. 7, Al Giffin, TE, Auburn. 9, Henry Jones, RB, Grambling. 10, Jim Smith, DB, Utah St. 11, Alan Pastrana, QB, Maryland. 12, Wes Plummer, DB, Arizona St. 13, John Sias, SE, Georgia Tech. 14, Gary Crane, LB, Arkansas St. 15, Errol Kahoun, G, Miami (O.). 16, Billy Woods, DB, No. Texas St. 17, Buster O'Brien, QB, Richmond.

1970—1, Bob Anderson, RB, Colorado. 2, Alden Roche, DE, Southern. 3, John Kohler, T, South Dakota. 4, Jerry Hendren, WR, Idaho. 5, Bill McKoy, LB, Purdue. 6, John Mosier, TE, Kansas. 7, R. Montgomery, DB, Weber St. 8, (KC) L. Porter, RB, Southern. 9, D. Washington, LB, Alcorn A&M. 10, M. Fullerton, DT, Tuskegee Inst. 11, Cleve Bryant, DB, Ohio University. 12, Greg Jones, RB, Wisconsin St. 13, Jim McKoy, CB, Parsons College. 14, Jeff Slipp, LB, Brigham Young. 15, Maher Barakat, K, So. Dakota Tech. 16, Bob Stewart, QB, Northern Ariz. 17, Frank Kalfoss, K, Montana St.

1971—1, M. Montgomery, OT, So. California. 2, Dwight Harrison, WR, Texas A&I. 4a, Lyle Alzado, DE, Yankton Col. 4b, C. Johnson, CB, Alcorn A&M. 6, Howard Phillips, C, Michigan St. 7, Doug Adams, CB, Ohio St. 8, Tom Beard, LB, Michigan St. 9, John Handy, LB, Purdue. 10, Carlis Harris, WR, Idaho St. 11, Roger Roitsch, DT, Rice. 12, Floyd Franks, WR, Mississippi. 13, Craig Blackford, QB, Evansville. 14, Tommy Lyons, C, Georgia. 15, Lawrence James, RB, Norfolk St. 16, Steve Thompson, DT, Minnesota. 17, Jack Simcsak, P-K, Virginia Tech.

ALL-TIME DRAFT CHOICES (CONTINUED)

1972—1, Riley Odoms, TE, Houston. 3, Bill Phillips, LB, Arkansas St. 4, (Minn.), Tom Graham, LB, Oregon. 5, (Phila.), Jim Krieg, WR, Washington. 8, Ronnie Estay, LB, LSU. 9, Floyd Priester, DB, Boston U. 10, Richard Wilkins, DE, Maryland St. 11, Larry Brunson, WR, Colorado. 12, R. McDougall, DB, Weber St. 13, Bob Warner, RB, Bloomsburg St. 14, Jerome Kundich, G, UTEP. 15, Skip Parmenter, DT, Massachusetts. 16, Tom Bougus, RB, Boston College. 17, Lou Harris, RB, Southern California.

1973—1, Otis Armstrong, RB, Purdue. 2, Barney Chavous, DE, S. Carolina St. 3a, Paul Howard, OG, Brigham Young. 3b, John Wood, DT, LSU. 4, Tom Jackson, LB, Louisville. 5, Charles McTorry, DB, Tennessee St. 7a, Mike Askea, OT, Stanford. 7b, John Grant, DE, So. California. 9, Lyle Blackwood, DB, Texas Christian. 10, Al Marshall, WR, Boise State. 11, Elton Brown, DT, Utah State. 12, Jim O'Malley, LB, Notre Dame. 13a, Ed Smith, DE, Colorado Col. 13b, Ed White, RB, Tulsa. 14, John Hufnagel, QB, Penn State. 15, Calvin Jones, DB, Washington. 16a, Oliver Ross, RB, Alabama A&M. 16b, Ken Muhlbeier, C, Idaho State. 17, Kenneth Morgan, TE, Elon College.

1974—1, Randy Gradishar, LB, Ohio State. 2, Carl Wafer, DT, Tenn. State. 3, Claudie Minor, T, San Diego St. 4, Ozell Collier, CB, Colorado. 6a, John Winesberry, WR, Stanford. 10, Charlie Johnson, CB, Southern. 11, Steve Buchanan, RB, Holy Cross. 12, Larry Cameron, LB, Alcorn A&M. 13, John Clerkley, DT, Fort Valley St. 14, Rich Marks, DS, No. Illinois. 15, Piel Pennington, QB, U. of Mass. 16, Darrell Austin, T, So. Carolina. 17, Boyd Brown, TE, Alcorn A&M

1975—1, Louis Wright, CB, San Jose St. 2, Charlie Smith, DE, N. Carolina Cen. 3a, (N.Y.G.) Mike Franckowiak, QB-KS, Central Mich. 3b, Drew Mahalic, LB, Notre Dame. 4a, (KC) Steve Taylor, DB, Georgia. 4b, Rick Upchurch, WR-Spec., Minnesota. 5a, Stan Rogers, T, Maryland. 5b, Rubin Carter, DT, Miami. 8, Steve Foley, S-QB, Tulane. 9, Roussell Williams, DB, Arizona. 10, (KC) Hank Englehardt, C, Pacific. 10, Steve Haggerty, WR, Nev.-Las Vegas. 12, Harry Walters, LB, Maryland. 13, Eric Penick, RB, Notre Dame. 14, Jerry Arnold, G, Oklahoma. 15, Ken Shelton, TE, Virginia. 16, Bubba Bridges, DT, Colorado. 17, Lester Sherman, Ret. Spec., Albany St.

1976—1, Tom Glassic, G, Virginia. 2, Kurt Knoff, S, Kansas. 4, Craig Penrose, QB, San Diego St. 5, Lonnie Perrin, RB, Illinois. 8, James Betterson, RB, North Carolina. 9a, Jim Czirr, C, Michigan. 9b, (St. Louis), Jim Lisko, LB, Arkansas St. 10, Art Gilliam, DE, Grambling. 11, Greg Pittman, LB, Iowa St. 12, Randy Moore, DT, Arizona St. 13, Donnie McGraw, CB, Houston. 14, Larry Evans, LB, Mississippi Col. 15, Wilbur Summers, KS, Louisville. 16, John Huddleston, LB, Utah. 17, Randy Cozens, LB, Pittsburgh.

1977—1, Steve Schindler, G, Boston College. 2, Rob Lytle, RB, Michigan. 4, Bill Bryan, C, Duke. 7, Larry Swider, P, Pittsburgh. 8, Calvin Culliver, RB, Alabama. 9, Charles Jackson, NT, Washington. 10, Orna Middlebrook, WR, Arkansas state. 11, Phil Heck, LB, California. 12, Scott Levenhagen, TE, Western Illinois.

1978—1, Don Latimer, DT, Miami (Fla.). 2, Bill Gay, TE, USC. 8, Frank Smith, OT, Alabama A&M. 10, Vince Kinney, WR. 11, Lacy Brumley, OT, Clemson.

ALL-TIME ROSTER

Bob Adams, TE, Pacific, 1975. Kenneth M. Adamson, G, Notre Dame, 1960-62. Steve Alexakos, G, San Jose St., 1970. Ted Allen, RB, Springfield College, 1969. Elihu (Buddy) Allen, HB, Utah ST., 1961. Donald R. Allen, FB, Texas, 1960. Henry Allison, OT, San Diego State, 1977. Vaughn S. (Buddy) Alliston, LB, Mississippi, 1960. Lyle Alzado, DE, Yankton College, 1971-77. David R. Ames, HB, Richmond, 1961. Robert Anderson, HB, Colorado, 1970-73. Lou Andrus, LB, Brigham Young, 1967. Otis Armstrong, RB, Purdue, 1973-77. LeFrancis Arnold, GC, Oregon, 1974. Mike Askea, T, Stanford, 1973. Billy Atkins, DB, Auburn, 1964. Frank Atkinson, DE, Stanford, 1964.

Jay Bachman, C, Cincinnati, 1968-71. Bill Bain, OT, Southern California, 1976. Ernie Barnes, G, North Carolina College, 1963-64. Walter Barnes, DE, Nebraska, 1969-71. Odell Barry, HB, Findlay, 1964-65. James Barton, C, Marshall, 1961-62. Rick Baska, LB, UCLA, 1976-77. Norman Bass, DB, Pacific, 1964. Tom Beer, OE, Houston, 1967-69. Behrman, Dave, C, Michigan St., 1967. Henry Bell, HB, No College, 1960. Frank Bernardi, HB, Colorado, 1960. Lee Bernet, OT, Wisconsin, 1965-66. Gordon Bowdell, WR, Michigan ST., 1971. Phil Brady, S, Brigham Young, 1969. John Bramlett, LB, Memphis St., 1965-66. Don Breaux, QB, McNeese St., 1963. Bob Breitenstein, OT, Tulsa, 1965-67. Marlin Briscoe, QB, Omaha, 1968. John W. (Red) Brodnax, FB, Louisiana St., 1960. Boyd Brown, TE, Alcorn A&M, 1974-76. Hardy Brown, LB, Tulsa, 1960. Willie Brown, DB, Grambling, 1963-66. Sam Brunelli, G, Colorado State College, 1966-71. Bill Bryan, G, Duke, 1977. Tom Buckman, TE, Texas A&M, 1969. Fred Bukaty, FB, Kansas, 1961. Bobby Burnett, RB, Arkansas, 1969. George Burrell, S, Pennsylvania, 1969. Gerry Bussell, DB, Georgia Tech, 1965. Bill Butler, LB, San Fernando Valley, 1970. George (Butch) Byrd, DB, Boston Univ., 1971.

Carter Campbell, DE, Weber St., 1971. Albert R. Carmichael, HB, Southern California, 1960-61. Paul Carmichael, HB, El Camino JC, 1965. Don Carothers, OE, Bradley, 1960. Kenneth L. Carpenter, E, Oregon St., 1960. Rubin Carter, DT, Miami (Fla.), 1975-77. Tim Casey, LB, Oregon, 1969. John E. Cash, E, Allen, 1961-62. Tom Cassese, DB, C. W. Post, 1967. Grady Cavness, CB, Texas-El Paso, 1969. Barney Chavous, DE, South Carolina St., 1973-77. Max Choboian, QB, San Fernando St., 1966. Tom Cichowski, OT, Maryland, 1967-68. Ralph Cindrich, LB, Pittsburgh, 1974. Don Coffey, E, Memphis St., 1963. Steve Coleman, DE, Delaware St., 1974. Ed Cooke, E, Maryland, 1964-65. Dave Costa, DT, Utah, 1967-71. Bill Cottrell, G. Delaware Valley, 1972. Larry Cox, DT, Abilene Christian, 1966-68. Eric Crabtree, FL, Pittsburgh, 1966-68. Gary Crane, LB, Arkansas St., 1969. Willis Crenshaw, FB, Kansas St., 1970. Ken Criter, LB, Wisconsin, 1969-74. Ed Cummings, LB, Stanford, 1965. Carl Cunningham, LB, Houston, 1967-70. Mike Current, OT, Ohio St., 1967-75.

Eldon V. Danenhauer, T, Pittsburg (Kan.) St., 1960-65. William A. Danenhauer, E, Emporia College, 1960. Dick Davis, RB, Nebraska, 1970. Jack T. Davis, T, Arizona, 1960. Marvin Davis, DT, Wichita St., 1966. Joe Dawkins, RB, Wisconsin, 1971-73. Albert E. Day, T, Eastern Michigan, 1960. Al Denson, FL, Florida A&M, 1964-70. John Denvir, G, Colorado, 1962. Wallace Dickey, OT, S.W. Texas St., 1968-69. Richard L. (Bo) Dickinson, FB, Southern Mississippi, 1962-63. Doug (Bucky) Dilts, P, Georgia, 1977. Hewritt Dixon, HB-E, Florida A&M, 1963-65. Joe DiVito, QB, Boston College, 1968. Jack Dolbin, WR, Wake Forest, 1975-77. Tom Domres, DT, Wisconsin, 1971-72. Richard A. (Skip) Doyle, HB, Ohio St., 1960. Tom Drougas, T, Oregon, 1974. Rick Duncan, K, Eastern Montana, 1967. Pete Duranko, DE, Notre Dame, 1967-74.

Booker Edgerson, CB, Western Illinois, 1970. Ron Egloff, TE, Wisconsin, 1977. Jim Elfrid, LB, Colorado St., 1961. John Embree, WR, Compton JC, 1969-70. George Hunter Enis, QB, Texas Christian, 1962. John P. Epperson, E, Adams St., 1960. Thomas D. Erlandson, LB, Washington St., 1962-65. Mike Ernst, QB, Cal-Fullerton, 1972. Terry Erwin, HB, Boston College, 1968. Jay Dale Evans, HB, Kansas St.,1961. Larry Evans, LB, Mississippi College, 1976-77.

Stan Fanning, E, Idaho, 1964. Miller Farr, DB, Wichita St., 1965. Billy Ray Fletcher, OE, Memphis St., 1966. Steve Foley, DB, Tulane, 1976-77. Garrett Ford, FB, West Virginia, 1968. Fred Forsberg, LB, Washington, 1968-73. Jason Franci, OE, Santa Barbara, 1966. Mike Franckowiak, RB, Central Michigan, 1975-76. James G. Fraser, LB, Wisconsin, 1962-64. Al Frazier, HB, Florida A&M, 1961-63.

George Gaiser, OT, Southern Methodist, 1968. Bob Gaiters, HB, New Mexico St., 1963. Drake Garrett, DB, Midhigan St., 1968-70. Charles E. Gavin, E, Tennessee St., 1960-63. Bob Geddes, LB, UCLA, 1972. Jack Gehrke, WR, Utah, 1971. Cookie Gilchrist, FB, No College, 1965-67. Scotty Glacken, QB, Duke, 1966-67. Glenn Glass, DB, Tennessee, 1966. Tom

ALL-TIME ROSTER (CONTINUED)

Glassic, G, Virginia, 1976-77. George Goeddeke, G, Notre Dame, 1967-72. Austin (Goose) Gonsoulin, DB, Baylor, 1960-66. John Gonzaga, G, No College, 1966. Brian Goodman, G, UCLA, 1975. Harvey Goodman, G, Colorado, 1976. Cornell Gorden, CB, North Carolina A&T, 1970-72. Randy Gradishar, LB, Ohio St., 1974-77. Tom Graham, LB, Oregon, 1972-74. John Grant, DE, Southern California, 1973-77. Charles Greer, DB, Colorado, 1968-74. James D. Greer, E, Elizabeth, N.C. St., 1960. John Griffin, HB, Memphis St., 1964-66. Bill Groman, HB-E, Heidelberg, 1963. Dick Guesman, T, West Virginia, 1964. Donald Gulseth, LB, North Dakota, 1966. Melwood N. (Buzz) Guy, G, Duke, 1961-62.

Dale Hackbart, S, Wisconsin, 1973. Mike Haffner, OE, UCLA, 1968-70. Steve Haggerty, DB, Colorado, 1975. Wayne Hammond, DT, Montana St., 1976. Billy Hardee, DB, Virginia Tech, 1976. Tony Harris, WR, Toledo, 1972. Dwight Harrison, WR, Texas A&I, 1971-72. Johnny Ray Hatley, T, Sul Ross St., 1960. Arthur A. Hauser, T, Xavier, 1961. Wendell Hayes, HB, Humboldt St., 1965-67. Abner Haynes, HB, North Texas St., 1965-66. Alfred Haywood, RB, Bethune-Cookman, 1975. Jerry Hendren, WR, Idaho, 1970. Gary Henson, E, Colorado, 1964. Lonnie Hepburn, CB, Texas Southern, 1974. George W. Herring, QB, Southern Mississippi, 1960-61. Bo Hickey, FB, Maryland, 1967. Walter Highsmith, C, Florida A&M, 1968-69. Jack Hill, HB, Utah St., 1961. George Hoey, DB, Michigan, 1975. John Hoffman, DE, Hawaii, 1972. Jon Hohman, G, Wisconsin, 1965-66. Gus Holloman, DB, Houston, 1968-69. Gordon Holz, T, Minnesota, 1960-63. Jerry Hopkins, LB, Texas A&M, 1963-66. Don Horn, QB, San Diego St., 1971-72. Paul Howard, G, Brigham Young, 1973-77. Bobby Howfield, K, No College, 1968-70. John Huard, LB, Maine, 1967-69. Robert Hudson, LB, Clemson, 1960-61. John Hufnagel, QB, Penn St., 1974-75. Bob Humphreys, K, Wichita St., 1967-68. Glenn Hyde, OT, Pittsburgh, 1976-77.

Martin Imhof, DE, San Diego St., 1976. Jerry Inman, DT, Oregon, 1966-73.

Bernard Jackson, DB, Washington State, 1977. Larron Jackson, G, Missouri, 1971-74. Richard Jackson, DE, Southern, 1967-72. Tom Jackson, LB, Louisville, 1973-77. Frank Jackunas, C, Detroit, 1963. Ray Jacobs, T, Howard Payne, 1963-66. Charlie Janerette, T, Penn St., 1964-65. Tom Janik, HB, Texas A&I, 1963-64. Pete Jaquess, DB, Eastern New Mexico, 1967-70. Jim Jensen, RB, Iowa, 1977. William Jessup, E, Southern California, 1960. Eugene Jeter, LB, Arkansas AM&N, 1965-67. William (Billy) Joe, FB, Villanova, 1963-64. Charley Johnson, QB, New Mexico St., 1972-75. Calvin Jones, CB, Washington, 1973-76. Henry Jones, RB, Grambling, 1969. Jimmy Jones, OE, Wisconsin, 1968. Larry Jordan, E-LB, Youngstown, 1962-64. Donald G. Joyce, E, Tulane, 1962.

Larry Kaminski, C, Purdue, 1966-73. Bob Kampa, DT, California, 1974. Bill Keating, DT, Michigan, 1966-67. Mike Kellogg, FB, Santa Clara, 1966-67. Jon Keyworth, RB, Colorado, 1974-77. Jim Kiick, RB, Wyoming, 1976-77. Donald W. King, E, Kentucky, 1960. Robert E. Konovsky, E, Wisconsin, 1961. Jim Krieg, WR, Washington, 1972. Gary Kroner, K, Wisconsin, 1965-67. Ray Kubala, C, Texas A&M, 1964-67. Frank W. Kuchta, C, Notre Dame, 1960.

Ron Lamb, FB, South Carolina, 1968. Gordon Lambert, LB, Tennessee-Martin, 1968-69. Patsy C. Lamberti, Jr., LB, Richmond, 1961. Dan LaRose, DE, Missouri, 1966. Carl James Larpenter, G, Texas, 1960-61. Bill Laskey, LB, Michigan, 1973-74. Isaac T. Lassiter, E, St Augustine, 1962-64. Jim Leclair, QB, C. W. Post, 1967-68. Roger LeClerc, C, Trinity (Conn.), 1967. Jacky Lee, QB, Cincinnati, 1964-65. Max Leetzow, DE, Idaho, 1965-66. Mike Lemon, LB, Kansas, 1975. Jack Lentz, DB, Holy Cross, 1967-68. Darrell Lester, FB, McNeese St., 1965-66. Herman Lewis, DE, Virginia Union, 1968. Hub Lindsey, HB, Wyoming, 1968. Pete Liske, QB, Penn St., 1969-70. Floyd Little, HB, Syracuse, 1967-75. Tommy Luke, LB, Mississippi, 1968. Fran Lynch, HB, Hofstra, 1967-75. Tom Lyons, G, Georgia, 1971-76. Rob Lytle, RB, Michigan, 1977.

Ernest G. (Pete) Mangum, LB, Mississippi, 1960. Brison Minor, DE, Arkansas, 1977. Bobby Maples, C, Baylor, 1972-77. Charles E. Marshall, HB, Oregon St., 1962. Paul Martha, S, Pittsburgh, 1970. Billy Masters, TE, LSU, 1970-74. Pat Matson, G, Oregon, 1966-67. Archie Matsos, LB, Michigan St., 1966. Jack Mattox, T, Fresno St., 1961-62. Marv Matuszak, LB, Tulsa, 1964. Andy Maurer, OT, Oregon, 1977. Ray May, LB, Southern California, 1973-75. Brendan McCarthy, FB, Boston College, 1968-69. John McCormick, QB, Massachusetts, 1963, 65-66, 68. Robert V. McCullough, G, Colorado, 1962-65. Ed (Wahoo) McDaniel, LB, Oklahoma, 1961-63. Lewis B. (Bud) McFadin, T, Texas, 1960-63. John McGeever, HB, Auburn, 1962-65. Bill McKoy, LB, Purdue, 1970-72. James R. McMillin, HB, Colorado State, 1960-62, 1964-65. Robert McNamara, HB, Minnesota,

237

ALL-TIME ROSTER (CONTINUED)

1960-61. Eugene Mingo, HB, No College, 1960-64. Claudie Minor, T, San Diego St., 1974-77. Tommy Earl Minter, HB, Baylor, 1962. Rex Mirich, DE, Northern Arizona, 1967-69. Alvin Mitchell, S-WR, Morgan St., 1970. Charlie Mitchell, HB, Washington, 1963-67. Leroy Mitchell, CB, Texas Southern, 1971-73. Marv Montgomery, T, Southern California, 1971-76. Randy Montgomery, CB, Weber St., 1971-73. Mike Montler, C, Colorado, 1977. Alex Moore, HB, Norfolk St., 1968. Leroy Moore, E, Fort Valley (Ga.), 1964-65. Randy Moore, DT, Arizona St., 1976. Craig Morton, QB, California, 1977. Haven Moses, WR, San Diego St., 1972-77. John Mosier, TE, Kansas, 1971. Bobby Moten, OE, Bishop College, 1968. Chip Myrtle, LB, Maryland, 1971-72.

Rob Nairne, LB, Oregon State, 1977. Ron Nery, E, Wisconsin, 1963. Lee (Mike) Nichols, C, Arkansas A&M, 1960-61. John Nocera, LB, Iowa, 1963. Tom Nomina, G, Miami (Ohio), 1963-65. Philip H. Nugent, HB, Tulane, 1961.

Tom Oberg, DB, Portland St., 1968-69. Riley Odoms, TE, Houston, 1972-77. Phil Olsen, C, Utah St., 1975-76. Harold Olson, T, Clemson, 1963-64. John Olszewski, FB, California, 1962. Jim O'Malley, LB, Notre Dame, 1973-75.

Chris Pane, DB, Chico St., 1976-77. Ernie Park, G, McMurry St., 1967. Charlie Parker, G, Southern Mississippi, 1965. Don Parish, LB, Stanford, 1972. Al Pastrana, QB, Maryland, 1969-70. Craig Penrose, QB, San Diego St., 1976-77. James W. Perkins, T, Colorado, 1962-64. Lonnie Perrin, RB, Illinois, 1976-77. Anton Peters, T, Florida, 1963. John Pitts, S, Arizona St., 1973-75. Dave Pivec, TE, Notre Dame, 1969. Bobby Ply, DB, Baylor, 1967. Dickie Post, RB, Houston, 1971. Randy Poltl, DB, Stanford, 1975-77. Eugene Prebola, E, Boston Univ., 1961-63. Steve Preece, S, Oregon St., 1972. James Price, LB, Auburn, 1964. Errol Prisby, DB, Cincinnati, 1967. John J. Pyeatt, HB, No College, 1960.

Frank Quayle, RB, Virginia, 1969.

Steve Ramsey, QB, North Texas St., 1971-76. Leo T. Reed, T, Colorado St., 1961. Randy Rich, DB, New Mexico, 1977. Bob Richardson, DB, UCLA, 1966. Frank Richter, LB, Georgia, 1967-69. Larry Riley, DB, Salem College, 1977. Joe Rizzo, LB, Merchant Marines, 1974-77. Alden Roche, DE, Southern Univ., 1970. William E. Roehnelt, LB, Bradley, 1961-62. Stan Rogers, OT, Maryland, 1975. David S. Rolle, FB, Oklahoma, 1960-61. Albert Romine, HB, Florence St., 1960. Oliver Ross, Rb, Alabama A&M, 1973-75. Tobin Rote, QB, Rice, 1966. Justin D. Rowland, HB, Texas Christian, 1962. John Rowser, CB, Michigan, 1974-76. Tom Rychlec, E, American International, 1963.

George Saimes, S, Michigan St., 1970-72. Ron Sbranti, LB, Utah St., 1966. Robert Scarpitto, FL, Notre Dame, 1962-67. Carl Schaukowitch, G, Penn St., 1975. Steve Schindler, G, Boston College, 1977. Mike Schnitker, G, Colorado, 1969-74. John Schultz, WR, Maryland, 1976-77. Lew Scott, DB, Oregon St., 1966. James H. Sears, HB, Southern California, 1960-61. Goldie Sellers, DB, Grambling, 1966-67. Jeff Severson, DB, Long Beach St., 1975. Don Shackelford, G, Pacific, 1964. Rick Sharp, T, Washington, 1972. George H. Shaw, QB, Oregon, 1962. Rod Sherman, WR, Southern California, 1972. Roger T. Shoals, T, Maryland, 1971. Jerry Simmons, WR, Bethune-Cookman, 1971-74. Leon Simmons, LB, Grambling, 1963. Mike Simone, LB, Stanford, 1972-74. Jack M. Simpson, LB, Mississippi, 1961. John Sklopan, HB, Southern Mississippi, 1963. Milton (Mickey) Slaughter, QB, Louisiana Tech, 1963-66. Tom Smiley, RB, Lamar Tech, 1969. Daniel Eugene Smith, HB, Northeast Oklahoma, 1961. Don Smith, G, Florida A&M, 1967. Ed Smith, DE, Colorado College, 1973-75. Harold Smith, T, UCLA, 1960. Hugh B. Smith, E, Kansas, 1962. James Smith, S, Utah St., 1969. Paul Smith, DE, New Mexico, 1968-77. Willie Smith, G, Michigan, 1960. Matt Snorton, E, Michigan St., 1964. Henry Sorrell, LB, Chattanooga, 1967. Jerry N. Stalcup, LB, Wisconsin, 1961-62. Bruce Starling, HB, Florida, 1963. James E. Stinnette, FB-LB, Oregon St., 1961-62. Jesse Stokes, DB, Corpus Christi, 1968. Don E. Stone, FB, Arkansas, 1961-64. Otto Stowe, WR, Iowa St., 1974. Robert J. Stransky, Hb, Colorado, 1960. David Strickland, T-G, Memphis St., 1960. Jerry G. Sturm, C-T-G, Illinois, 1961-66. Jim Summers, DB, Michigan St., 1967. Neal Sweeney, OE, Tulsa, 1967. Bob Swenson, LB, California, 1975-77. Gene Sykes, DB, Louisiana St., 1967.

George Tarasovic, DE, Louisiana St., 1967. Jerry L. Tarr, E, Oregon, 1962. Lionel T. Taylor, E, New Mexico Highlands, 1960-66. Steve Tensi, QB, Florida St., 1967-70. Jim Thibert, LB, Toledo, 1965. Earlie Thomas, DB, Colorado St., 1975. Bill Thompson, CB, Maryland St., 1969-77. Jim Thompson, DT, Southern Illinois, 1965. Dave Tobey, LB, Oregon, 1968. Jerry Traynham, HB, Southern California, 1961. Frank Tripucka, QB, Notre

ALL-TIME ROSTER (CONTINUED)

Dame, 1960-63. Godwin Turk, LB, Southern Univ., 1976-77. Clem Turner, RB, Cincinnati, 1970-72. Jim Turner, K, Utah St., 1971-77. Maurice Tyler, S, Morgan St., 1973-74. Richard Tyson, G, Tulsa, 1967.

Rick Upchurch, WR, Minnesota, 1975-77. Olen Underwood, LB, Texas, 1971.

Bill Van Heusen, WR-P, Maryland, 1968-76. Bob Vaughan, G, Mississippi, 1968. Lloyd Voss, OT, Nebraska, 1972.

Bob Wade, CB, Morgan St., 1970. Clarence Walker, HB, Southern Illinois, 1963. Dave Washington, LB, Alcorn A&M, 1971. Dave Washington, OE, Southern California, 1968. Gene Washington, WR, Michigan St., 1973. Norris Weese, QB, Mississippi, 1976-77. Theodore A. Wegert, FB, No College, 1961. Bill West, CB, Tennessee St., 1972. Willie West, HB, Oregon, 1964. Max Wettstein, OE, Florida St., 1966. Jim Whalen, TE, Boston College, 1970-71. Andre White, OE, Florida A&M, 1967. Jim White, DE, Colorado St., 1976. Harold Williams, HB, Miami (Ohio), 1961. Wandy Williams, RB, Hofstra, 1969-70. Nemiah Wilson, DB, Grambling, 1965-67. Malcolm Richard Wood, QB, Auburn, 1962. James Earl Wright, HB, Memphis St., 1964. Lonnie Wright, DB, Colorado St., 1966-67. Louis Wright, DB, San Jose St., 1975-77.

William G. Yelverton, E, Mississippi, 1960. Joseph A. Young, E, Arizona, 1960-61. Robert Young, G, Howard Payne, 1966-70.

E. Robert Zeman, HB, Wisconsin, 1962-63.